Foreign and Commonwealth Office
54020000054539
AF843700

ECONOMIC, SOCIAL AND CULTURAL RIGHTS

SOUTHAMPTON STUDIES IN INTERNATIONAL POLICY

Published by Macmillan in association with the Mountbatten Centre for International Studies, University of Southampton

General Editor: John Simpson

Other academic members of the editorial board: Martin Alexander; Ralph Beddard; Dilys M. Hill; Stevan K. Pavlowitch

The series was established in 1986 to encourage the publication of multidisciplinary studies of those public policies with significant international components or implications. Areas of special interest include arms control and defence policies, energy policies, human rights, maritime and space issues, Third-World development questions and the EEC.

Published Titles

Ralph Beddard and Dilys M. Hill (*editors*)
ECONOMIC, SOCIAL AND CULTURAL RIGHTS: Progress and Achievement
Dilys M. Hill (*editor*)
HUMAN RIGHTS AND FOREIGN POLICY: Principles and Practice
Dilys M. Hill, Raymond A. Moore and Phil Williams (*editors*)
THE REAGAN PRESIDENCY: An Incomplete Revolution
Darryl Howlett
EURATOM AND NUCLEAR SAFEGUARDS
Mark F. Imber
THE USA, ILO, UNESCO AND IAEA: Politicization and Withdrawal in the Specialized Agencies
Caroline Thomas and Paikiasothy Saravanamuttu (*editors*)
THE STATE AND INSTABILITY IN THE SOUTH

Forthcoming Titles

Stuart Croft
THE END OF SUPERPOWER: A Reappraisal of British Conceptions of a Changing World, 1945-51
Ian Forbes and Mark Hoffman (*editors*)
INTERNATIONAL RELATIONS, POLITICAL THEORY AND THE ETHICS OF INTERVENTION
Joseph J. Hogan
BUDGETING IN AN ERA OF DEFICITS: The 1980s and Beyond
Darryl Howlett and Martin Navias
BALLISTIC MISSILE PROLIFERATION AND REGIONAL STABILITY IN THE 1990s
John Simpson
THE INDEPENDENT NUCLEAR STATE, Third edition
John Simpson and Anthony G. McGrew (*editors*)
WESTERN PERSPECTIVES UPON THE NUCLEAR NON-PROLIFERATION SYSTEM: Challenges and Choices
Joanne Spear
CARTER, REAGAN AND ARMS TRANSFERS

Economic, Social and Cultural Rights

Progress and Achievement

Edited by

Ralph Beddard
Senior Lecturer in Law, University of Southampton

and

Dilys M. Hill
Reader in Politics, University of Southampton

FOREIGN & COMMONWEALTH OFFICE LIBRARY

M
MACMILLAN

in association with THE CENTRE FOR INTERNATIONAL POLICY STUDIES UNIVERSITY OF SOUTHAMPTON

1001609141DS
JC 571
8 MAY 1992

©Ralph Beddard and Dilys M. Hill 1992

All rights reserved. No reproduction, copy or transmission of this publication may be made without written permission.

No paragraph of this publication may be reproduced, copied or transmitted save with written permission or in accordance with the provisions of the Copyright, Designs and Patents Act 1988, or under the terms of any licence permitting limited copying issued by the Copyright Licensing Agency, 33-4 Alfred Place, London WC1E 7DP.

Any person who does any unauthorised act in relation to this publication may be liable to criminal prosecution and civil claims for damages.

First published 1992

Published by
MACMILLAN ACADEMIC AND PROFESSIONAL LTD
Houndmills, Basingstoke, Hampshire RG21 2XS
and London
Companies and representatives
throughout the world

Printed in Hong Kong

British Library Cataloguing in Publication Data
Economic, social and cultural rights: progress and achievement. – (Southampton studies in international policy, ISSN; 0956–5043).
1. Human rights
I. Beddard, Ralph, *1939-* II. Hill, Dilys M. (Dilys Mary), *1935-* III. University of Southampton *Centre for International Policy Studies* IV. Series 323

ISBN 0–333–52196–X

Series Standing Order

If you would like to receive future titles in this series as they are published, you can make use of our standing order facility. To place a standing order please contact your bookseller or, in case of difficulty, write to us at the address below with your name and address and the name of the series. Please state with which title you wish to begin your standing order. (If you live outside the United Kingdom we may not have the rights for your area, in which case we will forward your order to the publisher concerned.)

Customer Services Department, Macmillan Distribution Ltd
Houndmills, Basingstoke, Hampshire, RG21 2XS, England.

Contents

The Mountbatten Centre for International Studies

The Mountbatten Centre for International Studies originated in the Centre for International Policy Studies which was established within the Department of Politics in the University of Southampton in 1983. It brings together members of the Departments of Adult Education, History, Law and Politics to foster interdisciplinary and multi-disciplinary research into the domestic and external dimensions of policy.

Members of the Centre are involved in research on a wide range of issues. Recently published works include volumes on the Falklands War, the Carter and Reagan Presidencies, the European Community, Human Rights, intervention, the international nuclear non-proliferation regime and the military use of nuclear energy in the United Kingdom. A major programme of research involving Centre members has investigated problems of North–South relations in the 1990s, using funds provided by the Ford Foundation of the United States. This has involved the Centre being granted observer status at international diplomatic conferences.

The Centre also sponsors research workshops and symposia on a range of subjects; recent topics have been human rights and foreign policy (aided by a grant from the Nuffield Foundation); nuclear non-proliferation policies in the 1990s (funded by the Ford Foundation), and information technology (funded by the Fulbright Commission).

Links have been established with the Centre d'Histoire Militaire of the University of Montpellier, and the Fondation Pour les Etudes de Défense Nationale, Paris. The Centre also participates in the work of the team on Political Culture in Eastern Europe at the Ecole des Hautes Etudes en Sciences Sociales and the Fondation Nationale des Sciences Politiques, Paris. Members of the Centre have participated in the work of the European Science Foundation, the European University Institute and the International Commission for the History of International Relations.

Preface

In 1988 the Human Rights Group of the Centre for International Policy Studies, Department of Politics, University of Southampton, held two workshops on Economic, Social and Cultural Rights. A total of 35 participants were involved in the two workshops. The first, entitled *Are Social and Economic Rights Human Rights? Are They Justiciable?* explored the philosophical and universal aspects of the issues and related them to national and international rights' regimes. The second workshop, *Universal Rights and Public Policy,* examined specific policy areas: health, education, equal opportunities and race relations, and the employment aspects of the European Social Charter. These concerns are reflected in the papers published in this volume. In addition, there was lively debate at the workshops on the issues presented in Sir James Fawcett, QC's session on 'The Place of the Judicial Process in Human Rights', with special reference to the European Commission on Human Rights, on Benedict Kingsbury's 'International Law and the Rights of Indigenous Peoples' and on Laurence Lustgarten's 'Advancing Equality for Ethnic Minorities: The Experience of the Race Relations Act 1976'. These debates are reflected in the present volume in the editorial chapters by Ralph Beddard and Dilys Hill. Part I covers the discussions and presentations on rights and their realisation, while Part II considers progress and achievement in a number of contemporary issue areas with particular reference to the United Kingdom.

The special feature of the Study Group and its workshops continues to be the opportunity it gives for academics, lawyers, public servants and activists, both from Britain and further afield, to exchange ideas and to advance knowledge and understanding. Membership of the Study Group is open to all those with a professional or academic interest in human rights; enquiries should be addressed to either Ralph Beddard or Dilys Hill.

Acknowledgements

The editors would like to thank Mrs K. M. Pack for her invaluable help in the preparation of the manuscript.

Workshop Participants

Two Workshops on *Economic, Social and Cultural Rights* were held in the University of Southampton in March and September 1988. The following people participated in one or both of the Workshops:

Michael Addo, Department of Law, Staffordshire Polytechnic
Susan Atkins, Faculty of Law, University of Southampton
Karen Babbage, University of Southampton
Jill Barrett, School of Oriental and African Studies, University of London
Ralph Beddard, Faculty of Law, University of Southampton
Alan Brier, Department of Politics, University of Southampton
Sufian Bakunira, School of Law, University of Warwick
Peter Calvert, Department of Politics, University of Southampton
Simon Crow, University of Southampton
Rose D'Sa, Commonwealth Secretariat
Sir James Fawcett, QC [President, European Commission on Human Rights, 1972-81]
Ian Forbes, Department of Politics, University of Southampton
Françoise Hampson, School of Law, University of Essex
Julia Häusermann, Director, *Rights and Humanity*
Dilys Hill, Department of Politics, University of Southampton
Benedict Kingsbury, Exeter College, Oxford
Julian Lonbay, Faculty of Law, University of Birmingham
Laurence Lustgarten, School of Law, University of Warwick
Jeremy McBride, Faculty of Law, University of Birmingham
Dominic McGoldrick, Faculty of Law, University of Liverpool
Jonathan Montgomery, Faculty of Law, University of Southampton
Sally Morphet, Foreign and Commonwealth Office
Bushra Musa, Bangladesh/Commonwealth Secretariat
Raymond Plant, Department of Politics, University of Southampton
Martin Raven, Foreign and Commonwealth Office
Margherita Rendel, Institute of Education, University of London
Michael Rubenstein, Editor, *Equal Opportunities Review*
Vivien Shrubsall, Department of Law, University of Nottingham
John Simpson, Department of Politics, University of Southampton

Peter Slinn, School of Oriental and African Studies, University of London

Caroline Thomas, Department of Politics, University of Southampton

Katarina Tomasevski, The Danish Center of Human Rights, Copenhagen

Rachel Trost, Faculty of Law, University of Southampton

Rachel Walker, Department of Politics, University of Southampton

Anthony Walters, Department of Philosophy, University of Southampton

Notes on the Contributors

THE EDITORS

Ralph Beddard is Senior Lecturer in Law, University of Southampton, and Tutor for Postgraduate Students. He is the author of *Human Rights and Europe*.

Dilys H. Hill is Reader in Politics, University of Southampton and Director of the Centre for International Policy Studies. She is the editor of *Human Rights and Foreign Policy* and author and co-editor of *The Carter Years: The President and Policy Making* (with Glenn Abernathy and Phil Williams) and of *The Reagan Presidency: An Unfinished Revolution?* (with Raymond A. Moore and Phil Williams).

THE OTHER CONTRIBUTORS

Michael K. Addo is lecturer in Law, Staffordshire Polytechnic

Ian Forbes is lecturer in Politics, University of Southampton

Julia Häusermann is an international human rights lawyer and Director of *Rights and Humanity,* an international humanitarian movement

Julian Lonbay is lecturer in Law, University of Birmingham

Jonathan Montgomery is lecturer in Law, University of Southampton

Sally Morphet is Head of the International and Commonwealth Section, Research Department, Foreign and Commonwealth Office

Raymond Plant is Professor of Politics, University of Southampton

Vivien Shrubsall is lecturer in Law, University of Nottingham

Part I
Rights and Needs
Definitions and Actions

1 Rights And Their Realisation

Dilys M. Hill

INTRODUCTION

The debate about economic, social and cultural rights is a lively and contentious one. Controversy centres on two problems. First, there is the alleged inherent difficulty in asserting that these concerns can in fact claim the status of rights. Second, and relatedly, there is the issue of whether they are justiciable, that is, can they be the subject of adjudication and enforcement? These two problems are inextricably intertwined. If, as many argue economic and social rights are not rights but goals and aspirations of human society, then they are not issues for the courts but for the policy process. At the same time, however, it can be argued that justiciability itself cannot be narrowly confined to the court process alone, but is more properly defined as a matter of review processes, and thus of enforcement and implementation.

In their turn review, enforcement and implementation are dependent on the existence of norms and standards, both within societies and internationally. This aspect of the debate is also contentious. To talk of norms and standards implies both their definition and their implementation. Here, rather than notions of justiciability, processes of consultation might be thought more appropriate, particularly in the international arena. Debate then centres on whether consultation is more properly thought of as a substitute for, rather than a form of, justiciability.

Finally, the claim of these human concerns to be rights is affected by the distinction which many commentators, particularly jurists, wish to make between notions of current realisability on the one hand and working towards full realisation on the other. On the basis of this distinction, a *right* is that which is, or ought to be, currently realisable. A right is extant. But if these human concerns can only be defined as desirable goals and aspirations then they are not rights but policy outcomes. If this is so, then it is not justiciability which is required but evidence that a society or government is working towards the full realisation of those policy outcomes. This distinction is not accepted by all commentators and justiciability and review again become intimately interlinked.

It is the complexity of definitions and practice with which this chapter is concerned: the grounding of rights, the universalism of human rights, the hopes for their realisation in general and in a given situation, the place of the judicial process and the concept of justiciability itself.

THE GROUNDING OF RIGHTS

Rights' theorists claim that there are basic and universal features of human life which can be recognised as existing within any moral, ideological or religious framework. Whatever the belief system, certain universal human rights can be recognised. Two criteria are crucial: universalism and moral relevance. The universal feature of humanity in terms of which rights should be recognised is, as Raymond Plant's chapter shows, the capacity of human beings for agency, deliberation, and choice.[1] Both universalism and moral relevance are satisfied on this basis since it is the capacity for agency which is the universal feature of human life and this capacity is always morally relevant.

The question that follows is how does agency, that is the capacity of human beings for reasoned action, bear on the question of social and economic rights? The critic can argue that all that the human capacity for agency requires, as a grounding for human rights, is forbearance on the part of others: freedom from interference is all that matters in realising the capacity for agency. Agency is to do with the lack of coercion, and gives no claim to resources. It cannot therefore be the basis for any claim for economic and social rights to be recognised as human rights. Critics of this position hold that any claim to resources, which is what these rights entail, has to be held against a background of scarcity. By contrast, negative rights – the right not to be killed and so on – are costless.[2] The inevitable existence of scarcity, however, implies that there has to be some kind of procedure for rationing on the basis of judgements. But to call on rationing and judgements is antithetical to the existence of a 'right': the claim to a right as such fails. The argument about the problem of resources can be taken further. Critics assert that there is a fundamental difference between acts and omissions. The right to life defined as absence of killing and the right to life based on the presence of the means to life is a crucial distinction, since there is a categorical difference between not killing and the withholding of life-saving resources.

It is clear that the debate surrounding these two criticisms bears directly on the issue of justiciability in relation to economic and social rights. The first criticism is that agency does not imply a claim to resources to enact rights. The second is that we can distinguish between acts and omissions in grounding human rights which are then seen as essentially based on forbearance, not positive action. Both criticisms are directly related to the issue of which economic and social rights would be capable of being justiciable, of giving the individual claim to redress through a public remedy procedure.

Many negative rights theorists state that while negative rights are costless, positive rights always make a claim on scarce resources. This distinction fails, however, since both sorts of rights have to be asserted against a background of scarcity. For example, Tomasevski makes the point that, in developing countries: 'Not only the universal primary education, but also an effective and independent judiciary necessitates resources'.[3] In all societies negative rights must be protected through the apparatus of state regulation by means of legislation, police forces and related controls and are thus not costless. For their part, positive rights are asserted against a scarcity of material resources. For both kinds of rights, judgements have to be made as to what kind of resources are going to be devoted to their protection. Both negative and positive rights are matters of scarcity and if categorical judgements can be made about negative rights, regarding them thereby as justiciable, then the same must be true of other rights.

Theorists of negative rights are not persuaded by this argument since acts and omissions can, they believe, be fundamentally distinguished: killing is one thing and withholding life-saving resources is another. They are morally different and the rights involved are morally different. The only circumstances in which omission enters into the rights situation is where inaction is the result of the failure to act in accordance with a contract or rule-governed situation. Aside from this exception, the individual has a strict or categorical right not to be killed but no right to resources. At most, the individual has a claim on the generosity, benevolence and altruism of others, not a claim to a right. To omit to act may be a failure of benevolence but it is not an infringement of a right. On this basis a right is a categorical, enforceable – thereby justiciable – thing, while benevolence is not. This position is rejected by those who hold that causation exists regardless of the existence of a contract. The individual can be causally responsible, through his inaction, for an outcome which infringes a right (the death of a child who could have been saved, for example) regardless of whether he had a contract or not. From this it follows that positive duties also exist. Given that this is so, no categorical distinction between negative and positive rights can be made. That is, negative rights are not a different species from social and economic rights. Otherwise the outcome would be, as Rehof puts it: '. . . why is it apparently more acceptable to die of hunger than to be shot?'.[4]

The theorists of positive rights assert that humans stand in quasi-contractual relations as it were with the rest of mankind based on both the shared capacity for rational agency and shared passions of sympathy.[5] Humans thus have a positive duty to act, beyond the existence of an explicit contract. The argument is essentially that if there is a commitment to negative rights then there is no reason in principle why that commitment does not similarly apply to economic and social rights. The same is true over the commitment of resources to the protection of a right. Judgements have to be made about the commitment of resources to protect rights. And this is true for both negative and positive rights. The resources needed may be much higher in the latter than in the former case, but this does not mean that there is a difference of principle between the two as negative rights' theorists claim.

A final crucial question follows from this conceptualisation of negative and positive rights under one rubric. What are the implications of the commitment of resources to the protection of rights: are there obligations to contribute to those scarce resources, and to refrain from abusing the scarce resources that do exist? This is clearly both a theoretical and a political question. There are those who hold, in the field of economic and social rights for example, that rights are asserted against a background of values in a particular society. It is these values which determine what is meant by the need on which the recognition of a right is based. For example, societal values which recognise the existence of want and privation, on which the right to social security is based. But, it could then be argued, such rights can only be granted if those who hold the right (to social security) are prepared to discharge a corresponding duty (participating in the culture of work which is part of society's values). Values, then, play a vital part in arriving at judgements about resources against which rights can be claimed.

THE CLAIMS TO UNIVERSALISM

The claim of human rights to be universal can be effectively examined, as Sally Morphet's chapter shows, in the context of the two United Nations Covenants.[6] Critics of the universal and comprehensive definitions of human rights have asserted that rights are a Western concept and that, furthermore, civil and political rights are completely different in nature from economic and social rights, with the notion of cultural rights being virtually ignored. In evaluating these issues it has to be acknowledged that the discussion of human rights is inevitably a political one. Governments have all kinds of motivations for being involved in the international human rights regime and this complexity must be recognised. It is still true to say, however, that the world community has accepted the Declaration and the Covenants as the international framework of human rights. Within this framework, although there is still debate over the precise nature of, and commitment to, rights, the Economic, Social and Cultural Rights Covenant provides a convenient basis of definition of these rights.

It is sometimes believed that the differences within the world community over the place of economic, social and cultural rights calls into question their universalism and moral relevance. In practice this has not been the case. The input to the establishment of the Human Rights Declaration came from many countries including, besides the West, the Arabic and Latin American nations, China, India and the USSR. There was also the move in Western countries, particularly in Europe and Scandinavia, to protect positive rights by means of a proactive welfare state. The United States also played a major part, through the influence of Eleanor Roosevelt, in the drafting of the UN Declaration on Human Rights. The status she commanded and her ability to maintain contact with American governmental and public opinion ensured that economic and social rights were able to maintain their place within the Declaration. The United Nations Declaration on Human Rights, agreed without any negative votes in December 1948, has acquired a pre-eminent status precisely because it encompasses the totality of rights. If the Declaration had not included economic and social rights then it is much less likely that some Third-World countries would have adhered to it.

Once the totality of rights had been established in the Human Rights Declaration the question then became that of defining them into law. What happened in practice was that the Covenants were separated. This was not because the rights were themselves significantly distinctive, but because it was believed at the time that some governments would only sign the civil and political rights Covenant. This pessimism was unfounded: no government has ratified only the civil and political Covenant alone.

The interest of the international community in the whole range of rights grew: the 1950s saw the negotiation on the draft articles of the Economic, Social and Cultural Rights Covenant and the emergence of the European Social Charter. These rights were not solely the concern of the Third World: the Europeans consistently demonstrated their acceptance of the whole range of rights and the European Social Charter is an important regional example of how such rights might be expressed and how they might be effected into law.

The 1960s saw the maturation of the international human rights regime. The Covenants were finally put in place; governments felt that they could not stand out against the Covenants and the regime took on an essentially cohesive nature.[7] The late 1960s was also the time when the international debate on the claims for, and enforceability of, economic rights as rights took on the wider challenge of the economic rights and duties of states. The political issue became that of the right of economically underdeveloped states to receive help from rich countries, and from the international community as a whole. This eventually culminated in the New International Economic Order (NIEO).

Again, what needs to be stressed about these developments is the extent to which they were not just the concerns of Third-World countries alone. Between 1973 and 1975 the United States participated in the Conference on Security and Cooperation in Europe (CSCE) process, which ranged over the whole spectrum of rights. This also involved the Second World in a need to change the way in which it looked at human rights, given that the issue was used politically to gain concessions from governments in the Second World.[8] The Soviet Union finally ratified both Covenants in 1973 and, under Carter's presidency, the United States included vital needs such as food, shelter, health care and education within its understanding of human rights (a position from which the Reagan administration retreated with some vehemence.[9]).

In 1976 the Covenants came into force. This raised the question of implementation, which has only really come to the forefront of debate in the late 1980s. From the political perspective, governments while endorsing a commitment to implementation had reservations about how it could be achieved, given that they would be both involved in submitting Reports and in trying to maintain their credibility and standing in the community of nations. This creates a real difficulty; the practical outcome has been that it is Non-Governmental Organisations (NGOs), not governments, which have taken the lead over issues of implementation across the whole spectrum of rights.

Since the end of the 1970s there has been an evolving approach which asserts that all human rights are indivisible and interdependent and that equal attention has to be given to the implementation, promotion and protection of all these rights. Governments believe that the system is effectively complete as it stands and that instead of seeking to establish further 'Third Generation' rights, the focus should be on implementation. The standard for implementation is that set by the Human Rights Committee and the new Economic, Social and Cultural Rights Committee has been established to meet this standard.

A number of unanswered questions remain. One is the claim that in the debate over the charter of the Economic Rights and Duties of States the existence of individual economic rights is in practice dependent upon the nature of the existing economic structure. Individuals, particularly those in developing countries, cannot realise their economic rights unless the Charter on the Economic Rights and Duties of States can be implemented. But this remains the subject of political divisions: though the Charter has been accepted by a majority of states at the United Nations, the opposition of a small number of nations, notably the United States and the United Kingdom, has blocked it.

A second question arises over enforceability of rights. An example here might be the attempt by the European Community to get legal provisions inserted into the Lomé Convention whereby certain aid provisions would be conditional upon the recipient countries having a good human rights record. This may be an example of a wider phenomenon, by which the true description of the international human rights regime is not a cohesive consensus over individuals' claims to economic and political rights but the self-interest which governs the foreign policy concerns of states. A third question follows from this recognition of self-interest. It is in the interest of many advanced countries not to politicise the human rights debate at the United Nations since they want to remain on friendly relations with important trade sources in the Third World. So they make gestures towards a consensus within the international human rights community.

The reality of the 1980s had undermined this assumed consensus. There has been a notable shift in the debate, particularly in the case of Britain and the United States, in favour of the efficacy of market forces as against intervention in support of claimed economic and social rights. Theorists in Britain and the United States have argued for a minimalist position: governments do have a concern with civil and political rights but they have no such direct concern with economic and social rights which are much better met by the free operation of the market. In a sense this leaves open the question as to whether these matters are properly 'rights' or not: in either case, government has no direct involvement in them.

It can also be argued that over the last decade these minimalist positions have had even more resonance internationally. The countries which dominate the international institutions like the IMF and the World Bank are the very states for whom the market debate is all-important. This can be seen in the American opposition to index linking and to regulation of the right of cartels in the debate on the Charter of Economic Rights and Duties of States.

A fourth question arises over the possible example which is afforded by the African Charter on Human and Peoples' Rights.[10] Because the African Charter is a wholly Third-World enterprise it may provide a better mechanism for self-regulation within that world, even though the geographical representation of both the Human Rights Committee and the Economic, Social and Cultural Rights Committee do try to avoid identification with First or Third-World traditions.

The international promulgation of human rights, in the Declaration, the Covenants, the European Social Charter and so on, also acts to provide leverage within countries. Political parties, pressure groups and individuals seek to bring pressure on their home governments. This has also created an interesting situation in some countries whereby government itself has used the existence of the Covenants to push for change – for example, in land reform – against wealthy groups within its own society. In other countries pressures both within government and from groups in the community raise sensitive issues about the human rights record. In these situations civil and political rights tend to become refocused in terms of economic and social rights.

Universalism and comprehensiveness, then, have come to be accepted as part of a cohesive international regime of human rights. Problems and lacunae still remain: over emphasis, over applicability, over the nature of government concern. In addition it can be argued that this universalism has failed in practice to meet the real challenge of poverty and the maldistribution of resources in the world. It is these failures which call into question the efficacy of the international human rights regime genuinely to address the real issues of basic economic and social rights.

THE REALISATION OF RIGHTS

The debate over the nature of economic and social claims has to address the challenge that if they are so frequently unrealised in a world haunted by extremes of poverty then there is little point in calling them rights. But to those involved with the practical issues of poverty, human rights are inherent in the dignity of humankind. That is, though rights may be confirmed by law, law is not the source of human rights. Human rights are fundamental in that they are a natural foundation on which laws can be based and which can then be a claim on resources both at the national and the international level, as Julia Häusermann's chapter shows.[11] For the positivist school of jurists, this causes difficulties since it, by contrast, takes the view that unless a right can be enforced in a court of law it cannot be considered to be a right at all. It is, and must be, justiciable. As Alston has put it: 'For positivists, an element of formal justiciability is an indispensible attribute of a right'.[12] As a result, economic and social rights, which are only imperfectly justiciable, cannot claim the status of rights. This is also the stance taken by the United States within the Helsinki process, in its assertions that economic and social issues are human aspirations, not rights.

The opposing point of view states that in the enjoyment of human rights it is impossible to divide the civil and political from the economic and social: they are interdependent and indivisible. This is borne out by the international regime. The Human Rights Covenant holds that there is a duty to take positive action to protect civil and political rights. The International Covenant on Economic,

Social and Cultural Rights, for its part, lays duties on states to recognise and take appropriate measures for the realisation of rights. Implementation is clearly crucial here. In a world in which many lack access to resources and services the ability to realise rights is harshly curtailed.

The potential for justiciability is grounded in the instruments, both international and regional, which govern economic and social rights: the Covenant of Economic, Social and Cultural Rights, European Community law, the Council of Europe's Convention on Human Rights, the European Social Charter, the African Charter. These instruments also highlight the issue raised above in the Introduction: the distinction between those matters which can be realised immediately – such as the non-discrimination principle in the Covenant – and which are clearly justiciable rights, and those which are seen as being implemented progressively, and thus whose claim to be a right is disputed. The realisation of rights involves implementation in both the national and international contexts. The state, in order to fulfil its obligations under international law, may incorporate provisions into national law. This is the point stressed by the Harare Declaration and the Bangalore Principles, which hold that:

> it is within the proper nature of the judicial process for national courts to have regard to international human rights norms – whether or not incorporated into domestic law and whether or not a country is party to a particular convention where it is declaratory of customary international law – for the purpose of resolving ambiguity or uncertainty in national constitutions and legislation of filling gaps in the common law.[13]

In the case of economic, social and cultural rights, however, this judicial incorporation is rarely sufficient: positive administrative action is also required. For example, the realisation of rights may be effected through the use of tribunals (as in the areas of race and sex discrimination and employment protection). Again, at national level, traditional and customary law may need to be re-examined (for instance, in relation to women's rights). But, both in the use of administrative practices and in the re-examination of traditional law implementation may be more a question of political will – decisions to allocate resources – than law. As a result it is often argued that rights are more an issue of social policy than of law and of questions of justiciability.

Social policy and administrative practices arise also in the realisation of basic needs. The right to food, for example, is not the right to be fed. It is essentially the right to the production of food, or of money income to buy food which is dependent on structural changes and subject to government policy decisions. Similarly the economic rights of underdeveloped countries should not be seen as a matter of donations to Third-World governments but rather as the right of poor countries to be able to negotiate fairly in terms of trade agreements and so on.

Within the international arena, implementation and supervision are matters of the reporting mechanisms of the Committees in which the emphasis is more on constructive dialogue with states than in adversarial confrontation (see the section on justiciability, below). Here an emerging issue is the existence of benchmarks and the setting of standards.[14] The Economic, Social and Cultural Rights Committee is starting to develop general comments in the tradition of the work of the Human Rights Committee which will assist in the evolution of normative standards. Such work depends, of course, on the Committees having access to appropriate, and appropriately analysed, documents. In this respect the international agencies (for example, WHO and UNICEF) and above all the NGOs have a major part to play.

The involvement of non-governmental bodies in the international regime in turn raises the question of the place of moral as well as legal obligations. While only the state is subject to international law, there is a moral obligation on individuals and NGOs to meet the demands for rights. It is also argued that this moral obligation can be extended to international actors such as the World Bank in relation to the human dimensions of major development projects. By extension, this moral obligation also devolves on the international economy itself, in ways which have led, (as we have seen) to demands for a new international economic order and a re-ordering of the international debt regime.

The interdependence of rights, and the pressing problem of their realisation in a world of massive disparities of basic provisions, calls for a very broad interpretation of law and legal instruments. It is not sufficient to view justiciability in terms of courts and the legal process, a point which is further developed below. What is required is a holistic approach to the protection of economic, social and cultural rights which adopts an enabling, solution-orientated, approach. Nor is it the case that what is being argued for is merely to extend the arena of consultations. The groups and countries affected are in effect requesting treaties and guarantees; concrete instruments which would in turn imply some element of justiciability to uphold claims to rights.

The realisation of rights can be illustrated by looking at the problem of indigenous peoples within international law.[15] This reveals, as Benedict Kingsbury argued at the workshop, the complications which are posed for normal assumptions about economic, social and cultural rights and their realisation by the nature of international law itself. Inherent in this debate are concerns about the relation of human rights law and international law *per se*. To legal sceptics, human rights law as it is read in the texts and in the Covenants takes an overly optimistic view that descriptive or operational statements are in fact law. Nevertheless, international law can itself offer grounds within which rights can be claimed, even though those grounds are not based on human rights' law as such. The subsistence fishing rights of New Zealand Maori peoples are a case in point, where claims based on economic zones within the 1982 Law of the Sea Convention were more important than strictly human rights' law considerations. The Convention has also been important in relation to coastline state jurisdiction affecting indigenous peoples in Papua-New Guinea.

The issue of how indigenous peoples can realise their rights also illuminates the doctrine of permanent sovereignty over natural resources and the related issue of the rights and duties of states. This is particularly relevant in relation to development. What are the distributional responsibilities of the state, both in relation to groups within its borders and to multinational companies and contracts? Here questions arise not just of legal claims but of preferential rights (to forest settlements, to fisheries) and of the allocation of resources.

The way law is applied is also pertinent to the claims of such minorities for their rights to be realised. Within the international law of the sea, and within international tribunals, there is a case for arguing that those whose communities, settlements and traditions depend on access to a livelihood (fishing in maritime zones defined between states, coastal settlements, traditional land areas such as forests) are right to insist that these factors are relevant. From this perspective, tribunals would have grounds for taking into account the economic circumstances and the need to maintain the dignity of the people or group. The same point can be made in relation to international law on the environment whereby any compensation money could be used to help those affected by environmental pollution, even though it might not be possible to speak of a right to environment as such in the human rights sense.

At international level the attempt to set juridical parameters to the rights of indigenous peoples started in the 1950s with the ILO's 1957 Convention on Indigenous and Tribal Populations. The ILO Convention was, however, assimilationist in thrust, laying the main emphasis on ensuring smooth integration of ethnic groups. The international emphasis has now changed to one of self-management and self-determination, and moves are currently underway to revise the ILO Convention. The modern concern to set standards and norms on the position of indigenous peoples expanded substantially in 1981-82 with the large UN study on the problem and the establishment of the United Nations Working Group. The Working Group is to be a part of the Sub-Commission on Discrimination and the Protection of Minorities, which in the summer of 1988 was working towards a draft Declaration on indigenous rights. The other main arena of activity is in relation to the World Bank, where lobbying by environmental groups and others is aimed at persuading the Bank to take account of the impact on tribal groups of the effects of large Bank projects.

It is pertinent to examine how such claims to human rights cases can be realised in practice. Anti-discrimination groups try to bring cases to a wide range of fora, including the Human Rights Committee of the United Nations and the Inter-American Commission on Human Rights. They also use the complaints procedure of the ILO. The majority of these cases are not primarily about civil and political rights in a traditional sense but arise over the control and use of land and the prevention of its exploitation by outside settlers, that is, matters of economic and social rights. The conclusion that emerges is that it is not sensible to make a harsh distinction between civil and political rights and economic amd social rights. It makes little sense also to seek distinctive procedural approaches to this range of rights, seeing one set as justiciable and the other more properly as a matter of social policy. The crucial point is, rather, the continuity between law and policy. In practice, justiciability cannot be divorced from the policy context in which much of the human rights regime exists and from which it derives much of its legitimacy. These questions are explored further in the sections below on the judicial process and the concept of justiciability.

The heart of the matter in this area as in all other areas of economic and social rights is the question of norms and standards. Norms tend to be expressed in very general terms: what is needed is greater moves towards internationally acceptable means of determining whether reasonable compliance is being achieved. To do that, more specific norms, and clearer mechanisms of monitoring, control and judgement, are needed.

It must be recognised, however, that not all states (and the United States is among them) accept this perspective. The counter argument is that while individuals are entitled to the enjoyment and implementation of universally-recognised civil and political rights, economic and social rights are by contrast societal goals to be progressively achieved. Though the international community might have a role in helping with such problems, the primary responsibility for economic and social issues rests with individual states.

Such a perspective appears to question the dominance of courts and of the legal process in determining the universal applicability of economic and social rights and their realisability in practice. What, then, might be the place of the judicial process in relation to these rights?

THE JUDICIAL PROCESS AND HUMAN RIGHTS

The starting point on the place of the judicial process in the field of human rights must be, as Sir James Fawcett QC stated, the status of the concept of justiciability itself.[16] It can be argued that the judicial process in Britain is generally inadequate in its scale and in its impact. In the international arena, however, there is a place for the judicial process, and it is the examination of the nature of that process which can illuminate its potential viability within the British context. Paul Sieghart has stressed the point that:

> legalism . . . in the field of human rights law is both necessary and important, for the ultimate legitimacy of any government depends on the legality of its acts . . . It is therefore supremely important to know whether a government does or does not comply with its legal obligations, and this can only be objectively established by the use of the lawyers' techniques.[17]

The judicial process can be understood to mean a decision by a recognised authority, normally a court, whereby it applies or declares a rule of law in a public situation. But we immediately have to confront what might be called collective issues and this raises the question not of the judicial process but the determination of social policy. It can be argued, therefore, that the determination of social, economic and cultural rights are matters of legislation, that is, of social policy, though the impact of the courts may be involved at some point.

Within the international arena, as it exists in the European example, there is a case for stating that the judicial process should be very limited. Though the judicial process may be inherent in Article 6 of the European Convention, the main body of the Convention does not make the Articles matters of judicial control but of reporting. While the United Nations Covenant on Civil and Political rights is in a sense judicial, the Economic, Social and Cultural Rights Covenant, and the European Social Charter of 1965 are not really judicially controlled: the issues are issues for parliament and for the public. There is a sense of evolution in the attempts to use these instruments as directives, as a means of control over action. For example, the European Social Charter is an attempt to direct Parliaments on the way that social policy should evolve.

The range of human rights has, therefore, developed historically on these twin tracks: a judicial process on the one hand and a social policy process on the other. This modality is reflected in European developments, with the two areas managed by two bodies, the Court and the Commission. It is important to the issue of justiciability, however, to recognise that this is not an absolute dichotomy, For example, the European Commission is concerned with how far states' policies match and fit the European Convention, but in *the process of investigating* the facts there is an element of a judicial process. Where there is some judicial element the Commission may send the case on to the Court. In any event the Commission makes a report to the Committee of Ministers, which then takes a decision. So the Commission process involves both a decision procedure and an input to social policy.

The notion of a Commission – which might be reflected also in the institution of the Parliamentary Commissioner for Administration in the UK (the Ombudsman) – is a very fruitful one. A Commission is a body that can investigate a situation and, because of its remit and experience, reach conclusions and make recommendations. In the case of the European Commission the process is one which investigates, forms judgements about social policies and makes recommendations. The existence of this standard setting and directive process then calls into question the need for an explicit judicial mechanism through the Court. The crux of the matter is that the judicial process through the Court is narrower than that which is needed for determining human rights – their value, their improvement, their acceptance. It can be asserted that this determination of the nature and scope of human rights is a matter for a commission process rather than a judicial process. This is the strongest argument for the Council of Europe's approach to the remit of human rights broadly conceived, in handling it through a consultative and investigative commission process and not solely through a court or strictly judicial regime.

At the same time it is important to recognise that there is a place for that judicialism which inheres in the authority of the European Convention to which states are parties. The European Court commands attention and possesses an authority which derives from the Convention. The Convention allows decisions of the Court to be given effect: the implication of the Convention is that the contractual states will effect the decisions of the Court. The judicial regime is thus an authoritative one but the real operation of the whole process inheres in practice in the Commission. The Commission is the driving force and it could be argued that within the human rights remit of the Council of Europe the role of the Court has added little to the Commission's prime effectiveness. Were the Court to be allowed to take individual applications (which would then be referred to the Commission for investigation) it would operate as a court in the normal way and give judgement. The burden on the system, however, would probably make it unworkable.

A further issue here is the nature of the judicial approach itself. In dealing with economic and social rights there is a question of the desirability of a legalistic approach as opposed to one based on dialogue and consultation. The European Convention again highlights this difficulty: while Articles 5, 6 and 3 are eminently justiciable (or are perceived as such by those seeking to bring cases) the rest are reliant on social policy issues and lend themselves less readily to a judicial process. The question of justiciability is thus a prime factor in examining the nature and status of economic and social rights.

THE JUSTICIABILITY OF RIGHTS

If, as this chapter has attempted to show, economic, social and cultural rights are now an accepted (if still debated) part of the human rights regime, can they be made justiciable in the way that civil and political rights are held to be? Asserting human rights, it is argued, depends on their being justiciable; only in this way can they be claimed to be rights and to be realisable.

In the area of asserting human rights, it is necessary to distinguish between the concept of judicialism and that of judiciability. Judicialism may entail justiciability but not all justiciability is judicial. Judicialism is directed to the court system, while justiciability essentially inheres in the idea of review – though this of itself does not exclude court processes. It is also necessary, when considering the nature and applicability of the concept of justiciability, to distinguish between it and enforceability. For many people the issue is whether an individual case can be presented; this then brings the debate back to the courts. For human rights cases at the national level, enforceability is a matter for the government, justiciability occurs through the courts. In the international arena the situation is different: domestic law courts and governments come together to enforce decisions while justiciability goes beyond the court system into the domain of the Human Rights Committee, the European Commission, and so on.

Similarly, there are different procedures in the domestic and international regimes. In domestic law, since justiciability is carried out by the courts, it entails the normal procedure of the filing of complaints and the contestation of the contents. In international law (though there may in certain cases be a court) the absence of a court system does not necessarily deny justiciability. Although some critics do want to restrict the notion of justiciability to a court system, others believe the crucial mechanism is that of review. In the international regime it is still possible to have a review system and hence, as Michael Addo's chapter argues, justiciability.[18] Review thus becomes the operative definition.

Within the concept of justiciability, two elements can be distinguished: the adversarial and the inquisitorial. Adversarial justiciability points to the mechanisms of court procedure, of complaint and defence. Inquisitorial justiciability is more concerned with those processes of review which examine the facts of a case, requiring reports and commenting on them. This involves, for example, the notion of assessing states' performance and states' compliance with their obligations and treaties.

In the international arena, inquisitorial justiciability is carried out mainly through the various reporting requirements, for example under the European Social Charter, the United Nations Covenant, the ILO. In relation to positive rights, states are required, under Part IV of the UN Covenant on Economic, Social and Cultural Rights to submit reports to the Secretary-General who passes them to the Economic and Social Council for consideration. The Council's Working Group of governmental representatives, which is concerned with the actual review process, had been seen as lacking dynamism; as a result it has been replaced by a group of independent experts. In so doing it has moved closer to something like the Human Rights Committee and thus has better potential to review the states' reports. The review power of the ILO is even more comprehensive. The Director-General of the ILO has the power to request certain information under a Convention, regardless of whether a state has ratified that Convention or not.

The problem of economic, social and cultural rights is exacerbated by the debate on the implications of the wording of the Covenant. It lays down that states should undertake steps with a view to progressively achieving the full realisation of rights. If demands are to be met through progressive realisation, then once again we are facing the assertion, as we saw in the Introduction above, that these are societal goals, not inherent rights *per se*. This is not the only difficulty. The whole concept of progressive realisation also raises the question of what steps states are to take and at what point the right will have been achieved; when will we know when we have got there? And is there then a point at which an economic or social right stops being such and becomes a civil and political right? If it does, is it then justiciable when before it was arguably not justiciable?

Some commentators, such as Philip Alston, hold that 'taking steps' can be understood to include the incorporation of the Covenant into domestic law and the adoption of the judicial process. The contrary view is that it is preferable to identify a certain minimum content of a right such that states have to take steps to achieve this minimum content. The issue of the nature of a right is also implied in the provision of the United Nations Covenant which lays an obligation on states to recognise a right. An obligation to recognise a right presupposes the existence of a right. This in itself does not imply action: an obligation may be a negative one, in the sense of abstaining from harm. More emphasis has been placed, however, on the positive connotation of obligation, in that the duty to respect a right is taken to cover positive undertakings.

The debate on economic, social and cultural rights does not stop with the issue of review or inquisitorial justiciability. It is still possible to have contestation over such rights and they are thus subject to adversarial justiciability. In the domestic law of states there are instruments – constitutions, statutes – that guarantee aspects of positive rights whereby the individual can seek redress through the courts (Social Security legislation in Britain is one example). Again, in the area of discrimination, recourse to the courts may be possible to seek the enforcement of an economic and social right to work. Thus there is a defence in domestic law based on statute; adversarial justiciability, therefore, does not have to depend solely on a constitutional provision.

Extrapolating from this position, it can be argued that, before the European Court of Justice, not just the constitutional aspects but the statutory aspects of member states can be issues of review. Thus economic and social rights become subject to adversarial justiciability. The position appears even more explicit in the case of the African Charter on Human and Peoples' Rights. The African Charter incorporates the whole range of human rights and subjects them to a uniform procedure by which they may be the subject of discussion or review by the African Commission. Again, there is no Court but there is provision for individuals to petition the African Charter over the violation of their economic and social rights. This is probably the first instance in which such rights are being individually addressed, and becoming explicitly justiciable.

CONCLUSION

How then might the problems and limitations of justiciability be evaluated? Philosophically, as this chapter began by arguing, economic and social rights have a claim to the status of rights. In practice, the issue becomes that of their realisation: inquisitorial justiciability centred on the review process in international and regional structures. A difficulty remains, in that whereas individuals can point to the right of fair trial as being the right to be heard and so on, it is much more difficult to associate the individual with similar benefits in relation to economic and social rights. For critics, this again raised the issue of the consonance of justiciability. To many, justiciability depends on a final decision of some kind. This in turn implies standards and mechanisms for determining whether the standard has been met.

The question can still be raised, however, as to whether at the international level this decision-making capacity on standards and norms is necessary before something could be said to be justiciable. Reporting and review mechanisms themselves do, arguably, meet the criteria. Those who reject this view of the international regime do so because of the problem that the very general nature of certain rights makes it extremely difficult to render them justiciable. Unlike the domestic arena, where judicial review decides if a contract has been complied with or a statute met, the contractual term of the international Covenants are so different, and the standards are so diverse, that concrete decisions over 'contractual' obligations become very hard to determine.

The result may be that we may have to accept various degrees of justiciability, with the ideal being a court system with all the powers and backing that that implies. In the international arena this ideal may not be reached, though review of obligations may still claim to be a form of justiciability. Admittedly, the ability of the review process to judge reports effectively depends on reliable and extensive information, on the activities of NGOs, and on the status in which the system is held. Here we can see positive value in the review process. The fact that governments accept their obligations and are willing to subject themselves to public review, and do so within a framework of lobbying and information provided by NGOs provides both publicity and the possibility of actual change. Narrow definitions of justiciability are not an insuperable barrier to the realisation of economic, social and cultural rights, and the claims of these rights to be accepted continues to dominate both the international human rights regime and the domestic affairs of nation states.

NOTES

1. Chapter 2, Raymond Plant, *A Defence of Welfare Rights*.
2. A position refuted by many authors who stress that traditional rights of freedom from government interference require state action involving resources for the administration of justice. See, for example, L.A. Rehof, 'Development Assistance From The Point Of View Of Human Rights', L.A. Rehof and C. Gulmann (eds), *Human Rights in Domestic Law and Development Assistance Policies of the Nordic Countries* (Dordrecht, The Netherlands: Kluwer Academic Publishers, 1989), p.12.

3. K. Tomasevski, *Development Aid and Human Rights* (London: Pinter, 1989), p.203. (Katerina Tomasevski was a participant of the 1988 Southampton Human Rights Study Group Workshop from which this Part of the present volume arose).
4. L.A. Rehof, 'Development Assistance From The Point Of View Of Human Rights', p.12.
5. R. Plant, op. cit.
6. Sally Morphet, 'Economic, Social and Cultural Rights: The Development of Governments' Views'.
7. Sally Morphet, op. cit.
8. See the discussion on Détente, and the chapter by Iain Elliot, in Dilys M. Hill (ed.), *Human Rights and Foreign Policy* (London: Macmillan, 1989).
9. See P. Alston, 'Making Space for New Human Rights: The Case of the Right to Development', M. Panner and W.J. O'Farrell (eds), *Human Rights Yearbook. Vol. 1. 1988* (Harvard, Mass.: Harvard Law School, 1988), pp.22, 27.
10. The Charter was adopted as a regional treaty by the Organisation of African Unity in 1981 and entered into force on 21 October 1986. By April 1989 35 African countries had ratified or acceded to the Charter.
11. Julia Häusermann, 'The Realisation and Implementation of Economic, Social and Cultural Rights'.
12. P. Alston, 'Making Space for New Human Rights: The Case of the Right to Development', p.33.
13. Judicial Colloquium on the Domestic Application of International Human Rights Norms, Harare, Zimbabwe, 19 – 22 April 1989, *Harare Declaration of Human Rights* (London: Commonwealth Secretariat, 1989), pp.4-5; Judicial Colloquium in Bangalore 24 – 26 February 1988, *Developing Human Rights Jurisprudence: The Domestic Application of International Human Rights Norms* (London: Commonwealth Secretariat, 1988).
14. For a discussion of implementation and supervision, and a critique of the problems of norms and standards, see P. Alston, 'Making Space for New Human Rights: The Case of the Right to Development', especially pp. 35–8 and p.31.
15. The round table debate on Indigenous Peoples was led by Benedict Kingsbury of Exeter College, Oxford.
16. The round table discussion on the judicial process was led by Professor Sir James Fawcett, QC, former President of the European Commission on Human Rights.
17. P. Sieghart, *The Lawful Rights of Mankind* (Oxford: OUP, 1985), p.xi.
18. Michael Addo, 'Justiciability Re-Examined'.

2 A Defence of Welfare Rights

Raymond Plant

It is frequently argued that social and economic rights, which in this chapter I shall collectively call Welfare rights, are not genuine rights because they are neither enforceable nor justiciable. In this they are thought to contrast sharply with civil and political rights. Civil and political rights are regarded as justiciable at least in principle, whereas welfare rights are not and this is so, the critic argues, because there are logical or categorical differences between the two sorts of rights which in fact account for their different legal standing. In this chapter I shall argue that the claim that there are these categorical differences between the rights is in fact ill founded. If this is so, then it will follow that the question of justiciability cannot turn on these alleged logical differences. On the view I advance here if civil and political rights are regarded as justiciable, then there is no reason of principle for regarding welfare rights as not being so. However, I shall not address the question of whether civil and political rights are justiciable. I shall take the liberal view that they are for granted and then argue that there is no sufficient logical difference between the two sorts of rights which could account for different attitudes to justiciability.

A fully developed theory of rights has to provide an account of at least four things:

(1) The agent to whom the rights are ascribed.
(2) The features of the agent which justify the ascription of such rights.
(3) The nature of the objects, resources, states of affairs, processes, or forebearances to which the rights are rights.
(4) The range of individuals or institutions who have the duties or obligations which correspond to the rights of other agents: that is, who or what has the duty to respect, implement, or satisfy the rights which individuals have.

Following Gewirth we might put these features into the following formula:

A has a right to X against B in virtue of Y.[1]

So we have to give an account of the agent, A; what it is about the nature of A that grants the right, Y; the nature of the right asserted, X; and against whom it is asserted, B. Can a theory of welfare as a basic right satisfy the various elements of this formula in a cogent and coherent manner? I shall argue that it can, basing the justification of the right on an account of the needs of a rational agent. However, as we shall see, such a view also challenges some generally accepted assumptions about the scope of the responsibilities and obligations which accompany rights. My strategy will be to consider ways in which arguments in relation to the four features mentioned in Gewirth's formula are deployed in relation to rights such as life or liberty and then try to show that there are corresponding and equally cogent arguments in the case of the rights to welfare.

Two elements (at least) of Gewirth's formula are interdependent – the account of the agent to whom rights are ascribed and the characteristics in virtue of which they are ascribed (that is, features A and X in the formula). Clearly these cannot be wholly separated because the features in terms of which rights are justified will have a clear bearing upon the identity of the agents to whom they are ascribed. So, for example, in thinking about point X of the formula we might be inclined to take the view that rights were ascribed in terms of either the possession of consciousness in general or some specific feature of consciousness such as an ability to form and express a view about the agents' interests. It would follow from such an argument that animals, for example, would not have these rights, nor might some human beings – the severely mentally retarded or those in persistent coma, just to take two instances. Alternatively, if we took the view that rights were grounded in the fact of human vulnerability so that the possession of rights might be seen as some defence of our existence in the light of this vulnerability, then there would, of course, be no reason why, if this is all there was to the justification of the rights in question, those rights should not be ascribed to animals. In view of this, the proper course is to develop an account of those features of existence which could act as a basis for the idea of rights and then to specify those beings which could at this point in the argument include animals, who could be taken as instantiating these features in their lives.

What might such features be? In answering this question it is, I believe, possible to apply two formal constraints upon any potential answer. First, if certain features of existence are potential grounds for basic rights then these features must be universal. That is to say, if they are to underpin a theory of universal rights then those features of life in virtue of which such rights are held must themselves be universal. By 'universal' here I mean not specific to culture, religion or ethnic origin and at this point in the argument not even specific to species. The second constraint is moral relevance. Because a set of rights specifies a range of rights, claims and duties which rights bearers can hold against one another, these rights presuppose some moral sensibility, an ability to claim rights and to recognise duties as binding in the light of rights. Since rights specify a sphere of moral relationships, those features of life which are held to ground rights must be morally relevant. Hence, while it might be a distinctive feature of human beings that they possess ear lobes, this could not be a ground for the ascription of rights because however biologically distinctive this feature is, it is not morally relevant! Given these two constraints, we can say that any account in virtue of what X's rights are will have to be both universal and morally relevant.

The criterion of moral relevance here can be taken in two ways. It could mean that a proposed criterion is part of a particular substantive morality, or it could mean that it is a presupposition of any possible morality. It is fairly clear that a theory of universal rights could only be compatible with the former view if this particular substantive morality could objectively and rationally be grounded so that other individuals accepting other moral outlooks would have to accept it as rational and fundamental. However, the history of moral thought since Plato does not give us any grounds for optimism for believing that such a foundational and acceptable moral theory could be arrived at. The diversity of values is so great that if the ground for ascribing rights to individuals could only be derived from a particular substantive moral code then while such a view of rights might be cogent and authoritative *within* that morality, its authority would only extend as far as the general authority of that morality. To provide the grounds for a general or universal theory of rights we must look at the other possibility. Instead of looking to a particular moral code or outlook, we should rather look at the question of whether, given the facts or moral diversity, there are still any universal features of human life which appear to be necessary presuppositions or conditions for morality, whatever such moralities may turn out to be. If there are any such features, then they would be universal and, as presuppositions of morality, necessarily morally relevant.

This basically Kantian way of posing the problem seeks a transcendental deduction of the grounds of rights by reflecting upon the necessary preconditions of morality. Kant,[2] of course, argued that such preconditions were to be understood in terms of rational, autonomous agency and the ability to formulate rules of universal scope. These features of existence would be very difficult to deny in terms of moral relevance in the sense that any moral code is presumably going to invoke ideas of ought/ought not, right and wrong, good and bad – all notions which presuppose a capacity for choice between alternatives, at least as they are envisaged *within* that morality. We might argue with Kant that rational agency could be seen to be a necessary condition of any moral code since such a code will prescribe ends to be followed and alternatives to be avoided, and these presuppose a capacity for agency. This does not mean that agency would of itself have to be rated highly or at all within the moral code in question, only that, recognised or not, it is implicitly assumed in the very activity of moral conduct.

On this view the capacity for rational agency might be regarded as both a universal and necessary condition for morality and therefore a possible foundation for a theory of rights. What sense of rights could the idea of rational agency or autonomy ground? One answer is rights to forebearances of various sorts. If we emphasise autonomy as the basis of rights, then it seems an easy thing to move to the Nozickian position[3] that the central way of protecting human inviolability is through a set of rights which impose constraints upon the possible range of interferences by others. In other words, rights are to be understood negatively as requiring the absence of interference, coercion, assault, killing, and so on.

This view would, of course, exclude the idea that agency could act as a ground for welfare rights understood as the positive right to resources, rather than the negative view of liberty. If agency and autonomy are universal, necessary features of a morality which could act as a basis for rights, then on a negative view of liberty this freedom and autonomy is only diminished by intentional coercion. My freedom to choose and to act is only constrained if there is an identifiable individual who is intentionally coercing me. A negative account of rights could then cope with these sorts of infringements of autonomy because such rights demand forebearance from coercion and interference of all sorts. However, on this view freedom and autonomy do not require resources and opportunities, merely the absence of coercion. Thus on this account of autonomy while it could ground a negative view of rights, that is, it is in virtue of their possession of autonomy that individuals should be protected by a set of rights against coercion and interference, it would not ground a more positive view of rights as rights to resources. On the negative view of liberty the absence of resources is not a restriction of freedom. The only restrictions on freedom arise from the intentional coercive actions of other agents.

This negative view of the requirements of autonomy is based upon the following considerations. It is argued that there must be a clear distinction drawn between freedom and ability in the sense that there is a wide range of things which I am unable to do which it would be absurd to regard as infringements of my liberty. These inabilities may be of all sorts:

(1) Logical inabilities: I cannot draw a picture of a mountain without a valley.
(2) Physical impossibilities: I cannot as a male bear a child.
(3) Inabilities arising from my own nature and character, so I am unable to become a creative mathematician.
(4) Episodic inabilities: I cannot ride my bicycle uphill today – the wind is too strong.
(5) Inabilities arising from my own earlier choices which have affected my present circumstances – I am now unable to become a Roman Catholic priest, I am unable to run in a marathon.

There are, no doubt, many other forms of inability which could be categorised in different ways, but in each of these cases the limitations on my power are not caused by intentional coercion, and while in each case my abilities may be limited, my freedom is not. I am free to do these things; I am unable to do them. This point is made very clearly by Hayek in *The Constitution of Liberty*:

> . . . we presuppose a human agent if we say that we have been coerced . . . Coercion implies both the threat of inflicting harm and the intention thereby to bring about certain conduct.[4]

Given this definition of coercion, autonomy does not require resources; on the contrary it requires the absence of intentional restraint and coercion. Autonomy is thus to be protected by negative rights and not by guaranteed rights to resources.

There is a subsidiary argument here, turning upon the intentional nature of coercion. Economic markets in particular are not to be seen as coercive in their outcomes for the worst off members of society. The poverty which an individual may experience as the result of the operation of a free market is not, on this view, to be construed as a limitation of liberty and autonomy. The reason for this is a conjunction of the points made above. First, the possession of resources, powers and opportunities is distinct from liberty which is freedom from coercion; second, the outcomes of markets are an unintended and unforeseen result of individual decisions to buy and sell, taken on all sorts of different grounds. Hence poverty is not caused by intentional action and is not a restriction of liberty. Sir Keith Joseph and Jonathan Sumption in their book on *Equality*[5] have clearly seen the point at stake here. In a chapter which is devoted to arguing that poverty is not unfreedom, they argue that the contrary view – that it is a limitation on liberty – would require coercive action on the part of the state to remove poverty in order to secure liberty as a basic right. Accepting the arguments stated above, they reject this approach.

Hence, on this view, while agency, autonomy and liberty are universal and necessary preconditions for any moral code, they do not imply any welfare rights. The demand for autonomy is to be left alone, an idea carried out in terms of rights to forebearance rather than rights to welfare. However, there are arguments which can weaken the force of these ideas. The first is the idea, due to Rawls, of the worth or value of liberty. In this context this argument would go something like this: if freedom is the absence of intentional coercion, we must surely be able to explain what the worth of liberty is to an individual. Why do we want to be free from coercion?

The answer must surely be that if we are free from coercion we shall be able to do more of what we want to do. In this sense the idea of ability, of being enabled to do more things, enters into the justification of the worth of liberty. So if we are interested in the worth and value of liberty to an individual person, we must also be concerned with what that individual is able to do. This would be the basis for saying that the value of liberty as an effective power to act requires resources and that the value of liberty would require not just rights against intentional coercion but also those resources, which would secure the same kind of value for liberty of each individual considered as a moral equal. If the power to do something is central to why we find liberty valuable, then if we believe in an equal right to liberty there is no clear reason why this should only be defined as an equal basic liberty to be free from coercion, as opposed to an equal right to those basic resources which are necessary for individual agency and which will secure an equal basic value for liberty between individuals.

These points about the interrelationship between liberty and ability or power are also reflected in our ordinary language distinctions. For example, if a person is freed from a clear, direct intentional coercion (for instance, the removal of handcuffs), we could say that this removal enabled him or her to do certain things (if s/he chooses) which s/he was not able to do before. On the other hand to place such coercion on someone is to render them unable to do what they were able to do before. There are therefore great dangers in arguing that freedom is one thing, to be protected by rights against coercion, and ability and power not to be protected at all by rights.

However, not all inabilities should be seen as a restriction of freedom. If they are then it would absurdly follow that the state could only protect my liberty if it could secure my omnipotence, because any restriction on my ability or power would be a limitation on my freedom. If we wish to provide a defence of positive freedom and the positive welfare rights which would flow from this, we will have to try to define a class of basic goods which are necessary conditions of agency, as such, and which should therefore be protected in terms of rights, and distinguish between these goods and all the other goods which a particular agent might desire.

This strategy has two advantages. First, it would meet the Hayekian objection that the positive libertarian cannot distinguish between freedom and omnipotence; it would also be more logically coherent with a theory of rights because it would be concerned with whether there are any basic goods of agency, autonomy and liberty, irrespective of the particular culture within which an individual might live and the individual conceptions of the good which an individual might be enabled to realise within that culture. In this sense, attempting to identify the basic goods which would be required by agency would meet the universalistic requirement implicit in a theory of rights.

One way of putting the point, and one which might make it sound less abstract would be to argue in terms of needs, or basic needs. The issue can be put thus: are there any needs which are basic to agency which can be defined independently of the specific needs which an individual may have in a particular culture or morality? If there are such needs they would then define the set of basic rights which would reflect such needs.

The needs of agency will plausibly include, first of all, physical survival in the platitudinous sense that an agent is unable to exercise agency without physical integrity and survival. But there is more to the physical needs of agency than mere survival – agency must also include some element of a worthwhile life or physical well-being, because it is very difficult to imagine how a life of rational agency could ever be pursued if the whole effort of a person's life is devoted to securing the bare minimum to survive. In this sense to secure the capacity for agency for individuals will require not just restrictions on coercion defined by negative rights but positive rights to those resources which will contribute to both survival and well-being. Hence, food, shelter and health care of a sort relevant to and effective in a particular society would constitute basic goods of agency. However, the capacity of agency will also require other kinds of basic goods such as education which, in the terms relevant to a particular society, will be needed to sustain a capacity for agency, choice and effective functioning.

The right to freedom being secured by rights to these sorts of resources is not a freedom to do any individual thing but rather a general set of conditions which will enable the individual to go on to the sorts of things s/he wants to do. Basic needs have to be satisfied in order to do anything at all; non-basic needs are for those goods an individual needs to fulfil one particular plan of life in *one person's* particular circumstances. Rights have to do with the former sorts of needs, but not the latter. The first are universally and morally relevant, the second are morally relevant but not universal.

So if the ideas of agency, autonomy and freedom are basic to morality then they could underpin a set of rights which would be both negative rights to freedom from coercion, but also to those positive resources which are necessary conditions of acting in a purposeful way at all. These conditions would ground a positive theory of rights. At the same time it would answer the Hayekian objection that there would be no difference between freedom and omnipotence. The difference would be in terms of defining a set of necessary basic goods for liberty, rather than the optimal set of goods required for a particular free action.

This kind of argument can, I believe, provide a basis for thinking about the coherence of positive rights and it answers the first point of the formula with which I began, namely the facts of life in virtue of which rights are grounded. It will also give us a way of characterising those who are bearers of rights, namely those who are capable of rational agency, or at least have the capacity for such agency.

However, when we move to other parts of the formula, the idea of positive rights to welfare runs up against a number of severe difficulties which will have to be countered before a conception of welfare rights can be regarded as morally defensible. If we concentrate attention first of all on what individuals have a right to (the X in Gewirth's formula quoted at the beginning) then it is clear that problems arise. On a negative view of rights, what the individual has a right to is a form of forebearance on the part of others, or abstaining from action. So the right to life is the right *not* to be killed, the right to freedom of speech is the right *not* to be interfered with (unless, in exercising my right, I am interfering with another's right). Because these rights are therefore rights that certain things *not* be done they are, so it is argued, costless and not subject to scarcity. Welfare rights, however, as rights to resources, always imply costs and scarcity. This, it is sometimes argued, entails a theoretical difference between negative and positive rights. More importantly, these considerations give rise to issues of practibility. Because negative rights are asserted to forebearances, they are costless and always practicable, whereas welfare rights always involve costs and may not be practicable. How can a theory of human rights consistently endorse a set of rights which may not be practicable, because the resources to meet them in a particular society may be too great? Charles Fried poses the problem as follows:

> A positive right is a claim to something – a share in a material good, or some particular good such as the attentions of a lawyer or doctor, or perhaps a claim to a result like health or enlightenment – while a negative right is a right that something not be done to cure, that some particular imposition be withheld. Positive rights are inevitably assigned to scarce goods and consequently scarcity implies a limit. Negative rights, however, the rights not to be interfered with in forbidden ways do not appear to have such material, such inevitable limitations. If I am left alone, the commodity I obtain does not seem to be a scarce or limited one. How can we run out of people not harming each other, not lying to each other, leaving each other alone?[6]

On this view, there is a major difference between the kinds of things to which rights are asserted as between negative rights and positive or welfare rights. The critic of welfare rights will also argue that these considerations actually strike at the heart of the rationale of rights. If positive rights are always rights to scarce resources then, by definition, such rights cannot be realised at the same level simultaneously by all right holders. If scarcity prevents this then there will have to be a rationing procedure to determine whose rights are to be realised to which resources in a set of given circumstances. The critic will argue that these decisions will typically be made on consequentialist or utilitarian grounds,[7] whereas the whole thrust and rationale of rights-based theories is against consequentialist and utilitarian considerations – that there are ways of dealing with people which are wrong irrespective of the calculation of consequences. However, the very fact of scarcity plunges us into consequentialist considerations. For example, if the right to life is construed as a right to resources rather than as the negative right not to be killed, then in circumstances in which there is only one life-saving resource with two persons having a right to it, then assuming there are no over-riding clinical means for giving the resource to one rather than the other, the distribution of the resource will be based upon consequentialist arguments such as cost-benefit analysis or whatever. In that sense, the positive right to life cannot be assigned or neglected without getting into utilitarian calculation. However, if the right to life is the negative one of not killing, then, so it is argued, the failure to give a life-saving resource to A does not, on his death, mean that he has been killed – he died of, for example, kidney failure, not as the intentional result of the failure to provide dialysis. Hence negative rights to the non-performance of actions implies no scarcity and an ability to steer clear of utilitarian calculation.

These are very cogent points and any theory of positive rights has to confront them. There are two basic issues here, the extent to which negative rights can be regarded as costless and the problems of acts and omissions in relations to forebearance. The first of these is easier to deal with than the second.

There is a common initial objection to the point which Charles Fried makes, namely, that negative rights are not costless because the appropriate amount of forebearance may not be present and will require legislation which is not costless, and sanctions, police, law courts, prisons, to secure the appropriate degree of compliance with forebearance and abstinence from action. In this sense, in the world as it is, negative rights are not costless, and indeed the decision of how far to go in the legal protection and enforcing of rights may well involve utilitarian calculation. However, the critic of welfare rights could still argue that there is a logical or conceptual difference in the sense that we would imagine a world, for example, a community of saints, in which there are always the degree of forebearance required to secure negative rights in a costless and unconstrained way, whereas even in such a world positive rights and rights to resources and will still involve utilitarian calculation. In such a possible world therefore we can see the logical difference between positive and negative rights, even though in the world in which we live the differences are less obvious in practice. However, this is a difficult thesis to sustain, not just because of its counterfactual basis – such arguments are often useful in philosophy when we are trying to clarify a distinction – but rather because a very similar counterfactual argument is open to the defender of welfare rights. It is open to him to argue that he could envisage a possible world without material scarcity and that in such a world the rights to welfare goods would be costless. This counterfactual argument reveals that they are both about scarcity. The first is imagining a world in which there is no scarcity in those forms of human motivation which underpin forebearance; the latter imagining a world in which there is no material scarcity. Both are equally logically possible but neither throws much light on the nature of rights. Indeed one would be inclined to say that in a community of saints, as in a world without material scarcity, rights would be irrelevant. What would be the point of insisting upon rights in such a world? This shows, I believe, that rights have a place in a world in which there is scarcity both of motivation and resources, and that if a theory of rights is of any point and purpose in life, it has to be capable of making sense in the world as we know it, marked as that world is by scarcity.

Having said that, it still remains the case that since both negative and positive rights are asserted against a background of scarcity of both motivation and material goods there may have to be procedures for dealing with priorities to claims to rights. If these are not to be dealt with on a consequentialist/utilitarian basis, which might undermine ideas of rights, then a rights-based theory has to be able to produce a decision procedure and a way of prioritising rights claims which will avoid utilitarian calculation. This is a very difficult theoretical issue but it is one which affects negative as much as positive rights, if my arguments in the previous paragraph are accepted as cogent. If the rights in question are supposed to be absolute, then reference to consequentialist or utilitarian considerations would be ruled out. However, this seems unrealistic since if all rights involve costs, there may have to be choices made. On the other hand, if the rights are thought of as *prima facie* rights which can be over-ridden by consequentialist calculations, then in what sense are they rights at all? Jonathan Glover in *Causing Death and Saving Lives* has argued this point:

> A doctrine of absolute rights goes further than this and excludes the possibility of ever justifying killing by its consequences. But the claim that we have only a prima facie right to life does not exclude this possibility.[8]

So is there a decision procedure within rights theory which could avoid the collapse of absolute rights into *prima facie* rights and these into utilitarianism? I certainly cannot construct such a procedure here, but in any event it would have to satisfy two criteria. It would first have to be developed out of a further elaboration of the grounds in virtue of which rights are ascribed in the first place. In terms of the theory offered here, this would be a development of the theory of needs and agency. If these needs can be ascribed in greater detail than I have attempted in this essay, then they could perhaps be put in order of priority in terms of the urgency of their satisfaction. So, for example, the need for survival would come before that of well-being and autonomy. However, there are difficult issues beyond this, but without confronting these, both negative and positive rights run the risk of collapsing into utilitarianism. The other strategy is to claim that rights can only be overridden by other rights:

> A theory of prima facie human rights could be to the effect that only rights, and never other values or consequences, can override rights. Such a prima facie rights theory would have no affinities at all with utilitarianism other than having a maximising calculus. However, it would be a calculus about maximising satisfactions of rights and only that. Such a theory could be one in terms of a hierarchy of rights, such that, solely by reference to the rights involved and their places in the hierarchy, we could determine what rights were absolute.[9]

Clearly such a hierarchical theory would have to develop its hierarchical structure from reflection upon, for example, the theory of needs on which rights are based. This seems to me to be perhaps the most urgent but soluble problem outstanding in theories of rights.

There is a further difference between the nature of the rights in negative and positive rights claims, which is often used by critics of welfare rights to assert that there is a categorical difference between the two sorts oi rights. It is argued that the sorts of resources to which positive rights are asserted are vague and indefinite so that it is difficult to specify the corresponding duty with any precision. In the case of negative rights the duty is clear and precise – it is abstinence from action, interference, killing, and so on. In the case of welfare rights these rights are asserted to physical well-being, education and the like. If there is a corresponding duty to satisfy these rights, based as they are upon an account of the needs of a rational agent, then it is very unclear how extensive this duty is. Any attempt to define the duty with more precision will be arbitrary. So, there is a basis here for a conceptual distinction between negative and positive theories of rights. For example, if we take the right to life on the negative view, it is the right not to be killed and this duty is plain and categorical; whereas if the right to life is taken to imply a right to the means to life then it is much less clear how far this duty extends – do I have a right to all those medical interventions and technologies which will keep me alive? If not, then the cut-off point will be arbitrary, probably based upon utilitarian calculation and will be inconsistent with the general theory of rights in question. This point is often made with reference to the idea of needs, which I have argued, provides us with the basic criteria in terms of which rights are ascribed. The argument here is two-fold. First of all, there is a claim that needs are insatiable and that they are essentially culturally relative, so that in the light of these two considerations it is impossible for a theory of needs to provide a basis for a clear duty corresponding to the rights claimed on the basis of such supposed needs. These features of needs, which yield such unclear duties, mean that institutions and authorities seeking to satisfy such needs as rights will be forced to act in an arbitrary and discretionary way just because a theory of needs cannot provide us with a watertight account of corresponding duties.[10] Such arbitrariness and unpredictability in relation to rights makes a nonsense of the whole idea of rights. Insofar as needs are culturally relative and relative to subcultures within a society, similar problems of corresponding duties will arise. Gray argues this thesis as follows:

> The objectivity of basic needs is equally delusive. Needs can be given no plausible cross-cultural content but instead are seen to vary across different moral traditions . . . One of the chief functions of the contemporary ideology of social justice may be, as Hayek intimates, to generate an illusion of moral agreement whereas there are in fact profound divergencies of values.[11]

This latter point can perhaps be answered first. The argument is that there is some objectivity of basic needs as a ground for rights and this objective content will be generated by arguing not about what are the necessary conditions for pursuing a view of the good as seen within this, that, or the other moral code, but rather by arguing that there are certain basic needs which will have to be fulfilled if *any* conception of the good is to be pursued. These needs will be both negative and positive, namely, freedoms from intentioned coercion and interference are necessary for agency, but so also are certain resources such as physical well-being and education. Now it may well be that what is thought to be appropriate in the way of resources to provide well-being and education may vary from society to society, but nevertheless the right to some standard in these cases provides a benchmark to assess the social responsibilities of government. It has, however, to be accepted that the exact content of these responsibilities in terms of the possession of goods and services cannot be settled in advance by reflection on the conceptual structure of the rights involved. However, although this is a concession to the critic, how serious is it, and does it mark a difference between positive rights to resources and negative rights?

If we accept the argument deployed earlier, that in the world as we know it, negative rights cannot just be based upon non-coerced forebearance but will have to involve positive protection by government in the way of police, courts, prisons, and so on, then it becomes very unclear that the concession does mark a difference. The degree of protection that may be required to secure negative rights cannot be excogitated from the nature of the rights in question any more than it can in the case of welfare rights. These are matters for policy and politics but nevertheless a right such as the right to privacy does not lose its force as a benchmark against which to assess governments any more than a right to welfare. But the extent of the institutional provision to protect a right of privacy is a contingent matter, not a conceptual one, and, furthermore, one which, like medical needs, will change with technological advances. Computers and information technology pose a range of threats to privacy which could not have been foreseen two or three decades ago, and the degree of protection needed to secure such rights will therefore vary with technological advance. Very similar kinds of arguments can be made about the nature of political and legal rights, assuming as I argued in principle earlier that such rights do require institutional forms of provision. Such forms will then be a matter of political negotiation and cannot just be 'read off' the nature of the rights in question.

This point can only be resisted if we were to take a purist view of negative rights, that they do not in fact require, as I have suggested they do, a positive form of protection by government. This point is argued in the following way by Charles Fried:

> My right to freedom of speech if not a right to be heard, much less a right to have my views broadcast and applauded. If my right implied these things, then certainly it would be equivalent to a positive right, and would run up against the limits of scarcity . . . But what if others would deprive me of my freedom of speech – a hostile mob for instance? Surely it is the case that in asking for protection against the mob I make an affirmative claim upon the scarce resources of the community. But this objection misses the point too, for the fact that I have a right to freedom of speech against the government does not mean that I have a right that the government protect any exercise of that right.[12]

However, if this is rejected so that the possession of a right implies a claim to the protection of that right, then the distinction between negative and positive rights falls, since all rights to the protection of rights are rights to resources. On the other hand, if we do not have a right to the protection of rights, then it is not clear what the point of rights is at all.

Fried goes on to argue that this type of argument which he is here criticising neglects the distinction between what is done to a person and what is allowed to happen. This point is crucial and as we shall see it has salience not only for the object of the right in Gewirth's formula but also for forming a coherent idea of against whom a right is asserted.

The point at stake in Fried's argument is that a negative right can be wholly satisfied by forebearance. The right to life is satisfied by not being killed, the right to privacy by not having my mail tampered with, the right to freedom of speech by not interfering with my exercise of it. The forebearance in question is a duty which is always capable of being discharged. Thus Trammel argues as follows:

> It is an empirical fact that in most cases it is possible for a person not to inflict serious physical injury on another person. It is also an empirical fact that in no case is it possible to aid everyone who needs help. The positive duty to love one's neighbour or help those in need, sets a maximum ethic which would never let us rest except to gather strength to resume the battle. But it is a rare case when we must really exert ourselves to keep away from killing a person.[13]

To extend rights to resources and aid extends our responsibilities in an irrational way and makes the duties connected with rights difficult to characterise and thus to discharge.

Clearly part of the answer to these claims rests upon what has gone before, namely that a theory of rights based upon needs is bound to imply that even so-called negative rights are going to imply the commitment of resources, and therefore the sharp distinction made by Fried and Trammel cannot be maintained. However, the more serious criticism of this view is about the definiteness of the duties of negative rights based upon the idea that we have a very clear idea of forebearance and omission and the responsibilities connected with these. However, particularly in the case of not killing, this can be doubted, and in doubting this we shall be forced to look briefly at the ethical issues of killing and letting die. The assumption of the argument is that there is a categorical moral distinction between the two, that the former involves the infringement of rights, whereas the latter does not, and that responsibility in the former case is clear and unequivocal; in the latter case vague and extensive. However, there are a number of reasons for coming to doubt the view that there is a simple moral distinction at stake here. The issues are very complex, but there is no clear distinction and the assumption about acts and omissions upon which it rests are not sufficient to account for a difference in the rights at stake in each case. If killing and allowing to die are, in certain circumstances, morally equivalent, then these acts and omissions cannot be correlated with rights in terms of forebearance and the provision of resources, because the failure to provide resources for life could then be regarded as morally equivalent to killing and thus an infringement of the right to life. A more general way of putting the point is this. If the fundamental duty implied by a negative right is the duty not to harm, then this may well imply positive duties because the failure to act (to forebear) can itself produce harm and indeed a degree of harm which is morally equivalent to the intentional infliction of harm. Certainly John Stuart Mill held this view when he argued in the *Essay on Liberty* that 'a person may cause evil to others not only by his actions but by his inaction and that in either case he is justly accountable to them for the injury'.[14] If this argument is accepted then it is difficult to maintain the idea of infringing a right as always an intentional action and that the right can always be rejected by the appropriate form of forebearance.

One way in which critics of positive rights attack this idea is by arguing that harm can only be caused by omission if there is an antecedent duty towards the person, of if the omission is performed by an agent who has some special responsibility towards the individual in question. So, for example, if there is a contractual relationship between X and Y so that if X omits an action he may say that Y has been harmed. Thus if a doctor has assumed responsibility for the care of a patient and then fails to fulfil his obligation we can say that his inaction has caused harm. Similarly, if a parent rejects a child, this inaction causes harm because there is an antecedent obligation to aid and care for one's children. In an example used by Gewirth in *Reason and Morality*,[15] he discusses the case of a signalman whose failure to pull a lever causes the train to crash and thus the harm to those involved. However, while it may be true in these cases that inaction causes harm and perhaps infringes the rights of the people concerned, this is only because there is an antecedent duty based upon contract (in the case of the doctor); a conventionally accepted set of expectations (in the case of the mother); or a rule book (in the case of the signalman). In these cases the individual who fails to act stands in a special relationship of duty with the person harmed, and it is in this case that we can say that the inaction and the forebearance causes harm. However, the critic will go on to argue that this provides the basis for rejecting such an obligation between people generally in society. Unless there is an antecedent basis for a duty which creates a corresponding right to benefit from the performance of such a duty, there can be no basis for accepting the rights in question.

Hence the argument here turns upon two factors. The first is whether omissions can only cause harm if there is a specific contractual or quasi-contractual relationship between individuals; the second is whether the theorist of positive rights has a cogent argument for saying that there is an antecedent duty to meet the needs of people more generally. If so, which people and how generally?

The first question raises a deep problem in not only political theory but also the philosophy of science because the issue is about negative causal responsibility: namely that a failure to act causes harm. This way of putting the point should alert us to the potential weakness in the critic's position. If X, in failing to act, is negatively causally responsible for the harm which befalls Y, then presumably as with all cases of causation, this will depend upon the state of the world. Yet how can X's moral relationship with Y, which for the critic is crucial, make a difference to the sequence of causation? The critic is prepared to say that in certain circumstances in which X and Y stand in a moral relationship then X by his inaction may cause harm to Y; however assuming that he does not stand in such a relationship to Z the same failure to act does not cause harm. If this is so then we have to be prepared to argue that a conventional relationship, of the sort that a contractual relationship is, may make a categorical difference to whether X causes harm to Y. Take the following example: in the first instance the mother of a child fails to rescue her child at no possible risk to herself from drowning in shallow water. In this case we would have to say that her failure to act caused harm and that she infringed the rights of the child because, given the moral relationship in question, the child had a right to expect protection in both positive and negative senses from its mother. In the second case imagine that a total stranger failed to save a child in similar circumstances knowing that he is the only person in a position to save the child. If he fails to save the child he has not caused it harm because there is no antecedent relationship between the child and the potential rescuer. Saving the child would be a meritorious act, but to fail to save the child does not mean that he has negative causal responsibility for the harm which befalls it. However, in each case the child ends up dead as the result of two forms of inaction and what is not clear, and what is vital to the critic's case, is how the issue of the moral relationship or the lack of it between the parties concerned makes any difference to the causal circumstances. These are obviously very large issues but I doubt whether a theory of antecedent moral obligation can enable us to draw the distinctions required in the categorical way assumed by distinction between negative and positive rights in the way the critic takes to be central. If, as Jan Narveson[16] argues, criticising Gewirth: 'the signalman's inaction is a cause because there is an antecedent basis for the positive duty . . .', we need to have a theory about how obligations can make a difference to causation.

The second crucial question is whether the positive rights theorist can in fact provide a basis for the obligation to aid. The negative rights theorist will argue that we only have a positive duty to aid when we stand in a specific moral, contractual or professional relationship with another individual and that we cannot generalise from these to other cases. So if the positive rights argument is to go through, we need to have antecedent grounds for the obligation to aid others even when we do not stand in such a self-assumed relationship with them. Part of the argument to be deployed by the positive rights theorist here will be to claim that part of the answer has already been given in terms of needs and the resource preconditions of rational agency. However, the critic of positive rights can still argue that this argument is insufficient, we still need arguments on which my supposed obligation to meet the needs of others as a right can be based. It may be true that rational agency requires these needs to be satisfied but that does not of itself yield a right to the resources of others. Why should I pay attention to the needs of others even though I recognise them? So what moral force if any, do needs have, and how do they relate to the claim that they can act on the basis of rights?

In making this criticism the critic is rejecting the argument imagined by Kant directed towards a positive theory of duties. He takes the case of a man who is:

> . . . himself flourishing, but he sees others who have had to struggle with hardships (and when he could easily help; and he thinks 'what does it matter to me . . .'). Now admittedly if such an attitude were a universal law of nature mankind could get on perfectly well . . .[17]

That is, I can see that others may need help from me to satisfy their needs, but I can still decline to accept the moral obligation to help them. However, Kant goes on to argue that such a position is not really consistent when he says:

> . . . it is impossible to will that such a principle should hold everywhere as a law of nature. For a will which decided in this

> way would be in conflict with itself, since many a situation might arise in which a man needed love and sympathy from others and in which, by such a law of nature issuing from his own will he would rob himself of all the hope of help which he wants for himself.[18]

A rational man may pursue ends that require cooperation of others with him if he is to secure those ends, and if so he has to will the means to those ends – the help of others. If this is universalised then he will require that men help one another to achieve those ends, which requires cooperation. On this kind of basis then, it would seen inconsistent with the Kantian premise to argue that a man has no duty to help those in need because in a similar situation he might be so deprived and needy that he could not achieve whatever ends he might have without the help of others to satisfy his needs. The principle of respect for persons, as an alternative formulation of the Categorical Imperative, would be consistent with such a principle of social cooperation. However, it does not actually require it, because the position need not be the only one open to a rational man. As Robert Wolff points out, it would be possible for a man never to set for himself an end whose achievement appears to require cooperation with others and to forswear any ends he has adopted as soon as it turns out that such cooperation is needed.[19] In addition, the actual upshot of Kant's discussion is unclear – it does not imply that such help in realisation of ends should be seen as a *right* as opposed to a *claim*; that it should not necessarily be seen as a strict obligation rather than as a matter of beneficence. Certainly it is possible to read Kant as implying a principle of help as a right, but in the case of Goldman this goes beyond the text;

> We undoubtedly not only would want to be helped or to be answered favourably when begging for help, but would want to be able to demand help as a right so that the need for begging with its additional degradation would not arise. We would want not to await the beneficence of others as a dog might do but to be able to demand satisfaction of basic needs as a right of human beings . . .[20]

As Goldman articulates the case, it is made to appear rather intuitive – a matter of what 'we' would not require in certain circumstances – and it could be argued that it may or may not be in the spirit of Kant's position. However, the argument could perhaps be made a bit tighter than Goldman presents it. If all Kant's argument shows is that general benevolence is a coherent universal principle for a rational agent to will, then an individual clearly would not have a right to benevolence. Also, it is not clear that an agent willing only generalised benevolence would have any expectation that others would help him. Benevolence for Kant is an imperfect duty – it is something that is desirable to do, but it is not obligatory for any particular individual in any specific amount. Consequently, if a rational agent is going to will a principle of cooperative help as Kant suggests, it might well be that he would will it as a right and as a correlative strict duty on the part of those who help, because otherwise a particular individual could have no confidence that people's benevolent impulses would be directed towards him.

On this interpretation, then, Goldman might be correct in arguing that the Categorical Imperative willed by someone who sought ends requiring cooperation would will such help as a right and would recognise a corresponding duty to help others in the pursuit of their ends. Then this could be a basis for rejecting Nozick's view that no entrenched principle, of need satisfaction as a right is consistent with the Categorical Imperative of which the principle of respect for persons is held to be an alternative formulation. However, this still leaves two issues entrenched. First, there is the difficulty posed by Wolff of purely individual ends which do not require cooperation. Is there any reason for thinking that the pursuit of such ends is impossible? Perhaps so; it is not an argument that the ends in question have to be cooperative, but rather that the pursuit of any ends, public or private, might require others' help. For example, the fulfilment of the basic needs of life and autonomy are central for the pursuit of any end, private or public. A man could hardly forswear any end that required cooperation if, in fact, he could not pursue any end at all, if he was able to supply his basic needs by himself. In this sense, therefore, perhaps reflection on Kant's example on his own terms might provide a basis for rejecting Nozick's claim that a recognition of need satisfaction as a right is inconsistent with the principle of respect.

Another way of putting the argument would be in terms of respect for persons and the place which this value might be thought to have about rights both in their negative and positive forms. That is to say, theories of rights are ways of institutionalising in specific form the duties and obligations which the idea of equal respect for persons requires. The Kantian idea of human beings as ends in themselves is close to the idea, central to rights, that individuals should not be made subject to utilitarian calculation and turned into means for the ends of others. If this idea of respect lies behind the negative idea of rights, it can be argued that it can be made to yield a positive theory. Again, we might turn to Kant for insight into this when he argues that:

> Now humanity could no doubt subsist if every body contributed nothing to the happiness of others, but, at the same time refrained from deliberately impairing their happiness. This is, however, merely to agree negatively and not positively with humanity as an end in itself unless everyone endeavours also, so far as in him lies to further the ends of others. For the ends of a subject who is an end in himself must, if this conception is to have its full effect in use, be also, as far as possible, my end.[21]

What seems to underpin this argument is that respect for persons is due to individuals because they are capable of rational agency, of seeking ends and, as we might now say, pursuing a conception of the good. If we respect a person as a person because of this capacity of rational agency then we cannot both respect him in virtue of this capacity and be indifferent to the question of whether he has the means of exercising that capacity. Hence the principle of respect for persons, which lies behind the negative idea of rights, combined with a limited argument in favour of positive liberty, would yield a set of positive rights to those resources which would satisfy the basic needs of agency. Of course, this would still require some grounding for the principle of respect for persons. However, in this chapter my aim has been more modest, to show that in so far as this principle is argued by negative rights theorists, it can be elaborated to secure a set of positive welfare rights.

We have to turn now to the final aspect of Gewirth's formula, namely the person, persons, or institutions against whom or which the right is claimed. On the face of it, if human rights are generally universal then they should be held equally as claims against every other person. In the case of the negative interpretation of rights, it is argued, sense can be made of this requirement. The reasoning here is parallel to the cases discussed earlier – that forebearance and abstaining from action are sufficient to satisfy negative rights. So insofar as I am not actively killing, assaulting and interfering with the rights of others, I am respecting their rights. So if we take the case of an individual who is poor and destitute, insofar as I did not intentionally cause his poverty I can respect his right merely by abstaining from action, and this is as true for a destitute member of my own society as it is for any other society. Hence, the idea of each having a duty to respect the rights of all other right holders individually is capable of fulfilment on this basis. However, it is not at all clear against whom social and economic rights are claimed. It would seem clear that while I have a strict duty to respect the negative rights of all other individuals simultaneously and given the nature of those rights this can be done in a costless way, nevertheless no single person can have a duty to fulfil the economic and social rights of other persons. As Narveson says:

> One could work twenty-four hours a day at the relief of suffering and could impoverish oneself contributing to charity, but it is felt that to require one to do this would be going rather too far.[22]

While I have a general moral duty not to harm and interfere with the lives of others and others have a right to claim such forebearance from me, I cannot have a general and strict moral obligation to provide resources to relieve the suffering of all who suffer, and they in turn have no right to my resources for such relief.

If this is so, then it would seem that welfare could not be a right just because the right could not be claimed against any particular person; no particular individual could be blamed for the non-fulfilment of the right, and no specific individual would be responsible for any claim to compensation falling due as the result of the failure to implement that right. It would seem that again it would be best to see welfare as a matter of humanity, generosity, altruism and therefore imperfect duty, to which there would be no corresponding right.

It might be thought that the answer to this would be that the right to welfare is a right to be claimed, not against individuals, but rather against society as a whole, or more specifically the government, and this is in part the answer that Narveson gives in his interesting utilitarian discussion of this question. However, this still does not go quite as far as the welfare right theorist wants to go. As Narveson himself says,[23] this move would still make the right in question an imperfect one, because if we go back to Mill's distinction[24] – an imperfect duty is one that is directed against no particular person – the case we are now considering is closely parallel to this, and the right to welfare would become a right against no one in particular and thus would, by parity of reasoning, be an imperfect right. In the same way as no specific right corresponds to an imperfect duty, so an imperfect right could not imply a specific duty on the part of anyone. To be forced into this position would be just about the same as having to recognise that there is no right to welfare.

However, it is possible, following the lead of Narveson, to take matters further than this. Consider what Narveson says:

> But a duty has to be someone's duty. It can't just be no one's in particular. Consequently the thing to do is to make it everyone's duty to do something, even if that 'something' is a matter of seeing that someone else does it. Those who are put on the business end, such as the police, medical people, firemen, etc, should, of course, be compensated for going to the trouble for performing these activities. The simplest solution is simply to make these professions supportable by the public.[25]

If this is accepted, and I think that there are good reasons for accepting it, then the strict or perfect duty of individuals would not be that of the personal provision of resources to deprived individuals, but rather the support of institutions, welfare agencies, social workers, and so forth, that attempt to meet social needs. As a strict duty this could then be required by government through taxation to support the meeting of social needs. In this way we could still see the welfare state in terms of rights and duties rather than in terms of institutionalised altruism. To see the human right to welfare as implying a duty to support government welfare measures would be equivalent to seeing due process of law as a human right. A specific individual has not the duty to provide such due process, but rather the duty to see that the procedures of due process are in fact carried out. The perfect duties corresponding to the rights of welfare are not then the personal provision of resources and services to individuals, but rather the duty to support governments and institutions that are organised to meet such needs. Hence my argument has been that if there are rights at all, then there are positive as well as negative rights, and that a positive theory of rights can be developed in such a way as to satisfy the cogent demands of Alan Gewirth's formula. Clearly the moral basis on which rights of any sort are grounded needs further elaboration. Nevertheless, it is a consequence of the argument deployed in this chapter that the case for negative and positive rights stands or falls together.

NOTES

1. A. Gewirth, *Human Rights* (Chicago: University of Chicago Press, 1982), p.3.
2. I. Kant, *Groundwork to the Metaphysics of Morals*, H.J. Paton (trans.) (London: Hutchinson, 1974).
3. R. Nozick, *Anarchy, State and Utopia* (Oxford: Basil Blackwell, 1974).
4. F.A. Hayeck, *The Constitution of Liberty* (London: Routledge & Kegan Paul, 1960), p.9.
5. K. Joseph and J. Sumption, *Equality* (London: J. Murray, 1979).
6. C. Fried, *Right and Wrong* (Cambridge, Mass: Havard University Press, 1978), p.110.
7. J. Glover, *Causing Death and Saving Lives* (Harmondsworth: Penguin, 1977).
8. J. Glover, *Causing Death and Saving Lives*, p.83.
9. H.J. McCloskey, 'Respect for Moral Rights versus Maximising Good' in R. Frey (ed), *Utility and Rights* (Oxford: Basil Blackwell, 1984), p.132.
10. J. Gray, *Hayek on Liberty* (Oxford: Basil Blackwell, 1984).
11. J. Gray, 'Classical Liberalism, Positional Goods and the Politicisation of Poverty', in K. Kumor and A. Ellis (eds), *Dilemmas of Liberal Democracies* (London: Tavistock, 1983), p.182.
12. C. Fried, *Right and Wrong*, pp.120 – 2.
13. R. Trammel, 'Saving Life and Taking Life', in B. Steinbeck (ed.), *Killing and Letting Die* (New York: Prentice Hall, 1980), p.168.
14. J.S. Mill, *Essays on Liberty* (London: J.M. Dent, 1910), p.74.
15. A. Gewirth, *Reason and Morality* (Chicago: University of Chicago Press, 1978), p.222.
16. J. Narveson, *Morality and Utility* (Baltimore: Johns Hopkins University Press, 1973), p.99.
17. I. Kant, *Groundwork to the Metaphysics of Morals*, p.90.
18. Ibid.
19. R. Wolff, *The Autonomy of Reason* (New York: Harper Torch Books, 1973), p.171.
20. A. Goldman, 'The Entitlement Theory of Justice', *Journal of Philosophy* Vol. 73 (1976), p.831.
21. I. Kant, *Groundwork to the Metaphysics of Morals*, p.48.
22. J. Narveson, *Morality and Utility*, p.235.
23. Ibid.
24. J.S. Mill, *Essays on Liberty*, p.305.
25. J. Narveson, *Morality and Utility*, pp.235 – 6.

3 The Realisation and Implementation of Economic, Social and Cultural Rights

Julia Häusermann

INTRODUCTION

This chapter aims to illustrate the importance of approaching the realisation of economic, social and cultural rights from a multi-disciplinary and pragmatic viewpoint, rather than a narrow academic legal perspective. It attempts to highlight the scope of the endeavours necessary to ensure the full realisation of these rights, particularly for the one fifth of humankind living in utter deprivation and poverty, and for whom these rights presently represent little more than pious aspirations. The analysis illustrates the importance of economic, social and cultural rights to the protection of life and of human worth and dignity, and suggests strategies for action aimed at improving the realisation and implementation of these rights. It is thus essentially a practical approach. It calls for a united effort by all those involved in social policy, welfare, development, law and human rights to work together to improve the lot of the economically and socially disadvantaged.

THE NATURE OF ECONOMIC, SOCIAL AND CULTURAL RIGHTS

Human rights are those rights inherent in every human being by virtue of his or her birth and human dignity. Human rights are frequently confused with legal rights. Whilst human rights may be confirmed by legal instruments, positive law is not their source. They are rights that precede law. Human rights are not granted by any authority or government, but are derived from the essential nature of humankind. They are not limited to civil and political rights, such as freedom from torture and physical oppression, or the rights to freedom of conscience, thought and belief. Human rights include economic, social and cultural rights such as the fundamental rights to adequate food, shelter and other necessities for life and dignity.

Following the atrocities of the Nazi era and of the Second World War, the member states of the newly established United Nations (UN), recognised the importance of the international protection of human rights. The Universal Declaration of Human Rights, adopted by the UN on 10 December 1948, confirmed a wide range of rights deemed essential for human worth and dignity. These were later incorporated into two legal instruments, the International Covenant on Economic, Social and Cultural Rights (ICESCR) and the parallel International Covenant on Civil and Political Rights (ICCPR). The two Covenants were adopted by the UN in 1966 and came into effect, between those states party to the instruments, ten years later.

The ICESCR protects such rights as the right to work or to obtain social security in the event of involuntary unemployment, the right to an adequate standard of living including food and housing, the right to education, to special protection for women and children, the right to participate in cultural life, the right to benefit from scientific progress and its applications, and the right to benefit from the protection of interests resulting from intellectual property. By Article 2(2) the rights are to be exercised without discrimination of any kind as to race, colour, sex, language, religion, political or other opinion, national or social origin, property, birth or other status. The prohibition of discrimination in the enjoyment of economic, social and cultural rights is further elaborated in the International Convention on the Elimination of all Forms of Racial Discrimination and the International Convention on the Elimination of All Forms of Discrimination Against Women.

At the European level, the 21 states of the Council of Europe have adopted two main human rights instruments, the European Convention on Human Rights and the European Social Charter. The European Convention, although predominantly an instrument protecting civil and political rights, protects some aspects of economic and social rights. The Social Charter, on the other hand, elaborates the labour rights contained in the ICESCR, but is less broad in the scope of rights protected. In addition, some economic and social rights are also protected by provisions in various EC texts.

The incorporation of economic, social and cultural rights into international human rights instruments, which impose legal obligations on states parties, underlines the belief that ensuring social welfare is part of government responsibility. This is a view held, at least at the most general level, by all nations. The increasing involvement of the state in various aspects of economic and social life, brings with it the obligation to ensure that its policies promote social welfare. There is wide agreement between proponents of both liberal welfare, and socialist, states that this is an important role of the state. The role is especially important now that so many people, particularly in industrialised countries, are no longer able to rely on their own production of food to meet their needs, but must rely on alternative means of livelihood. Throughout the world, in richer as well as in less-economically developed countries, members of disadvantaged sectors of society face overwhelming obstacles in meeting their daily needs.

In the oft-quoted words of Leopold Senghor, former President of Senegal, 'human rights begin with breakfast', The obvious necessity for human survival of access to adequate food, shelter, healthcare and other essentials confirmed as human rights in international instruments has not, however, prevented considerable debates about the nature of economic and social rights, and the responsibility of states to ensure their realisation. Indeed, there is probably more controversy over this aspect than any other, and, despite their incorporation into international human rights instruments, some Western commentators still argue that these rights are not 'human rights' at all, but merely aspirations of society.

This restricted view of human rights is particularly prominent among lawyers of the positivist school. They postulate that rights are limited to legal rights which can be enforced by legal processes. The lack of clear definition of some economic, social and cultural rights causes them to assert that these rights are not justiciable and thus cannot be considered to be 'human rights' at all (issues that are considered further in Michael Addo's chapter). Positivists regard provisions confirming such rights in international instruments as no more than statements of objectives or desired goals.

The view has been expressed both by theorists and politicians. For example, Maurice Cranston, the British philosopher and political scientist, argues in his book *What are Human Rights?*:

> I believe that a philosophically respectable concept of human rights has been muddled, obscured, and debilitated in recent years by an attempt to incorporate into it specific rights of

> a different logical category. The traditional human rights are political and civil such as the right to life, liberty, and a fair trial. What are now being put forward as universal rights are economic and social rights, such as the right to unemployment insurance, old-age pensions, medical services and holidays with pay. There is both a philosophical and a political objection to this. The philosophical objection is that the new theory of human rights does not make sense. The political objection is that the circulation of a confused notion of human rights hinders the effective protection of what are correctly seen as human rights.[1]

Whilst it is true that some of the provisions of the ICESCR, such as that protecting the right to paid holidays, may be of a less fundamental or universal nature than others, the former should not be taken as undermining the authentic and vital nature of other economic and social rights such as those protecting human survival. Tarzie Vittachi (until his recent retirement, UNICEF Deputy Executive Director for External Relations) argues that 'it is the need of human beings as individuals and in their social collectives, to protection from abuse, particularly from the instruments of power, which are embodied in laws relating to human rights'.[2] Throughout history, rights have been claimed as a restriction on abuses of power by those in authority – monarch, prince or government – and thus human rights set parameters in the treatment of individuals by those in authority. But it is not just political power that requires restraint. It is equally essential that economic or social power should not be permitted free reign to dispossess the less fortunate of the ability to feed and clothe themselves, nor should it be allowed to obstruct them in their attempts to obtain education or employment.

The debates as to whether economic and social rights are of the same nature as civil and political rights have raged since the early days of the drafting of the International Bill of Rights. It was originally intended that the Bill would be in two parts, the Universal Declaration of Human Rights, which would be followed by a legal instrument which would cover all those rights set forth in the Universal Declaration. However, during the drafting process, it was decided to divide the legal instrument into two separate covenants, one protecting civil and political rights and the other, economic, social and cultural rights.

The reasons for this decision were complex, but reflected the differences of opinions about the nature of the different human rights, and the appropriate means of ensuring their enforcement. Some states considered the nature of economic, social and cultural rights as different from civil and political rights, because whilst the latter could be protected immediately by law, it was felt that the former required programmes of action over time before they could be fully realised. It was argued, for instance, that a different approach would need to be taken by a state in order to protect the right to health, than that necessary to protect the right to a fair trial. Similarly, whilst an international monitoring body could be envisaged to deal with alleged violations of civil and political rights, a court-like body would not be appropriate to enforce such rights as the right to work or to enjoy an adequate standard of living.

Another factor was that by the time the covenants came to be drafted the Cold War had led to increased politicisation of the differences of emphasis and priorities in human rights inherent in the political systems of the East and West. There was a fear among some government representatives, that if economic and social rights were included in the same covenant as civil and political rights, many Western states would fail to ratify it. However, the fear that Western states would not ratify an instrument including economic, social and cultural rights has proved ill-founded (see Sally Morphet's chapter, below). In fact, to date more states have ratified the ICESCR than the ICCPR. As of 1 September 1987, the former had been ratified by 90 states, 86 of which had also ratified the political covenant.

The debate concerning the nature of the two branches of human rights has surfaced again in the context of the Helsinki Accords. During the 1986 Vienna follow-up meeting, US Ambassador Zimmerman explained that the United States had not emphasised economic and social rights during the Helsinki process, 'because we do not believe they concern matters of basic human rights. Rather these "quality of life" issues concern basic human goals and aspirations'.

Similarly, some jurists argue that they lack precise content and that the international instruments fail to impose specific obligations on states. In their view, such claims as the right to an adequate standard of living including food and housing (protected by Article 11 of the ICESCR) are not justiciable in a court of law, and cannot therefore be considered legal rights. The Dutch jurist Vierdag, for example, argues that the right to food is not an individual right, but rather a broadly formulated programme for governmental policies in the economic and social fields. For him, the 'implementation of [economic, social and cultural rights] including Article 11, is a political matter, not a matter of law, and hence not a matter of rights'.[3] But it is the exception rather than the rule that norms of international law can be enforced through courts of law, and there is nothing in principle to prevent a right being an international legal right even if it is not individually justiciable. To insist otherwise is to confuse the nature of human rights. As the Helsinki Final Act reminds us, human rights derive from human dignity, not justiciability.

Whilst it is true that many of the legal provisions protecting economic and social rights may not have been drafted with the same precision as those protecting civil and political rights, there is nothing to prevent the further enunciation of the former and their corresponding obligations. Labour rights, for example, have been specifically expounded in numerous instruments adopted under the auspices of the International Labour Organisation (ILO). Further, it is possible, when the will is there, to determine the specific content of the rights and obligations using indicators from outside the legal field. The right to adequate food may appear vague to a jurist, but is perfectly clear to a nutritionist, and has been articulated by international bodies such as the World Health Organisation (WHO) and the UN Children's Fund (UNICEF).

The wording of Article 2 of the Economic and Social Covenant, by which states parties undertake 'to take steps . . . with a view to achieving progressively the full realisation of the rights recognised in the Covenant', is sometimes cited in support of the view that States Parties are not under any immediate obligation to protect economic, social and cultural rights. Yet some provisions clearly impose precise obligations of immediate application. For example, Article 2(2) prohibits discrimination in the enjoyment of the rights protected by the Covenant. Thus, whatever the level of economic and social development of a State Party, the Covenant prohibits discrimination in access to available services and benefits. Prohibition of such discrimination could, and therefore should, be made justiciable immediately.

The meaning of Article 2 and the obligations it imposes were discussed at a meeting of experts in international law held at the University of Limburg, the Netherlands, in June 1986. The experts adopted a concluding document known as 'the Limburg Principles', which stated, *inter alia*,

> . . . the obligation 'to achieve progressively the full realization of the rights' requires States Parties to move as expeditiously as possible towards the realization of the rights. Under no circumstances

shall this be interpreted as implying for States the right to defer indefinitely efforts to ensure full realization. On the contrary all States Parties have the obligation to begin immediately to take steps to fulfil their obligations under the Covenant.[4]

The indivisibility and interdependence of the two sets of human rights is a fundamental tenet of the United Nations' approach to human rights,[5] frequently affirmed by various human rights bodies. The importance of both branches of rights has also been confirmed by the Foreign Ministers of the EC Member States. In a Declaration on Human Rights of 21 July 1986, they stated:

> The Twelve deplore the fact that countless people around the world suffer hunger, disease and lack of opportunity, thus being denied the enjoyment of the most basic economic and social rights. The promotion of economic, social and cultural rights as well as civil and political rights is of paramount importance for the full realisation of human dignity and for the attainment of the legitimate aspirations of every individual.

But whilst respect for economic and social rights is clearly vital for the life and dignity of the individual, these rights should not be regarded as having priority over civil and political rights, any more than civil and political rights should take priority over economic, social and cultural rights. The two branches of rights are of *equal* importance. In the past it has been argued by some socialist and developing countries that the economic and social circumstances in their countries do not yet permit the enjoyment of civil and political rights. In human terms this argument is spurious.

The recognition of this interdependence of the two branches of rights clearly reflects reality. A political prisoner is denied the right to work, the right to enjoy family life, the right to cultural expression – a far wider range of abuse of rights than merely the right to be free from arbitrary imprisonment. The homeless, lacking an address, are frequently unable to vote or in other ways to take part in civic activities. They suffer diminished opportunities to find work, and their children may be deprived of access to education. Furthermore, a denial of economic, social and cultural rights frequently stems from discrimination and subsequent lack of opportunity.

It is sometimes argued that since the states throughout the world have such different economic and social systems it is impossible or inappropriate to regard economic and social rights as universal. However, to discuss the enjoyment or denial of these rights does not require an analysis of the manner in which they are achieved. That economic and social rights must be protected is a matter of law and humanity. How a state ensures their implementation is a question of political choice. As the Limburg meeting concluded:

> the achievement of economic, social and cultural rights may be realised in a variety of political settings. There is no single road to their full realisation. Successes and failures have been registered in both market and non-market economies, in both centralised and de-centralised political structures.[6]

Another argument frequently heard is that the two branches of rights are of a fundamentally different nature, as civil and political rights impose proscriptive obligations on states, whilst economic and social rights impose positive duties. However, this is an oversimplification. State obligations frequently combine positive and proscriptive duties. For example, the right to life, protected by Article 6 of the Civil and Political Covenant, not only implies a prohibition on arbitrary killing by the state, but also requires states to protect their citizens from unlawful killing by others through the establishment of police forces and criminal justice processes. The complementary nature of both branches of rights has been recognised by the UN Human Rights Committee, responsible for reviewing States Parties' reports under the ICCPR. In a General Comment it has stated:

> The right to life has been too often narrowly interpreted. The expression 'inherent right to life' cannot properly be understood in a restrictive manner and the protection of this right requires that states adopt positive measures. In this context, the Committee considers that it would be desirable for states parties to take all possible measures to reduce infant mortality and to increase life expectancy, especially in adopting measures to eliminate malnutrition and epidemics.[7]

Conversely, the obligations of states to ensure economic, social and cultural rights should be interpreted as including a prohibition of any action which violates or negates rights or creates an obstacle to the enjoyment of these rights by its population or a section of the population. This point is particularly pertinent in the context of ill-advised 'development' projects which adversely affect the livelihood of sectors of the population, considered more fully below.

Despite the controversy surrounding the nature of economic, social and cultural rights, considerable benefit may be gained from insisting that they are human rights, as the term 'rights' infers a claim on resources both international and national, and the imposition of duties on states and other organs of society, as well as on individuals. Human rights are fundamental in the sense that they are the natural foundation on which other rights created by positive law can appropriately be based. The differences between the various rights and the obligations they impose should not obscure recognition of their equal importance for the protection of human worth and dignity. Whilst debates about the nature of economic and social rights might be of philosophical interest, it is difficult to regard them as credible or of any pragmatic value in the light of the constant inclusion of these rights in international legal instruments.

Human rights are built on the twin essential principles of justice and non-discrimination, and yet it is the inability of a substantive proportion of the world's population to benefit from access and resources and services available to other sectors of society that prevents them from benefitting from the full realisation of their human rights and dignity. Thus, before considering the means of implementing economic, social and cultural rights, it is worth reminding ourselves of the extent of the violations of these rights, in order that we do not, by focusing on legal provisions, lose sight of human reality and the enormity of the abuse of human rights caused by economic and social injustice, and by the denial of cultural rights.

THE REALITY

A report on food security prepared for the World Commission on Environment and Development began with these chilling words:

> We live in a world of cruel paradox. Nearly one fifth of our people live in absolute poverty, in conditions of utterly unacceptable deprivation, squalor and misery. They struggle for survival, but they lack basic resources. They have no land on which to produce food, nor money with which to buy it. They are caught in a poverty trap from which they cannot escape and they suffer a hunger they cannot satisfy.[8]

The Hunger Project reminds us of the extent of the unnecessary deaths caused by hunger. 'Every year 13 to 18 million people die as a result of hunger and starvation – 24 every minute, 18 of whom are children under five years of age. No other disaster compares to the devastation of hunger. More people have died of hunger in the last two years than were killed in World War I and World War II together'.[9] For 500 million people throughout the world hunger is a daily reality. Hunger is debilitating, it literally drains the life out of people. Children facing malnutrition in their infancy and adolescence may suffer irreparable brain damage, or other serious consequences to their health and stamina for the rest of their lives. The effects of hunger cannot, therefore, be judged solely in terms of number of preventable deaths. We must also count the cost to those who survive.

The areas of rapid growth are not the areas experiencing agricultural growth. In fact the reverse is true. Whilst so many people go hungry in some parts of the world, mountains of food pile up in others. Some industrialised countries, and indeed some developing countries, face a severe problem of over-production and surpluses. The majority of the world's hungry people live in poverty in the shanty-towns of the world's poorer countries or struggle to survive on unproductive marginal land. Before the year 2000, it is estimated that the world's population will increase by approximately 1500 million. More than three quarters of that increase is expected to be added to urban populations. Many millions of these people will be unable to find jobs in the swollen cities, and will face grave difficulties in buying adequate food.

Hunger results from poverty. There is a growing discrepancy between rich and poor nations, and, in many countries, between rich and poor individuals. Hunger, like poverty is increasing not only in the poorer countries of the world, but also in industrialised countries. On the streets of our big cities there are people with nothing – no food, no shelter, no hope. Many have slipped through the state's welfare net. There are old people struggling to survive on a fixed pension constantly devalued by inflation – many are hungry, cold and alone.

A symptom of the increasing poverty in less-developed countries is the growing number of children being forced out onto the streets through economic need. Many have had to abandon their education in order to seek some means of livelihood – often through selling or providing services on the streets. Their lack of education almost certainly ensures them an adult life of abject poverty. The problem will grow with them, not disappear.

In an effort to draw attention to the appalling problems of homelessness throughout the world, the United Nations designated 1987 as the International Year of Shelter for the Homeless. Never has there been such an urgent need to protect the right to shelter and make provision for this basic human need. It is astounding that in the latter part of the twentieth century an estimated one fifth of the world's population lacks adequate shelter. Yet, as Pérez de Cuéllar, Secretary-General of the United Nations, stated at the launch of that year, 'shelter is a basic human right and necessity'.[10]

The poor and disadvantaged, whether in rural or urban areas, are in double jeopardy of suffering abuse of their fundamental human rights: first, they daily suffer abuse of their right to an adequate standard of living in accordance with human dignity; second, their disadvantaged position makes them particularly vulnerable to other abuses of their human rights. Poverty stems from under- or unemployment, insufficient income and other abuses of labour rights. It is frequently associated with illiteracy and powerlessness. The poor lack a political voice and are invariably the first to suffer in times of famine or national disaster, and from the effects of environmental pollution. December 1987 saw the third anniversary of the Bhopal gas disaster in which 5000 died and 250 000 were injured. It is a sorry reminder to us of the threats of hazardous industries and pollution, and the tendency both of siting dangerous production in areas populated by the inarticulate poor, and of forcing the poor to live on marginal land which is unsafe and/or uneconomic to develop or farm.

The extent of the abuse of fundamental rights to food and shelter is so vast that it cannot be seen simply in legal terms. Political will on the part of all governments is clearly essential. It will require a concerted effort to ensure adequate allocations of budgets to the solution of the underlying problems giving rise to poverty and social injustice. The cost of providing shelter, education, health care and social services to the world's poor has been estimated at US$ 4.5 billion per annum. It is a massive sum, but roughly the same figure that the world spends on arms in just two weeks. This obscenity denies one fifth of the world's population their fundamental human rights to survive and live in human dignity.

Throughout the world there are indigenous populations and ethnic minorities denied their cultural rights. Some suffer policies tantamount to genocide; others face discrimination, prejudice and social rejection. Much remains to be done to ensure equal enjoyment of rights by all peoples as well as every individual.

LEGAL PROTECTION OF ECONOMIC, SOCIAL AND CULTURAL RIGHTS

It is clear that the implementation of the fundamental rights protected by the International Covenant on Economic, Social and Cultural Rights needs to be strengthened as a matter of urgency. This is primarily a question of political will, yet law can also play a role.

Continuing Development of International Protection

Although much has been done to develop international standards for the protection of human rights, since the adoption of the Universal Declaration of Human Rights (UDHR) 40 years ago, it is clear that if economic, social and cultural rights are to be adequately protected by law greater precision needs to be given to the normative standards. The ICESCR was drafted in general terms on the understanding that it would be for the competent specialised agencies of the UN to elaborate the detailed obligations required for the realisation of the rights it protects, as the ILO had begun to do in the field of labour rights. Article 23 of the Covenant provides:

> The States Parties to the present Covenant agree that international action for the achievement of the rights recognised in the present Covenant includes such methods as the conclusion of conventions, the adoption of recommendations, the furnishing of technical assistance and the holding of regional meetings and technical meetings for the purpose of consultation and study organised in conjunction with the Governments concerned.

In addition to ILO conventions and recommendations, additional protection provisions have been drafted by the United Nations Educational, Scientific and Cultural Organisation (UNESCO). Member states have adopted several international instruments which protect human rights within UNESCO's field of competence, for example, those relating to copyright, to the protection of cultural property during armed conflict, and to the prohibition of discrimination in education.

Greater precision is still required to expand other economic, social and cultural rights, and several initiatives are presently being undertaken in this respect. The Commission for Human Rights has been considering the special needs associated with the realisation of these rights for some time and its Sub-Commission on the Prevention of Discrimination and Protection of Minorities, for example, has recently appointed a Special Rapporteur to report on the implementation of the right to food. The report, prepared by Norwegian jurist Asbjorn Eide, was presented to the Sub-Commission at its session in August 1987.[11] Having analysed the right and the obligations it imposes, the report calls for further elaboration of the right to food. It draws attention to the work being carried out in this regard by a working group of the International Law Association, which is considering the drafting of an appropriate international instrument to enhance the protection of the right to food.

The UDHR recognises that motherhood and childhood are entitled to special care and assistance (Art 25(2)). This is expanded as far as healthcare for children is concerned in the ICESCR (Art 12(2)). However, it has long been recognised that it is not only in the field of health care that children are in special need of protection and the United Nations is presently drafting a Convention on the Rights of the Child which covers the whole range of children's rights, including their economic, social and cultural rights.

The rights of migrants and aliens has also been recognised. The need to protect the rights of individuals who are not natives of the country in which they live was given additional emphasis in a Declaration by that name adopted by the General Assembly in December 1985.[12] Several provisions relate to social and cultural rights. Article 5(d) confirms the right to choose a spouse, marry and found a family, and 5(f) the right to retain their own language, culture and tradition. Article 8 brings the protection of the right to safe and healthy working conditions into line with those protected for nationals. The Declaration does not impose binding legal obligations, but goes some way to providing more detailed enumeration of these rights.

Another important initiative in the field of economic and social rights is the adoption by the UN General Assembly in December 1986 of the Declaration on the Right to Development,[13] by which the relationship between the enjoyment of all human rights, civil and political, economic, social and cultural, and development was recognised. Article 1 defines the right to development as:

> an inalienable human right by virtue of which every human person and all peoples are entitled to participate in, contribute to and enjoy economic, social, cultural and political development, in which all human rights and fundamental freedoms can be fully realized.

Article 8 requires states, *inter alia*, to ensure 'equality of opportunity for all in their access to basic resources, education, health services, good housing, employment and the fair distribution of income'. Recognising one of the weaknesses of past development policies the Article continues, '[e]ffective measures should be undertaken to ensure that women have an active role in the development process', and ends with the sweeping statement '[a]ppropriate economic and social reforms should be made with a view to eradicating all social injustices'.

National Practice

The main obligation of States Parties to international human rights instruments is to ensure that the rights protected by international law are implemented within the national context. This may be done by including the rights in the constitution or specific national legislation. But the enunciation of rights in law is meaningless unless effective means are also introduced by which the enforcement of these rights might be sought. This may be achieved by providing an appropriate legal remedy for violation of the right. However, in the case of economic, social and cultural rights this is often more effectively achieved by administrative policies.

The obligation on states to ensure enjoyment of economic, social and cultural rights must also be seen as extending to the removal of any obstacles to the enjoyment of rights. Thus there is a need to consider existing law and practice (including traditional and customary laws and practices), to determine whether they act as obstacles to the full enjoyment of human rights, so that adequate reforms can be made. This may be a particular problem in the case of the rights of women in those developing countries where customary law frequently limits the enjoyment of their rights with respect to inheritance and land ownership, where traditional practices abuse the physical integrity of women and girls, or where social taboos restrict the enjoyment of their rights to education and work.

The provision of a legal right is not, however, always sufficient to ensure its realisation. To take another example from developing countries, even in countries where the law grants the right of girls to equal access to education, cultural traditions or financial constraints might mitigate against girls being sent to school, particularly at the secondary stage. In such circumstances, additional policies are required to ensure equal access. In some countries positive discrimination policies have been implemented to encourage parents to send their daughters to school.

It has already been noted above that some provisions of the ICESCR, such as the prohibition of discrimination, are of an immediate binding nature, whilst other provisions are to be progressively achieved. Anti-discrimination legislation is now common particularly in the industrialised countries, and may, as in the UK, be enforced through tribunals. Tribunals have also been found to be an effective forum for the implementation of employment and social security rights where these have been introduced into national law.

But whilst access to courts and tribunals might be an effective way of implementing some rights, others are less a question of law than of social policy. The allocation of a sufficient proportion of the state budget to social needs is essential. It has sometimes been argued that it is only the richer states that can afford to provide such services as free education and health care to all its inhabitants. But the experience of such countries as Costa Rica, Sri Lanka and Cape Verde illustrate that where there is a political will to give such services priority in national expenditure, considerable advances can be made despite low per capita incomes.

International Supervision of States' Obligations

Although there is no international right of individual petition in the case of economic, social and cultural rights, several procedures have been established to supervise state compliance with obligations imposed by international texts. For example, supervision of the provision of the European Social Charter is provided for in the Charter itself. States Parties are obliged to submit biennial reports on the steps taken by them to implement their rights in the Charter. These reports are subjected to a complicated procedure, first being submitted to a Committee of independent experts, then to the Governmental Committee on the Social Charter, next to the Parliamentary Assembly of the Council of Europe, and finally to the Committee of Ministers, which may make Recommendations to States Parties. These recommendations are not legally binding. However, they have usually been taken seriously by governments, and states have frequently changed their national laws and practices to conform with the Charter.

Until recently the international supervision machinery under the ICESCR was notoriously weak. Unlike the Social Charter and the ICCPR (which established the Human Rights Committee to review reports from States Parties) no supervisory body was provided for in the economic and social covenant. Instead, the UN Economic and Social Council (ECOSOC) was charged with the task of reviewing state reports. It set up a Sessional Working Group for this purpose, but this was composed of governmental representatives who, being members of the diplomatic missions in New York, frequently lacked the relevant expertise or the time to devote to the consideration of state reports. These weaknesses, which had been recognised for some years, led to a series of reforms, culminating in 1985 in a change of name and composition of the group. It is now known as the Committee on Economic, Social and Cultural Rights, and its members are selected from 'experts in the field of human rights serving in their personal capacity' rather than as representatives of the States Parties.[14]

The Committee met for the first time in March 1987 and held its second session in February 1988. It has already made considerable improvements as compared to the work of its predecessor. It has attempted to improve the procedure so that it might make more effective use of the limited time available to it to examine state reports. In considering these reports it has requested governments to identify any groups who may not be benefitting fully from the services provided by the state or from the protection of its law. The Committee thus plays an important role by focusing the attention of States Parties on the most disadvantaged sectors of society and the priority which needs to be given to meeting their needs.

The Committee has adopted a strategy of entering into 'constructive dialogue' with representatives of states presenting reports, so that it might examine with them how the full realisation of the rights protected by the Covenant might best be achieved. It has recognised the difficulties involved in ensuring realisation, particularly in the case of less-developed countries. The committee has called upon states to develop 'benchmarks' or 'indicators' by which they might determine whether the obligations under the Covenant have been met adequately. It has also recognised that in the regional context of Europe, for example, consensus has already been reached on many standards, through EC and Council of Europe legislation and regulations. The Committee aims to develop General Comments (along the lines of those of the Human Rights Committee), which could set out its view on particular rights, such as the legal obligations imposed by the right to shelter. In this way the Committee would contribute to the development and recognition of more precise normative standards.

Like its predecessor, the Committee is a subsidiary of ECOSOC, to which it reports, and thus non-governmental organisations (NGOs) in consultative status with ECOSOC are entitled to submit written statements to the Committee. However, to date, this opportunity has been taken up by only a handful of NGOs. It is to be hoped that other NGOs will take a more active interest in the work of the Committee – not just human rights groups, but also organisations involved in development work and other aspects of promoting economic and social justice – for their expertise could be of assistance both to the Committee and to States Parties. The Committee's work would also be strengthened by the production of appropriate documentation from other UN bodies, such as the ILO, WHO, UNICEF and UNESCO.

This approach of assisting governments to implement their obligations rather than merely condemning their failures, has also been discussed in the context of the Convention on the Rights of the Child presently being drafted by the UN. This envisages an innovative procedure which will involve UNICEF, as the main UN agency responsible for child welfare, and enable it to offer technical assistance to governments having difficulties in meeting their obligations under the Convention.

There have been constant requests for more effective international enforcement mechanisms in the field of human rights, ranging from a call for an international court of human rights, to the establishment of the position of a UN High Commissioner for Human Rights. In the field of economic and social rights the need for improving supervisory machinery is perhaps less urgent than the development of more just international and national economic and social systems, such as those envisaged within the context of the New International Economic Order.

STRATEGIES FOR STRENGTHENING THE IMPLEMENTATION OF RIGHTS

Recognising the scope of the responsibility of all individuals and organs of society

Human rights law is a branch of public international law which binds states rather than individuals. It is thus often erroneously assumed that the responsibilities which are the corollary of human rights are borne solely by states. Whilst it is true that states bear the primary international legal responsibility, every individual and organ of society has the obligation to respect the rights of others. This duty is confirmed in the preamble to the UDHR and of the two Covenants. The latter states 'the individual, having duties to other individuals and to the community to which he belongs, is under a responsibility to strive for the promotion and observance of the rights recognised' in the two Covenants.

Frequently these responsibilities of individuals are covered by municipal criminal or civil law, and as such are legally enforceable. But, as we have seen, legal provisions alone are not always sufficient. In combating racism and sexism, for example, concrete steps need to be taken to educate individuals so that they do not succumb to prejudice and intolerance. The obligation of individuals is to ensure that their actions do not unjustifiably interfere with the enjoyment of human rights by other people, and it is part of the obligation of the state to ensure that provision is made within national law to prohibit such an unjustifiable interference.

Organs of society other than governments are also under an obligation to respect human rights. However, legal enforcement of these obligations is particularly weak, and in some cases non-existent. Far greater accountability is required with respect to the actions of multinational companies and international bodies. Such bodies are frequently involved in projects which adversely affect the rights of large groups of people. For example, projects to build dams may cause the large-scale displacement of populations, and cut them off from their traditional lands and eco-systems on which they are dependent for their survival and cultural identity. Similarly, the introduction of large-scale cash cropping may have serious consequences for food production, and thus for the enjoyment of the right to food, particularly by the poorest members of society.

Writing about a joint project between the World Bank and the Indian State of Gujarat for the building of the Narmada dam, the American jurist, Clarence Dias, has questioned:

> Is it legal for the Bank to finance projects which will clearly violate human rights protected by both national and international human rights guarantees . . .? Should not the Bank insist, from the very beginning, that this (or any) project will be carried forward in strict compliance with this law? Should not the Bank put itself under law by prescribing procedures, to be followed at every stage of a project, which will assure protection of those rights which international law holds to be 'universal' and presumably binding on international organisations?[15]

International obligations to ensure a just international economic system

Article 28 of the Universal Declaration of Human Rights states: 'everyone is entitled to a social and international order in which the rights and freedoms set forth in this Declaration can be fully realised'. Articles 55 and 56 of the UN Charter itself spell out this international obligation to co-operate in meeting economic and social needs, and the ICESCR also envisages international assistance and cooperation in the realisation of the rights it protects. The full text of Article 2 (1) referred to above provides:

> Each State Party to the present Covenant undertakes to take steps, individually and through international assistance and cooperation, especially economic and technical, to the maximum of its available resources, with a view to achieving progressively the full realization of the rights recognized in the present Covenant by all appropriate means, including particularly the adoption of legislative measures.

Despite these provisions, the inequalities between richer and poorer nations continue to grow, and amount to a major stumbling block to the enjoyment of economic and social rights by many millions of people living in destitution. In a scathing condemnation of the present injustice of the international economic system and its effect on the enjoyment of human rights by the poor and disadvantaged sectors of world society, the *New Internationalist* stated in an Editorial:

> the greatest offender against human rights in global terms is undoubtedly the world's economy itself. This is the great 'free market' which makes the poor world pay back more than it receives in loans or aid; which has allowed the commodity prices that developing countries depend on to sink to their lowest level for 30 years; and which insists, through its agent the International Monetary Fund [IMF], on Third World governments pursuing economic policies that will mean destitution and even death for the poorest members of society.[16]

The economic adjustments sometimes imposed by IMF requirements to cut governments spending on such programmes as food subsidies, and the provision of health care, education and other welfare services, inevitably have a severe effect on the living conditions of the poorest members of the society concerned. It is essential that priority be given to the realisation of the fundamental rights and basic needs of the poorest sectors of society. Indeed, this is the main thrust of the ILO's approach, WHO's primary health care programme, and UNICEF's global strategies for the care of children.

The injustices of the international economic system have been highlighted by a UNICEF statement accompanying its 1988 State of the World's Children Report in the following evocative words:

> In many nations children are without food or health care or schooling because of financial famine which cannot easily be captured by television cameras. In 1981 the net transfer of resources from rich to poor worlds was over $40 billion. By 1985 the position had almost reversed.

The figures for that year were $27 billion from rich to poor in the form of aid and loans, and a staggering $54 billion back from poor to rich in the form of debt repayments and interest! Following the October 1987 stock-market crash, this inequality is likely to deteriorate rather than improve in the immediate future as the industrialised world tightens its economic belt.

It comes as no surprise therefore that a high priority on the agenda of less economically developed countries is insistence on the establishment of a New International Economic Order. In 1974 at the instigation of the political grouping of developing countries known as the Group of 77, the UN General Assembly adopted the Charter of Economic Rights and Duties of States.[17] The Charter is designed to 'constitute an effective instrument towards the establishment of a new system of international economic relations based on equity, sovereign equality, and interdependence of the interests of developed and developing countries'. A first and urgent step is the cancellation or restructuring of the debt burdens of developing countries.

Cutting arms expenditure

Just as it is impossible to separate the lack of realisation of economic and social rights from economic underdevelopment, so too is the enjoyment of these rights restricted by the vast amounts spent on armaments and defence. A comparison between required expenditure on global economic and social welfare and that spent on armaments has already been alluded to above. This relationship was also recognised by the Declaration on the Right to Development. The Preamble reaffirms that:

> there is a close relationship between disarmament and development and that progress in the field of disarmament would considerably promote progress in the field of development and that resources released through disarmament measures should be devoted to the economic and social development and well-being of all peoples and, in particular, those of the developing countries.[18]

Such statements, although not legally enforceable, are a step in the right direction, and strengthen the arguments of the peace lobby and campaigners promoting social welfare and justice.

Implementing appropriate development policies

The aim of development aid projects should be to meet the needs of the poorest of the poor rather than to develop prestige projects which all too frequently hamper the enjoyment of the rights of disadvantaged people. Mention has already been made of projects which uproot people from their land or dislocate food production. In order to ensure that persons are not adversely affected by development programmes their active participation in the planning and implementation of projects is essential.

The need to involve the beneficiaries of development policies has been recognised for some time by sensitive development workers, and was highlighted at a world conference on agrarian and rural development in 1979, sponsored by the Food and Agricultural Organisation. The conference concluded that:

> participation of the people in the institutions and systems which govern their lives is a basic human right and also essential for realignment of political power in favour of disadvantaged groups and for social and economic development. Rural development strategies can realise their full potential only through the motivation, active involvement and organisation at the grassroots level of rural people with special emphasis on the least advantaged strata, in conceptualising and designing policies and programmes and in creating administrative, social and economic institutions including cooperative and other voluntary forms of organisation for implementing and evaluating them.[19]

Empowering the poor and disadvantaged to seek their own rights

Poor and disadvantaged people need to be encouraged in their attempts to seek justice and respect for their human rights. But such efforts are not always successful. Work among disadvantaged communities in India and the Philippines has shown that disadvantaged groups who have spoken out against government policies which deny them their economic and social rights may be frequently harassed and silenced, denying them also their civil and political rights of freedom of speech and assembly. The full realisation of economic, social and cultural rights, therefore, cannot be seen merely in terms of the protection afforded these rights by international human rights law, but also includes state obligations to permit the enjoyment of such civil rights as the right to freedom of speech and assembly. Once again, it is impossible to consider the enjoyment of one branch of human rights in isolation from the other. What is required is a recognition of the breadth of the issues involved, and the adoption of an integrated approach to development and the protection of economic, social and cultural rights.

The need to empower the poor and disadvantaged applies not only to the deprived in less economically developed countries, but also to those destitute members of our own societies, who so frequently have lost hope and self-respect. Ensuring the realisation of human rights is about finding ways of empowering people and encouraging them to seek their rights in reaffirmation of their human worth and dignity. This requires identification of the obstacles preventing the enjoyment of rights; the raising of public awareness and understanding of human rights and responsibilities and the means by which they might be sought and implemented; the development of self-help strategies to assist those whose rights are abused; as well as the establishment of just national and international economic, legal and political frameworks which will ensure the enjoyment of human rights by all.

Adopting a new approach

A new approach to the protection of human rights is required. It must be holistic and recognise the interdependence of human rights with other fields such as environmental protection, peace and development as well as law. It must be a positive, solution-oriented approach. In the language of UNICEF, we need to forge a Grand Alliance between many disciplines and professions involving first and foremost the poor and disadvantaged themselves, as well as UN bodies, voluntary agencies, policy-makers, religious bodies, academics, the mass media, trade unions, indeed all sectors of society.

Education in human rights should be considerably extended both in the formal and non-formal spheres. As is illustrated by the present study group organised in Southampton, universities have an important role to play in analysing and increasing the understanding of economic, social and cultural rights and in disseminating principles of human rights and responsibilities.

It is not only at the international and government levels that changes are required, but at the grassroots and community levels also. Lest we should lose heart in the face of the enormity of the problem and challenges, let us take courage from the growth of grassroots movements, such as the Indian Chipko Movement and the Green Belt Movement of Kenya, and those in South America working to assist the poor and oppressed.

Addressing the Causes of Abuse

Part of this new approach must be a determination to identify and tackle the causes of abuse of rights, not only in terms of structural injustices, but in terms of those factors leading individuals to violate the rights of others. Ali Mazuri, the African historian, has stressed that the greatest danger to human rights is the dichotomy between 'us' and 'them' which is the most persistent theme in human perceptions, not only between individuals but also between states.

At the individual level, intolerance is a principal cause of human rights violations: the unwillingness to accept a person different from ourselves, or a point of view different from our own. This all too frequently leads to oppression of religious or cultural minorities, and to racism in all its ugliness. Anthropologists today reject the concept of race as a way of demarcating people. As Clyde Kluckholm writes '[I]f all living people were ranged in a single sequence according to degree of resemblance, there would be no sharp breaks in the line, but rather a continuum where each specimen is different from the next by an almost imperceptible variation'. It is essential that measures to combat racism and intolerance should focus on our common humanity. Education must play an important role, but projects designed to build bridges between estranged communities and to promote dialogue are equally essential.

Other causes of violations can be identified including greed, lust for power, and insecurity. The abuse of economic and social rights of the deprived sectors of our society is exacerbated by the refusal of the privileged to give up their benefits, and owes much to the greed which causes the blind pursuit of increased profits without due regard to the detrimental effects this might have on the poor and disadvantaged, or on the environment on which we are all dependent.

The link between social and economic injustice and violations of civil and political rights has been emphasised above. The experience of Latin America teaches us that when the deprived and oppressed start seeking their rights, the threatened élite may react out of insecurity, increasing police power, and brutally repressing those seeking change. To a lesser extent we can see signs of this process in the UK, with a greater emphasis being placed on strengthening law enforcement agencies than on understanding and addressing the underlying causes of the social tensions giving rise to such phenomena as inner city riots.

Strengthening the Role of NGOs

The role of individuals and voluntary agencies is very important. Indeed, many would argue that much of the progress made in the human rights field is due to non-governmental initiatives. The concern of governments for human rights issues is frequently hampered by political alliances or by military or economic considerations. NGOs, on the other hand, can carry out research and fact-finding investigations and offer balanced and impartial reports which are not influenced by political expediency. Unfortunately, in order to ensure efficiency, most human rights organisations deal either with a limited number of issues, or with specific countries. Thus it is sometimes difficult to see the overall picture, and to recognise the linkages between cause and violation.

As David Matas, a Canadian human rights lawyer, asserts, we need to go beyond merely collating information on violations and penetrate the arena of ideas. We must, for instance, identify those ideologies which promote racism and totalitarianism, and attempt to find ways of lessening their negative impact on the respect for human rights. The human rights movement as a whole needs to move on from merely monitoring and protesting violations, and start tackling the causes of those violations. In doing so we need to use those techniques, such as impartiality and political balance, which have already been used successfully.[20]

This is one of the rationales for my own organisation, Rights and Humanity. It is particularly concerned with identifying the obstacles to the full enjoyment of human rights, especially by economically and socially disadvantaged people, such as the destitute and socially rejected. Its work is aimed at empowering such people to seek their own rights, and promoting just national and international societies by education and public awareness of human rights and responsibilities.

CONCLUSION

There is now a coherent body of law protecting economic, social and cultural rights, and whilst continued efforts are required to strengthen the law, the main focus needs to be shifted from normative development to ensuring the actual implementation of these rights. In order to ensure in full the enjoyment of economic, social and cultural rights tremendous structural changes are required, not only in the international economic system, but also in national societies. It is essential that those presently holding economic and social power should recognise their human responsibilities to permit these changes so that all members of the human family can live in dignity.

In capitalist and mixed economies, ways must be found to ensure that an unfettered free market economy does not dispossess the poor and less articulate members of society from enjoyment of an adequate standard of living. In centralised economies, renewed efforts are required to ensure that state policies do not hamper individuals in the enjoyment of their individual rights, including the right to respect for their cultural and religious identity and integrity. Developing countries must balance their desire for economic growth against the human priority of ensuring the enjoyment of the basic rights and needs of all members of their societies.

The full realisation of economic, social and cultural rights requires a holistic approach which takes into account the linkages between the enjoyment of these rights and social justice, development and the protection of the environment, as well as peace and disarmament. Far greater attention needs to be given to addressing the root causes of disadvantage. The law provides the framework: what is now required is joint action aimed at establishing just international and national societies in which the fundamental human rights of every man, woman and child are fully protected and realised.

NOTES

1. M. Cranston, *What are Human Rights?* (London: The Bodley Head, 1973), p.65
2. V. Tarzie Vittachi, *Children's Rights: A Question of Obligations* (New York: UNICEF, 1985).

3. E. Vierdag, 'The Legal Nature of the Rights Granted by the International Covenant on Economic, Social and Cultural Rights', Netherlands Yearbook of International Law, Vol. VI, IX, 1978, p.103
4. The Limburg Principles on the Implementation of the International Covenant on Economic, Social and Cultural Rights, submitted as a *Note Verbale* dated 5 December 1986 by the Netherlands to the Commission on Human Rights, UN Doc. E/CN.4/1987/17, 8 January 1987, para. 21.
5. See, for example, UN General Assembly Resolution 32/130.
6. The Limburg Principles, op.cit., para 6.
7. General Comment 6(16) HRC (1982), UN Doc. A/37/4-, p.93.
8. S. Muntemba, *Food Security*, background paper prepared for the World Commission on the Environment and Development, the Brundtland Commission, 1986.
9. The Hunger Project, *Ending Hunger*, 1985, p.7, building on data compiled by UNICEF.
10. UN Secretary-General's Speech, 1 January 1987, inaugurating the International Year of Shelter for the Homeless, quoted in *Rights and Humanity Journal*, Vol. 1, No.2, Summer 1987, p.4.
11. A. Eide, 'Report on the Right to Adequate Food as a Human Right', UN Doc. E/CN.4/Sub.2/1987/23.
12. Gen. Ass. Res. 40/144 of 13 December 1985.
13. Gen. Ass. Res. 41/128.
14. ECOSOC Res. E/1985/17.
15. C. Dias and J. Paul, 'Developing Legal Strategies to Help Combat Rural Impoverishment: Using Human Rights and Legal Resources' in *International Context of Rural Poverty in the Third World* (New York: Council on International and Public Affairs, 1986), p.266.
16. C. Brazier, 'Running for Rights: A New Internationalist Olympics', *New Internationalist*, 1 January 1988, p.6.
17. Gen. Ass. Res. 3281 (XXIX), 12 December 1974.
18. Gen. Ass. Res. 41/128.
19. World Conference on Agrarian Reform and Rural Development, convened by FAO in Rome, 12-20 July 1979: *Food Strategy Guidelines*.
20. C. Kluckman, *Mirror for Man* (1949), p.117 quoted in D. Matas, *The Ideological Foundations of Human Rights Violations*, op. cit., text delivered at Malik Ghulam Jilani Human Rights Convention, Lahore, Pakistan, 25 October 1986.

4 Economic, Social and Cultural Rights: The Development of Governments' Views, 1941–88

Sally Morphet[1]

INTRODUCTION

The subject of economic, social and cultural rights is a complex one though unfortunately oversimplifications in the discussion of it abound. This chapter traces the development and changes in governments' thinking on the subject since President Roosevelt espoused freedom from fear and freedom from want as two of the four main human freedoms in his address to Congress in January 1941. It argues that representatives of the main protagonists in the debate (the First, Second and Third Worlds) can be seen in action as early as the 1940s. It suggests that the differences within each group have often been just as fierce as those between groups, and that each of the groups as well as the individual states within the groups, have been affected both by the debate and subsequently by the existence of the Human Rights Declaration (1948) and two Covenants on Economic, Social and Cultural Rights and Civil and Political Rights (which were opened for signature in 1966 and came into force in 1976). It will also note that all three instruments were designed to have worldwide significance and to cross ideological and cultural barriers. As a result there is a certain ideological neutrality and eclecticism about all three which enabled them to serve as a common focus for numerous states and individuals.[2]

Although this chapter concentrates on governmental views on economic, social and cultural rights, it also attempts to show the ways in which Third-World and even Second-World countries, have accepted civil and political rights in order to show that the simplistic view that both sets of countries are alike in paying no attention (at least theoretically) to civil and political rights does not stand up to scrutiny. It will also touch on the development of Third-World views on the economic duties owed to them by other states seen most recently, some suggest, in the 1987 Declaration on the Right to Development but at its political zenith in the early 1970s, and how this has obscured the other debate. The chapter will also note the main developments on economic, social and cultural rights in the postwar period (not all, of course, the work of governments), and will highlight the common ground in the continuing three-cornered interrelationship between the West, East and the Third World.

The international human rights debate has been carried on at numerous levels and for many reasons, and it has always had a strong political content. It makes sense therefore to suggest, as Philip Alston[3] has done, that the international human rights system can be described as 'a somewhat obfuscatory generalization which artificially collects under one umbrella a wide range of differing conceptions of rights, a cast of actors of immense diversity in terms of motivation and understandings, and an enormous variety of processes'.

The complexities of the debate are also in evidence if one turns to questions of how economic, social and cultural rights can be defined and whether and how they differ from civil and political rights. Everyone agrees that economic, social and cultural rights form part of the Human Rights Declaration: there is less agreement on what they are. One commentator[4] has argued that economic and social rights comprise Article 17 (the right to own property) and Articles 22-7 (the right to social security; the right to work; the right to rest and leisure; the right to an adequate standard of living; the right to education and the right to freely participate in the life of the community) and Article 20 interpreted as the right to form and join trade unions. A recent commentator[5] suggests that Articles 21–24 are economic rights; that social rights are covered by Articles 26 and 27; and that Article 25 covers subsistence rights, particularly the right to food and the right to a standard of living adequate for the health and well-being of oneself and one's family.

The negotiation of the two Covenants, despite the fact that they have certain articles in common, has led many to assume that the two sets of rights are more different than alike. This is arguable. It has, for instance, been suggested that the categories in which rights are presented are not always distinct.[6] One of the principal draftsmen of the Declaration considered that economic and social rights did not belong to an inferior category even though they depended on varying conditions and were too vague to be legally definable.[7] Other rights, such as the right to defend oneself before the law, also depended on varying conditions, while the rights to property and to individual freedom were not always capable of being the subject of a legal action. Economic and social rights could also be the subject of a judicial claim as soon as they had been defined within a country.

THE SECOND WORLD WAR AND THE HUMAN RIGHTS DECLARATION, 1948

It seems unlikely that the Human Rights Declaration would have come into existence without the support of the United States. The Declaration itself is intimately related to Roosevelt's address to Congress in January 1941. In this he looked forward to a world founded on four human freedoms: freedom of speech and expression; freedom of worship; freedom from want; and freedom from fear. The two latter freedoms were reaffirmed in the Atlantic Charter of August 1941 as a statement of Anglo–American goals. The third freedom was elaborated in a further message to Congress in January 1944:

> We have come to a clear realisation of the fact that true individual freedom cannot exist without economic security and independence . . . In our day these economic truths have become self evident. We have accepted, so to speak, a second Bill of Rights under which a new basis of security and prosperity can be established for all regardless of station, race or creed . . . .[8]

This language was mirrored in the second preambular paragraph of the Human Rights Declaration.

The continuing pressure in this area was not primarily due to governmental intervention. As John Humphrey, the first Director of the UN's Division of Human Rights, has pointed out,[9] the 1944 Dumbarton Oaks proposals on the United Nations contain only a general reference to human rights. 'The relatively strong human rights provisions of the Charter were largely, and appropriately, the result of determined lobbying by non-governmental organizations and individuals at the San Francisco conference' which were supported by the United States Secretary of State at the last minute. The main governmental protagonists of an international bill of rights were Cuba, Chile and Panama. Latin Americans were not then regarded as part of the Third World but it is interesting to see their distinctive voice begin to emerge both through the adoption of the 1948 American Declaration on the Rights and Duties of Man (which dealt only with civil and political rights) nine months before the Human Rights Declaration, and through their contribution to the final debates in the Third Committee in 1948. Mr Humphrey notes that it seemed at times that the chief protagonists in the conference room were the Roman Catholics and the Communists, with the latter a poor second.[10]

John Humphrey, who was responsible for the first draft of the Human Rights Declaration in 1947, maintains that the best of the texts from which he worked was the one prepared by the American Law Institute. This had been the text unsuccessfully sponsored by Panama both at San Francisco and later in the General Assembly. It needs to be noted by those who consider the Declaration solely a Western creation that it had been drafted in the United States during the war by a distinguished group 'representing many cultures' including Arabic, British, Canadian, Chinese, French, pre-Nazi German, Italian, Indian, Latin American, Polish, Soviet Russian and Spanish.[11] Humphrey's own support for economic and social rights was a further crucial factor. 'I did not' he writes[12] 'need to be told that the former [civil and political rights] can have no meaning without the latter [economic, social and cultural rights]. It is by no means certain that economic, social and cultural rights would have been included in the final text if I had not included them in mine'.

The French representative, M. Cassin, maintained reference to economic, social and cultural rights in the draft text he submitted to the drafting committee (again not all Western – Australia, Chile, China, France, Lebanon, the Soviet Union, United States, United Kingdom) in June 1947. The most fervent advocate of economic and social rights on the committee was, not surprisingly, the Chilean representative. The draft was subsequently discussed at three sessions of the Commission chaired by Eleanor Roosevelt. She is credited with using 'her influence to win compromises in the form of six articles on economic/ social rights' in the draft but ensuring that these 'were so worded as to present standards, rather than prescribe governmental action' as the Russians had wished.[13] The revised draft went to the General Assembly in 1948. It was referred to the Third Committee, which devoted 81 meetings to the text. However, the final text was very similar to the one that had been prepared by the Commission.

The Declaration was adopted on 10 December 1948 by 48 votes to none with abstentions from Byelorussia, Czechoslovakia, Poland, Saudi Arabia, South Africa, the Soviet Union, the Ukraine and Yugoslavia. Delegates from Honduras and Yemen were absent.

The timing of the adoption of the Human Rights Declaration was crucial. The politicisation brought about by the Cold War subsequently made confrontation rather than partial cooperation the rule. Cold War rhetoric had already been given a boost in Eleanor Roosevelt's speech on the preservation of human freedom at the Sorbonne during the Paris General Assembly of 1948, in which she argued that the abstentions by four communist UN members on the Declaration in the Commission pointed to the 'fundamental difference in the conception of human rights as they exist in these states and in certain other members of the UN'. This has been described as a tactical move to take the conflict with the Soviet Union 'out of context of traditional great power rivalry and put it into the more sublime perspective of a moral struggle between freedom and oppression'.[14]

THE DIVISION OF RIGHTS IN THE DECLARATION INTO TWO COVENANTS, 1949–52

Despite the Cold War, the Human Rights Commission began to focus on the question of putting the Human Rights Declaration into a legal form in 1949. The representatives of Australia and the Soviet Union proposed that the Covenant should include social and economic rights: others opposed this. This question was referred to in the General Assembly in 1950, which after a bitter debate on a Yugoslav amendment by 38 for, seven against and 12 abstentions (Resolution 421 (V)), decided to include them in one Covenant. Subsequently India, France, the United Kingdom, the United States and Uruguay requested the General Assembly to reconsider its decision: and the General Assembly decided in early 1952 (Resolution 543 (VI)) by 27 for, 20 against and three abstentions, that there should be two covenants, one on political and civil rights, and the other on economic, social and cultural rights, which should be opened for signature simultaneously.

This compromise had the advantage of treating both sets of rights equally and recognising the Cold War political realities. It had become increasingly obvious that the US Senate would be unlikely to agree to adhere to international covenants. The Eisenhower administration helped defeat the contentious Bricker amendment in part by announcing in April 1953 that the United States did not intend to become party to any human rights Covenant. John Humphrey[15] has suggested that the General Assembly rationalised its decision, by suggesting civil and political rights could be given effect to immediately, while economic, social and cultural rights were objectives to be achieved progressively. 'The real reason for the decision probably was therefore, that while they favoured the principle of unity, a number of governments were willing to agree to the separation in order to make it possible for certain countries, which were opposed on principle to the international codification of economic and social rights, to ratify at least a covenant on civil and political rights.'

The initiative in the human rights field was now primarily in the hands of the 13-strong Arab/Asian group[16] which had worked together in the context of the Korean war since 1950 and had made a major Third-World contribution to the Covenants by proposing that both should affirm the right of self-determination of peoples during the 1951/52 General Assembly. Their growing interaction with like-minded Latin Americans is illustrated by their attitude to Chile's amendment, which sought to stop the two Covenants from being drafted separately. The close rejection of this by a roll call vote of 29 – 25 – 4 in February 1952 is worth noting. Those voting for (Arab/Asian group italicised) were *Afghanistan*, Argentina, *Burma*, Byelorussia, Chile, Columbia, Cuba, Czechoslovakia, Ecuador, *Egypt*, Ethiopia, Guatemala, Haiti, *Indonesia*, *Iran*, Israel, Mexico, *Pakistan*, Poland, *Saudi Arabia, the Soviet Union, Ukraine, Yemen*, Yugoslavia; those voting against were Australia, Belgium, Bolivia, Brazil, Canada, China, Costa Rica, Denmark, France, Greece, Honduras, Iceland, *India*, *Lebanon*, Liberia, Luxembourg, Netherlands, New Zealand, Nicaragua, Norway, Paraguay, Peru, Sweden, Thailand, Turkey, United Kingdom, United States, Uruguay and Venezuela; those abstaining were the Dominican Republic, Panama, *Philippines* and *Syria*. They were supported, as can be seen, by representatives of the Second World but they were, nevertheless, determined to fight their own battles and they were at odds over the question of international implementation procedures. These procedures were supported by many of the Third-World countries, including the Chairman of the Commission (Malik of Lebanon); they were not supported by the Second World.

WESTERN EUROPE'S CONTINUING ACCEPTANCE OF ECONOMIC, SOCIAL AND CULTURAL RIGHTS IN THE 1950s

The Commission's discussion of the articles on economic, social and cultural rights after the General Assembly decision of 1950 was affected by the attitude of specialised agencies, particularly the ILO, which for its own reasons supported the United States position.[17] The Commission submitted the draft texts to ECOSOC and the General Assembly in 1954 and during 1956–58 the Articles relating to economic and social rights were approved with little major amendment. These negotiations undoubtedly had an effect on the concomitant negotiations then going on to complement the European Convention on Human Rights with a European Social Charter. The list in the Covenant and that in the Social Charter is similar though the Social Charter lists 19 economic and social rights distinguishing between some that are grouped together in the Covenant. The Social Charter was opened for signature in 1961 and came into force in 1965. The First World (apart from the United States) has been particularly consistent about accepting civil and political and economic, social and cultural rights.

REPORTING ON HUMAN RIGHTS FROM ALL THREE WORLDS 1956–58

A new United States initiative was, however, taken by Secretary of State Dulles to compensate for his announcement that the United States would not become a party to the Covenants.[18] The three-pronged initiative sought *inter alia* to ensure that ECOSOC asked member governments to report annually on developments regarding human rights. The initiative bore fruit in 1956 when ECOSOC initiated a system of periodic reporting on progress achieved in human rights. The first series of reports had to cover 1954–56. Governments were asked to provide material on rights enumerated in the Human Rights Declaration (that is, civil and political, and economic, social and cultural rights) and the right of peoples to self-determination. By the end of 1958 41 governments from all three major groups had submitted reports. However self-propagandising in tone, these reports, covering rights of concern to all three worlds, can be said to constitute the beginning of a monitoring process which continues today.

THE BURGEONING THIRD WORLD CONTINUES TO ACCEPT ALL KINDS OF RIGHTS, 1955–63

The non-aligned movement began in 1961, a year after 16 African states had joined the United Nations. Previously all members of the Arab/Asian group plus 11 others who attended the conference (including the Peoples Republic of China) were able to subscribe to the Bandung Declaration of 1955, which not only supported the principle of self-determination as set out in the UN Charter, but also noted the Human Rights Declaration as 'a common standard of mankind'. This commitment was subsequently recognised in the 1960 General Assembly Declaration on Colonialism and the 1963 Declaration on the Elimination of Racial Discrimination. With the exception of South Africa all the countries from the Second World which had abstained in 1948 had now voted for the acceptance of the Declaration.

THE COVENANTS ARE OPENED FOR SIGNATURE 1966

Discussions in the Third Committee in 1962 and 1963 mainly centred on the introductory Articles to the Covenants (namely, the obligation of states to respect the rights enunciated, with particular reference to the question of whether the obligation was of immediate or progressive effect).[19] Little attention was paid to the Covenants in 1964/65 because the Third Committee was primarily concerned with the Convention on the Elimination of all Forms of Racial Discrimination. In 1966 work on the Covenants was completed through the discussion of measures of implementation. The fairly weak provisions for the Covenant on Economic, Social and Cultural Rights were that States Parties would undertake to submit reports on the measures which they had adopted and the progress made in achieving the observance of the rights was recognised in the Covenant. These reports were to be transmitted to ECOSOC for consideration. ECOSOC could then transmit them to the Commission for study and for general recommendations as appropriate. The Covenant also provided for the appropriate participation of the specialised agencies. Both Covenants were adopted unanimously (including the United States), by, in the case of the Economic and Social Rights Covenant, a vote of 105 – 0.

THIRD WORLD INITIATIVES ON THE ECONOMIC RIGHTS AND DUTIES OF STATES 1964–74

The late 1960s it can be argued, was a time of radicalisation in the Third World in part because of problems of economic development, the increasing strength of OPEC, the 1967 Arab–Israel war and the lack of change in Southern Africa. References to the Human Rights Declaration continued to be made in the context of the resolution on South Africa but even more emphasis was laid on the right of economically underdeveloped states to receive help from the international community. As early as 1964 the second Non-Aligned Summit had stressed that economic development was an obligation of the whole international community and that it was 'the duty of all countries to contribute to the rapid evolution of a new and just economic order under which all nations can live without fear or want or despair and rise to their full stature in the Family of Nations' (it can be seen that this bears a strong relationship to Article 28 of the Human Rights Declaration). This concern with economic questions was taken further by the Group of 77 (an alliance of the Latin-American, Asian and African regional groups, many of them non-aligned, at the United Nations) which had been formed in 1963, and played a major role at the first UNCTAD conference which produced the Algiers Charter of Economic Rights of the Third World in October 1967.

The same year the Ukrainian Chairman of the Human Rights Commission had proposed that the Commission should include a new agenda item on the question of the realisation of economic and social rights contained in the Universal Declaration. This was followed by the adoption of a GA resolution in 1968 requesting the UN Secretary-General to prepare a preliminary study of issues related to the implementation of the Declaration and the Covenant on Economic, Social and Cultural Rights. Subsequently the Conference in Tehran, which had been organised to celebrate Human Rights Year (1968) and to examine progress made since the adoption of the Declaration, called on all states to sign and ratify the Economic, Social and Cultural Rights Covenant. It also expressed the view that these rights should receive due and increasing attention in the activities of the UN in view of the increasing importance of realising these rights in the modern world. The Tehran Conference produced a Proclamation which declared that the primary aim of the United Nations as regards human rights was 'the achievement by each individual of the maximum freedom and dignity', and placed this obligation on the state. It then called *inter alia* for help to close the economic gap between developed and developing countries.

The next year (1969) the Commission by 30 – 0 – 1 (United Kingdom) appointed an Iranian Special Rapporteur to submit a comprehensive report on the realisation of economic, social and cultural rights 'taking particular account of the special problems of developing countries in this regard'.[20] These pressures continued. By early 1972 the Group of 77 ensured that the third session of UNCTAD (1972) had agreed to establish a working group to draw up the text of a draft Charter of Economic Rights and Duties of States. The fourth Non-Aligned Conference (Algiers 1973) stated in its Political Declaration that 'international security cannot be achieved if it does not include an economic dimension which guarantees to all countries the right to implement their development programmes free from economic aggression and any other form of pressure'. It also spoke of 'the right of states to recover their natural resources and develop them for the benefit of their peoples within the framework of a freely chosen development programme'. This pressure, combined with the raising of oil prices, led to the convening of the sixth special session of the General Assembly in 1974 at the request of President Boumedienne.

During this period the Group of 77 and the non-aligned countries worked extremely closely together. The Group of 77 tabled two documents for the session: a draft Declaration on the Establishment of a New International Economic Order; and a draft Programme of Action. The eventual documents were adopted by consensus though a number of Western states had particular reservations on the Programme of Action. This referred to the proposed Charter of Economic Rights and Duties of States as of vital importance. It 'shall constitute an effective instrument towards the establishment of a new system of international economic relations based on equity, and interdependence of the interests of developed and developing countries'. The Charter was adopted on 12 December 1974 by 120 – 6 (Belgium, Denmark, Germany (Federal Republic), Luxembourg, United Kingdom, United States), with ten abstentions (Austria, Canada, France, Ireland, Italy, Israel, Japan, Netherlands, Norway and Spain). Chapter 1 of the Charter gives a list of principles which should govern economic as well as political and other relations among states. These 15 principles include both (g) equal rights and self-determination of peoples and (k) respect for human rights and fundamental freedoms. Chapter II on Economic Rights and Duties of States provided *inter alia* for the right of every state to choose its economic system (Article 1), and for the right to permanent sovereignty over wealth, natural resources and economic activities (Article 2).

This Charter has been discussed in terms of another Bill of Rights by James Fawcett.[21] He states that in places it reads like an extension of human rights to states, and suggests that 'the notion of their each having economic rights and duties as elaborated in it, reflects . . . first the widely held conviction that the LDCs (less developed countries) have as such inherent rights, at present denied them in full or in part to equal or equitable treatment in the fields of trade, payments aid and development; second, the assumption that it is possible by intergovernmental agreement and collaboration to manage international economic relations both efficiently and fairly, and even to establish a 'new international economic order''. This campaign, spearheaded by Algeria, overlaid but did not conflict with the previous acceptance by many Third-World countries of the rights set out in both Covenants. By the end of 1976, the year in which both Covenants came into force, both had been ratified or acceded to by seven First-World countries, nine Second-World countries and 23 Third-World countries.

A RENEWED UNITED STATES INTEREST IN HUMAN RIGHTS, 1973–81

It was the Congress that sparked off a renewed United States interest in civil and political rights in the 1970s because certain members considered that aspects of US policy in, for instance, Vietnam and Latin America had contributed to human rights violations. Democratic Congressman Fraser was Chairman of the Sub-Committee on International Organizations and Movements (later renamed the Sub-Committee on Human Rights and International Organizations) which adopted a report in 1974 called *Human Rights in the World Community: A Call for US Leadership*. This contained 29 recommendations regarding human rights as a factor in US foreign policy as well as ways and means of protecting human rights through governments and international organisations.[22] Congress also tried to influence the protection of civil and political rights by amending legislation linking aid and human rights.

Economic, social and cultural rights could not easily be ignored. The United States participated in the Conference on Security and Cooperation in Europe (July 1973 – August 1975) with European members of the First, Second and Third Worlds. Although not a Treaty, the participating states declared their determination to respect and put into practice a number of principles of primary significance guiding their mutual relations. These include Principle VII, *Respect of Human Rights and Fundamental Freedoms*, including the freedom of thought, conscience, religion or belief (which bore a close relationship to principle (k) of the Charter on Economic Rights and Duties of States) under which they *inter alia* declared their determination to promote and encourage the effective exercise of civil, political, economic, social, cultural and other rights and freedoms, all of which derive from the inherent dignity of the human person and are essential for his/her free and full development.

The commitment of both superpowers to both Covenants (the Soviet Union had ratified both in 1973) came nearer after President Carter came into office in January 1977. Carter took the question of economic and social rights more seriously than Congress had done in the early 1970s. His Secretary of State, Cyrus Vance, defined human rights in May 1977 as meaning the right to be free from governmental violation of the integrity of the person; the right to the fulfilment of such vital needs as food, shelter, health care and education, and the right to enjoy civil liberties. The first *Country Reports on Human Rights Practices* issued by the Carter administration contained a section relating to the fulfilment of such vital needs as food, shelter, health care and education.[23] In October 1977 President Carter signed both Covenants.

THE COMING INTO FORCE OF BOTH COVENANTS AND DISCUSSION OF THEIR IMPLEMENTATION, 1976–88

With the coming into force of the two Covenants in early 1976 the focus of discussion began to turn to the question of their implementation. The continuing concern for both rights set out in both Covenants (some of which are, of course, identical) can be seen by the fact that by 1987 only four states (Greece, Honduras, Solomon Islands and Uganda) were party to only one Covenant, that on economic, social and cultural rights, while the other 86 were parties to both Covenants. In 1977 the continuing concern, particularly of the Third World, with the realisation of economic, social and cultural rights, was demonstrated by the Senegalese insertion of a paragraph in a resolution dealing with this issue at the Human Rights Commission. The insertion asked the Secretary-General to undertake a study on the international dimension of the right to development. This concern was followed up at the General Assembly by Resolution 32/130, which was passed by 123 – 0 – 15 (Austria, Belgium, Chad, France, German Federal Republic, Ireland, Israel, Italy, Ivory Coast, Luxembourg, Netherlands, Paraguay, Spain, United Kingdom, United States).

This ragbag resolution had been the subject of much controversy.[24] It decided that the approach to future work on human rights within the United Nations system should take eight concepts into account. The first two were concerned with the relationship between civil and political and economic, social and cultural rights. 1(a) asserted that all human rights were indivisible and interdependent,[25] and that equal attention should be given to the implementation, promotion and protection of both civil and political, and economic, social and cultural rights. 1(b) noted that the full realisation of civil and political rights without the enjoyment of economic, social and cultural rights was impossible. Lasting progress depended on sound and effective national and international policies. 1(d) stressed the relationship between collective and individual rights. Human rights questions should be examined globally, taking into account both the overall context of the various societies in which they present themselves as well as the need for the promotion of the full dignity of the human person and the development and well-being of the society. 1(e) stated that priority should also be given to the realisation of the New International Economic Order (NIEO).

The concern expressed about aspects of GA Resolution 32/30 had to some extent been allayed by the time the Declaration on the Right to Development, which had been influenced by two successive French rapporteurs, was passed by the General Assembly in 1986 by 146-1 (United States), with eight abstentions (Denmark, Finland, Federal Republic of Germany, Iceland, Israel, Japan, Sweden, United Kingdom). In this formulation the first part of Article 1 noted that the right to development was an inalienable human right by virtue of which every human person and all peoples were entitled to participate in, contribute to and enjoy economic, social, cultural and political development, in which all human rights and freedoms could be fully realised.

Meanwhile a determined and reasonably successful effort has been made to ensure that the implementation machinery for the Covenant on Economic, Social and Cultural Rights became more like that of the Human Rights Committee for the Covenant on Civil and Political Rights. This Committee (composed of independent experts) can examine states reports, consider inter-state complaints and express views on complaints submitted by individuals from the few states that have so far ratified or acceded to the Optional Protocol. They have also begun to make general observations on Articles of the Covenant. From 1979 to 1986 the reports due under the Covenant on Economic, Social and Cultural Rights were examined by a Sessional Working Group of ECOSOC which met annually for three weeks. This proved inadequate and in 1985 the Council decided to establish a new Committee composed of 18 experts elected in their personal capacity on the basis of an equitable geographical distribution. The first session took place in March 1987. In this session 'Eastern European expert members revealed a strong and unequivocal resistance to the adoption of any procedural innovations which would make the Committee more effective and more relevant to the problems of the real world'.[26] This attitude reflected that taken by the Second World in the discussion on implementation in the early 1950s. Despite this, Second World states were participating with others in the deliberations of this Committee and even more unexpectedly those of the Human Rights Committee. And even more openness prevailed at the 1988 Session when the former Soviet expert on the Committee resigned while other experts took 'a significantly more open and progressive approach'.[27]

CURRENT GOVERNMENTAL ATTITUDES TO ECONOMIC, SOCIAL AND CULTURAL RIGHTS

The United States

Under President Reagan human rights continued to play an important part in US foreign policy, but attention was very much focused on the shortcomings of Second World countries. This led *inter alia* to less emphasis being placed on economic, social and cultural rights. The US State Department 1981 *Country Reports* stated that economic and social rights were excluded because this idea 'is easily abused by repressive governments which claim that they promote human rights even though they deny their citizens the basic rights to the integrity of the person, as well as civil and political rights. This justification for repression has in fact been extensively used. No category of rights should be allowed to become an excuse for the denial of other rights. For this reason, the term economic and social rights, is for the most part not used in this year's Reports'.[28]

The format of these reports has been modified over the years, though in the view of the UK independent expert on the Human Rights Committee they need to be treated with a certain reserve.[29] The President of the International League of Human Rights stated in his evidence to Congress in 1987 that they considered the reports had become more comprehensive and more candid and objective than in the first years of the Reagan Administration. They are now focused on discrimination, an aspect of economic and social rights heretofore ignored. The Director of the Lawyers Committee for Human Rights, however, stated that 'The international human rights laws developed in the last forty years are explicit in considering economic, social and cultural rights as well as civil and political rights. While conceptions of these rights may differ, it weakens the reporting process to neglect any reference to these matters'.[30] The United States remains relatively unengaged on this question.

The Soviet and East European View

The old political dimension of the human rights discussion is apparent in a 1987 article by V. Chkhikvadze, a corresponding member of the USSR Academy of Science. He states:

> The significance of the human rights covenants is hard to overestimate. These are practically the first comprehensive international legal acts in world history imposing on the states which have ratified them obligations to ensure the proclaimed rights and freedoms, in the first place, the right to life. Human life and opportunities for all-round development of the individual represent the highest value. The historic documents adopted twenty years ago envisage the creation of material and spiritual conditions that ensure life with dignity for every individual and for all nations.[31]

The current human rights debate in the Soviet Union has been given new impetus and direction under President Gorbachev. More convergence between the First and Second Worlds is now noticeable as economic decision-making in the East becomes more market-oriented and as Soviet law has been developed to enforce the justiciability of economic and social rights.[32]

The European Community

The European Community Foreign Ministers in their Declaration on Human Rights issued under the British Presidency in July 1986 remain consistent about the interrelationship between civil and political and economic and social rights. They note:

> The Twelve deplore the fact that countless people around the world suffer hunger, disease and lack of opportunity, thus being denied the enjoyment of the most basic economic and social rights. The promotion of economic, social and cultural rights as well as of civil and political rights is of paramount importance for the full realisation of human dignity and for the attainment of legitimate aspirations of every individual. Neither lack of social and economic development, nor any persuasion of ideology may serve as a justification for the denial of civil and political rights. The Foreign Ministers affirm that in the development of their relations with non-member states as well as in the administration of aid the European Community and its Member States will continue to promote fundamental rights so that individuals and peoples will actually enjoy to the full their economic, social and cultural rights and their civil and political rights.

The Third World

Third World countries (57 of which had become parties to both Covenants by September 1987) are on the whole united in their attitude to economic and social rights, including the right to development interpreted as a personal and a group right. But this does not mean that they attach no importance to civil and political rights. Many affirm their indivisibility and interdependence, and they have often in the 1980s worked with Western states on the civil and political rights as well as economic, social and cultural rights. As one commentator noted, 'a core coalition of states drawn from the industrialized democracies and from the truly non-aligned Third World have repeatedly acted together to maintain the United Nations human rights regime and to try to embarrass states that violate its rules'.[33]

CONCLUSION

All the Three Worlds discussed over this period have demonstrated their acceptance of the civil, political, economic, social and cultural rights package through acceptance of the Human Rights Declaration and over 50 per cent of all states have now adhered to both Covenants. This important consensus has been obscured by inevitable politicisation and the separate but linked debate about the rights and duties of states at both the international and regional level which was particularly prominent in the 1970s and which concentrated (though not exclusively) on the subject of economic rights. What these commitments mean in practice is not the subject of this chapter, but is explored in related work in this volume.

NOTES

1. The opinions expressed are the author's own and do not necessarily represent those of the Foreign and Commonwealth Office.
2. P. Alston and G. Quinn, 'The Nature and Scope of State Parties' Obligations under the International Covenant on Economic, Social and Cultural Rights', *Human Rights Quarterly*, No.9, 1987, pp.160, 221.
3. P. Alston, 'The Nature of International Human Rights Discourse: The Case of the "New" Human Rights', Paper presented at Oxford University, May 1987, p.7.
4. J. R. Green, *The United Nations and Human Rights*, (Washington DC: The Brookings Institution, 1956), pp.30-2.
5. J. Donnelly, 'International human rights: a regime analysis', *International Organization*, Summer 1986, pp.606-7.
6. C.J. Friedrich, 'Rights, Liberties and Freedoms; A Reappraisal', *American Political Science Review*, 1963, pp.841-5.
7. R. Cassin, 'Twenty Years after the Universal declaration', *Journal of the International Commission of Jurists* – part one – Special Issue 1968, pp.11-12.
8. J.F. Green, op. cit., p.14.
9. J.P. Humphrey, *Human Rights and the United Nations: a great*

adventure (Dobbs Ferry, New York: Transnational Publishers Inc., 1984), pp.12-13.
10. Humphrey, op. cit., p.32.
11. American Law Institute Committee, Statement of Essential Human Rights, *The Annals of the American Academy of Political and Social Science*, January 1946, p.18.
12. Humphrey, op cit., p.34.
13. A.G. Mower, *The United States, The United Nations, and Human Rights, The Eleanor Roosevelt and Jimmy Carter Eras* (Westport, Conn: Greenwood Press, 1979), p.55.
14. Mower, op. cit., p.34.
15. J.P. Humphrey, *The United Nations and Human Rights*, pamphlet, Canadian Institute of International Affairs, 1963, p.10.
16. Humphrey, 1984, op. cit., p.159.
17. P. Alson, 'The United Nations' Specialized Agencies and Implementation of the International Covenant on Economic, Social and Cultural Rights', *Columbia Journal of Transnational Law*, Vol. 18, No.1, 1979, pp.79-118.
18. Humphrey, 1984, op. cit., p.176.
19. P.Alston and G. Quinn, op. cit.
20. The United Kingdom emphasised the UK's concern to promote economic, social and cultural rights, but drew attention to the work already being done by the specialised agencies, regional economic commissions and UNCTAD. It considered that the study should be undertaken by the Secretary-General.
21. J.E.S. Fawcett, 'UNCTAD IV: Another Bill of Rights', *World Today*, April 1976.
22. D.D. Newson (ed.), *The Diplomacy of Human Rights*, (Washington DC: Georgetown University Press, 1986), pp.14-19.
23. Op. cit, Mower, pp.89-91.
24. J. Donnelly, 'Recent Trends in UN Human Rights Activity: Description and polemic', *International Organization*, Winter 1981; P. Alston, 'The alleged demise of political human rights at the UN: a reply to Donnelly'; J. Donnelly, 'The human rights priorities of the UN: a rejoinder to Alston', *International Organization*, Summer 1983.
25. GA Resolution 421 V had stated that 'the enjoyment of civic and political freedoms and of economic, social and cultural rights are interconnected and interdependent'.
26. P. Alston and B. Simma, 'Report on First Session of the United Nations Committee on Economic, Social and Cultural Rights, *American Journal of International Law*, vol. 81, No.3, 1987.
27. P. Alston and B. Simma, 'Second Session of the UN Committee on Economic, Social and Cultural Rights', *AJIL*, Vol. 82, No.3, 1988.
28. D.P. Forsythe, 'Socioeconomic Human Rights: The United Nations, The United States, and Beyond', *Human Rights Quarterly*, 1982, p.436.
29. Ms R. Higgins, QC, 'Human Rights and Human Policy', *Colloquy: Democracy and Human Rights* (Thessaloniki: Council of Europe, 1987), p.13.

30. Hearing before the subcommittee on Human Rights and International Organizations of the Committee on Foreign Affairs, 19 February 1987, p.98; p.132.
31. V. Chkhikvadze, 'Covenants on Human Rights: Their Historical Significance', *International Affairs*, January 1987, p.55.
32. Alston and Simma, on. cit., *AJIL* Vol. 82, No. 3, 1988, p.613.
33. D.P. Forsythe, 'The United Nations and Human Rights 1945 – 1985', *Political Science Quarterly*, Summer 1985, pp.268-9.

5 Justiciability Re-examined

Michael K. Addo[1]

INTRODUCTION

Numerous attempts have been made to address the question of whether economic, social and cultural rights (ESCRs) are justiciable.[2] Unfortunately, however, none of the existing analyses of the subject are investigated outside the broader context of comparing such rights with civil and political rights (CPRs). Thus the shortcomings inherent in such an approach inevitably affect the reliability of the conclusions on justiciability.

Furthermore, the overwhelmingly close identification of ESCRs issues with matters of policy has restrained, perhaps unduly, the analyses of their justiciability, for there is a commonly-held view that matters of policy are not entirely suitable candidates for judicial or other litigation.[3] There may be an element of truth in such a view but only in so far as it arises in a limited context. After all there is a sense in which all human rights' issues including CPRs are matters of policy; and to assume that for that reason alone they cease to be justiciable is difficult to sustain.

Despite the difficult theoretical and practical questions raised by the protection of human rights in general and by the ESCRs in particular, the view that economic, social and cultural rights are not justiciable seems sufficiently widespread to have contributed to the existing timid and compromising attitudes[4] to those rights. The present chapter will be devoted to a re-examination of the justiciability of ESCRs. Although a different approach will be proposed, this will be done within the context of the shortcomings of the existing analyses of the subject.

THE EXISTING APPROACHES TO JUSTICIABILITY

Existing conclusions on the justiciability of ESCRs may be summarised as generally unfavourable, denied in as far as most of the analysts have denied the justiciability of such rights. These conclusions are based on broad theoretical approaches, some of which are only partially correctly applied or evidently incorrect. Two of these main theoretical bases of the conclusions which run through most if not all the existing analyses are:

(1) The nature of the meaning attributed to the concept of justiciability as applied in the context of ESCRs.
(2) The subsumption of the subject of the justiciability of ESCRs under the broader analysis of ESCRs *vis-à-vis* CPRs.

In both cases, there are obvious errors concerning the conclusions that have been made and are thus deserving of re-examination.

The Meaning of Justiciability as a Concept

The notion of justiciability connotes more than a mere descriptive term of art. Indeed, it embodies an essential and indispensable purpose dimension. It is thus distinguishable from similar terms such as enforceability. In addition the application of justiciability may differ in different contexts and may necessarily assume a variety of formal characteristics. The primary aim and purpose of justiciability, however, remains essentially unchanged in its different forms and fora. These important characteristics of the concept of justiciability are either ignored and/or confused in its application to ESCRs.

The confusion about the nature of the justiciability of ESCRs is very obvious in its correct synonymous usage with enforceability of those rights. The Dutch jurist, E.W. Vierdag, for instance, has argued that:

> It is submitted that in the practice of international law the enforceability of a right appears to be considered an essential element in it. In this connection, saying a right is 'enforceable' is intended to mean that an authority of the state (or, for that matter, an international authority) is competent to receive complaints about violations of the right by anyone – executive state organ, official or private person – and to give redress by cancelling or rectifying the violating act or regulation, or by awarding compensation for damage, or both. If the authority in question is a court of law, the term 'justiciable' may be preferred.[5]

There is no denying the relationship that exists between the two terms, but as juridical concepts, they have different effects and are accomplished by different means.

Enforcement of human rights deals with the execution of the legal regime created by human rights instruments. This is usually done by a state body (the government) or its agents. The central theme of the enforceability of human rights is the identification of the entitlements and duties created by the legal regime which have to be maintained and executed. There is normally a degree of subjectivity involved in enforceability to the extent that the exact dimension of the legal regime to be put into effect leaves discretion to the person or body undertaking the execution. Justiciability, on the other hand, has a direct derivation from the administration of justice. As justice in its various forms is the goal of justiciability, the mechanism of review is standard to it; which presupposes that non-compliance with the terms of the legal regime will require some form of redress. Justiciability ideally therefore calls on the role of a person or body with no interest in the controversy giving rise to the review. There is, however, a relationship between justiciability and enforceability in as far as the former is a direct follow-up to the latter. Justiciability is a juridical mechanism triggered off by the inadequacies in the enforceability or execution of human rights.

In domestic law, the enforcement of any legal regime, including that of human rights, is carried out by the executive branch of government. A human rights regime which bestows rights and guarantees the interests of people and bodies other than the government is likely to raise elements of controversy in the process of its execution. State authorities may inappropriately perceive the terms of their executory powers and hence this power of enforcement is subject to review by an independent judiciary. The role of the judicial process in domestic law justiciability is at this stage irreplaceable. In domestic law, effective justiciability is supported by varying degrees of sanctionary measures. These range from fines to terms of imprisonment. In some cases, the determination of a violation of rights is followed by a call for rectification which may include the restoration of interests and the payment of compensation to the victim. The judicial concepts of enforceability and justiciability in domestic law influence their application in international law. The aims of the two concepts are similar in international law but their contents are different. In the field of international human rights law, for instance, the enforcement and execution of human rights which is a matter for a domestic forum is in the domain of contracting parties. States are expected as part of the enforceability process to respect and ensure (the respect of) rights in human rights treaties. This process includes all the aspects that have been identified above in domestic law as constituting enforceability and justiciability, including the decisions of the domestic courts. This underlies the need in international human rights law to exhaust domestic remedies.

The justiciability of international human rights law is usually undertaken by bodies which resemble, in varying degrees, the domestic court system. It needs emphasising that despite the influence of domestic law conceptions of justiciability, international review bodies need not be courts to carry out their duties effectively as some writers have suggested.[6] That is to say, judicialism, although important to justiciability in domestic law, is not always necessary in the international law forum. In practice, the restriction of justiciability to a court in international law would confront us with the interesting scenario of looking to the International Court of Justice for effective justiciability. In this case, considering that the Statute of the ICJ restricts access to states only,[7] it would be almost futile to seek the redress of violations of all human rights including civil and political rights. This is because, for there to be an effective protection of all human rights, there is an absurd yet implicit situation in which a state acts both as an applicant and a defendant before the court when it violates the rights of its own citizens. The only possible justiciability of rights before the International Court of Justice exists in the form of actions on behalf of the citizens of a particular state against another state. This form of justiciability alone does not constitute full and effective protection of human rights.

The bodies responsible for ensuring compliance with human rights obligations in international law by necessity differ from those in domestic law:

(a) The parties seeking justiciability may differ from those in the domestic forum;
(b) The decisions of international review bodies are not binding as in the domestic law sense;
(c) Whereas effective justiciability in domestic law relies on a sanctionary system this is not always the case in international law. There is a great degree of reliance on good faith, and in the few cases where some form of sanctions are evident, they may be indirect and subtle.

Nevertheless, justiciability in international human rights law has a number of similarities with that conception in domestic law:

(a) They both are review mechanisms to ensure state compliance with its obligations;
(b) The eventual beneficiary in either fora, whether directly or indirectly, is the individual.

The application of justiciability domestically has enormous analogous relevance to justiciability in an international form. The closer international justiciability can get to the domestic law model the better if for no other reason than that the domestic law model manifested in judicialism has been tried over a long period of time. However, an independent conception of justiciability in international human rights law which does not completely align with the domestic law model should not be ignored if it addresses the relevant issues of review and justice in a more effective way.

Adversarial and Inquisitorial Justiciability

A fuller understanding of justiciability needs to address the question of procedure. In domestic law, court procedure for the review of alleged violation of rights does not differ from that already laid down for other cases. In most jurisdictions, this involves the filing of a complaint by the victim followed by attempts to prove the particulars of the violation. The violator of the rights is then called upon to contest the complainant's allegations. On the basis of the available evidence, the domestic court reaches a conclusion and makes a determination as to whether there has been a violation or not and if so what follow-up orders are appropriate. This form of review mechanism is individual-oriented and rights-based and constitutes *adversarial justiciability*. Here again, in the desire to transplant domestic legal regimes into international law, adversarial justiciability has characterised most international human rights procedures.[8] This procedural form of justiciability is mainly used in international human rights instruments dealing with civil and political rights. Vierdag and others have concluded that since justiciability is properly restricted to a court mechanism, then the use of adversarial justiciability for civil and political rights in international human rights law entails the conclusion that only civil and political rights are justiciable.[9]

The limitation of justiciability in the international form to civil and political rights alone is, however, a grave error. It is an error attributable to the restrictive understanding of justiciability as it ignores and sacrifices the substantive aspects of review and the attainment of justice which underlie justiciability. It cannot be denied that adversarial justiciability exists in both domestic law and international law, and that that form of justiciability is important. However, the restriction of justiciability to the adversarial procedure may prove unworkable, for example, in international human rights treaties which do not have an adversarial justiciability procedure. Such treaties include the United Nations Covenant on Economic, Social and Cultural Rights[10] and the European Social Charter.[11] It would seem inconceivable, however, that the critics desire to restrict economic, social and cultural rights solely to these instruments. It would therefore be misleading to imply that the absence of adversarial justiciability under these particular instruments means their absence and inapplicability in other instruments or indeed as evidence of the non-justiciability of all economic, social and cultural rights.

In addition, because of the absence in international law of the types of judicial authority that exist in domestic law, other forms of justiciability which do exist and are equally effective need to be recognised and used. *Inquisitorial justiciability*, which involves the institution of an enquiry mechanism as undertaken by bodies such as the Human Rights Committee when it examines state reports is equally important. The discussion of state reports is aimed *inter alia* at seeking to identify the extent to which contracting parties have complied with their human rights undertakings. In cases where states fall short of their undertakings, they are accordingly informed and in some cases promises are sought and given as to rectification. It is clear from this process that inquisitorial justiciability is obligation-based (in contradistinction to rights-based)[12] and is a parallel and supplementary mechanism for the justiciability of human rights in international law. It is a redress or review mechanism not directly aimed at individual violations of rights, but generally benefits all those whose rights are, or are likely to be, adversely affected. Indeed, inquisitorial justiciability, unlike adversarial justiciability, has a preventive ring to its application. Instead of securing redress after the violation of the right, inquisitorial justiciability also seeks to prevent violation by ensuring state compliance with human rights obligations. Justiciability can be said to be achieved in this case where the benefit is to more than one individual and where the violation is addressed on behalf of beneficiaries instead of by them.

The modes of effectively ensuring the enforcement of international human rights obligations may fall short or indeed lack, in procedural terms, certain aspects common to domestic law. This, however, should not be seen as a compromise on justiciability. The significant aspect of justiciability in international law is the attainment of an effective protection of human rights. Individual redress, although important and indeed of the essence of effective protection of human rights, should not be seen as necessarily determinative. This is especially so in international human rights law where the individual's access to the international review body is not always automatic (as in domestic law) but dependent on the approval of the state party.[13] In the same vein, whereas the prevention of violation of rights may not be considered a significant part of justiciability in domestic law, in international humans rights law (which aims to regulate sovereign state behaviour), a mechanism designed to prevent human rights violations can in certain circumstances be considered the essential part of a process of justiciability.

The significance of inquisitorial justiciability in international human rights law (civil and political as well as economic, social and cultural rights) is compelling. Aimed at preventing violations, it is a better mode of safeguarding some human rights the violation of which may fully be determined after the occurrence of the action. Examples of these include the right to life and the prohibition of torture. In ordinary terms, the determination of a violation and the provision of some form of compensation are the redresses available. The restitution of life is impossible and hence the right must be safeguarded by prevention. Further, adversarial justiciability – by which state action is directly contested – may not be the best action in international law where state power to determine individual access to international tribunals is virtually unlimited. In such circumstances, inquisitorial justiciability offers a better mode of safeguarding human rights.

The Comparison of ESCRs and CPRs Justiciability

A considerable amount of the existing conclusions on the non-justiciability of ESCRs are based on an integrative comparison with CPRs. This is done by using the provisions and procedures in existing international instruments on the subject. Such an analysis is not necessarily an erroneous one if the constraints of such a limited approach are recognised and admitted.

In broad terms, there is a general conclusion that ESCRs as identified in various treaties are non-justiciable.[14] These conclusions are based on a strict separation of the issues raised by the two categories of rights. This is an obvious practical shortcoming in view of the evident overlap of the provisions of different treaties, and the consequent overlapping of issues. A number of examples illustrate the artificiality of the separation. In the United Nations, the right to education is identified as an ESCR[15] and thus not justiciable. The same right is protected in Protocol I and the European Convention of Human Rights and Fundamental Freedoms[16] and thus has been the subject of litigation[17] before the European Commission and Court of Human Rights, and thus by implication, domestic judicial litigation. These procedures made education a justiciable right. The right to self determination,[18] the freedom to form and join trade unions[19] and protection for the family and children[20] are further instances of overlapping treaty provisions. The result of these overlaps make it absurd to insist that depending on the treaty in which they appear, the issues they raise may or may not be justiciable.

A distinction usually identified between civil and political rights and economic, social and cultural rights relates to the preciseness of the definition of the rights in the international instruments. It is sometimes argued that civil and political rights, unlike economic, social and cultural rights, are capable of, and indeed have been the subject of, precise definition, and are thus easily justiciable.[21] It is usually unclear from the writings of these advocates, which concept of justiciability (adversarial or inquisitorial or any other) is being referred to. The implication in these writings is that the reference is to adversarial justiciability. There is little or no reference to inquisitorial justiciability such as the discussion of state reports, and in the process an important aspect of the justiciability of economic, social and cultural rights is lost sight of.

The question of the precision of definitions has further implications. It is implicit in much of these analyses that the difference lies not so much in an identifiable, precise definition but in the absence of an exhaustive tabulation of the prescriptions and prohibitions required by the terms of the economic, social and cultural rights treaty instruments. There is some confirmation of this in a number of the international human rights instruments. For example, while Article 9 of the International Covenant on Economic, Social and

Cultural Rights[22] provides only that states recognise the right to social security, the provision on equality before the law in Article 14 of the International Covenant on Civil and Political Rights[23] tabulates a detailed list of its constituent elements.[24] A detailed tabulation of the constituent elements of human rights eases the work of the bodies responsible for their justiciability, but the problem remains that there are varying degrees of elaboration for different rights. In fact, an attempt to standardise the content of all human rights provisions is impossible due to the degree of relativism that appears in the application of different rights. This does not invalidate the argument, however. The bearing of detailed elaboration on justiciability is no more than incidental and should not be seen as determinative.

In addition, it is incorrect to say, as would seem to be implied from the above analysis, that all civil and political rights are elaborated in detail whereas economic, social and cultural rights are not. Article 11[25] and Article 16[26] of the International Covenant on Civil and Political rights make only provisions for the rights they guarantee without further elaboration, whereas provisions in Article 8,[27] Article 10[28] and Article 13[29] of the International Covenant on Economic, Social and Cultural Rights have relatively detailed elaboration of their constituent elements. It would then be logical to claim that some, rather than all civil and political rights are justiciable (as is now asserted), and that the same is true for economic, social and cultural rights. The error in associating justiciability solely with full elaboration of the constituent elements of human rights is even clearer in the context of the European Social Charter. The Charter is the European equivalent of the International Covenant on Economic, Social and Cultural Rights in the United Nations. Its provisions in Part II,[30] including that on social security,[31] have detailed elaboration of their constituent elements, making the work of interpretation much easier. It would be ludicrous to assert, as do advocates who determinatively correlate elaboration with justiciability, that the rights in the European Social Charter in general, and the right to social security in particular, are in some way justiciable while similar rights in instruments such as the International Covenant on Economic, Social and Cultural Rights are not.

Another set of alleged differences between the two groups of human rights which affects their justiciability relates to the nature of state obligations. It has been argued that state obligations arising from civil and political rights require abstention on the part of states to ensure full compliance, while the obligations arising from economic, social and cultural rights require positive acts and above all the commitment of financial resources.[32] These apparent differences in state undertakings underlie the belief that civil and political rights involve immediate obligations whereas economic, social and cultural rights which require policy action have relativism and aspirationalism built into them. A number of authors suggest that this distinction makes it easier to subject civil and political rights to justiciability but not economic, social and cultural rights. There is some merit in this argument to the extent that it eases the work of determining human rights violations from the angle of negative obligations (that is, forbearance or restraint). However, the association of negative obligations with civil and political rights and positive obligations with economic, social and cultural rights is superficial and hence its use to determine justiciability is equally superficial. The traditional fair trial provision of the International Covenant on Civil and Political Rights,[33] for instance, requires States Parties to provide special services to protect that right fully. These include, in appropriate cases, the provision of interpreters and sometimes defence counsels. Civil and political rights do have positive dimensions, as Alston aptly points out:

> In today's world, ensuring the free exercise of civil and political rights will often involve significant state intervention and the incurring of considerable public expenditure in order to establish a system of courts, to train police and other public officials, and to establish a system of safeguards against potential abuse of rights by state officials themselves.[34]

Positive and negative obligations thus do cut across both civil and political rights and economic, social and cultural rights. This points to the need for immediate action or immediate inaction on the part of states in relation to both categories of rights,[35] and hence the opportunity for the justiciability of both sets of rights.

A final distinction of civil and political rights from economic, social and cultural rights, which affects their justiciability, is the determination of a violation and its redress. The relevance of this distinction for justiciability lies in the relationship between the precise determination of violation of rights and the provision of remedies as being primarily the theme of justiciability. A human rights regime which does not address the issue of violation of the rights it creates (especially in individual terms) is not justiciable.[36] Economic, social and cultural rights have been judged as not providing this link between the determination of violation and its remedy. This line of reasoning is incorrect unless the concept of violation and redress of rights is seen principally and exclusively from the individual libertarian point of view. From this standpoint, it may be possible to view justiciability in its adversarial mode, as is reflected in civil and political rights. Although the violations of economic, social and cultural rights may have evident implications for individuals, it is usually perceived as the violation of the rights of groups (or people). But violating the rights of more than one individual at a time does not make economic, social and cultural rights any less subject to review and redress. In ordinary domestic law adversarial justiciability is possible in the form of group actions. In international human rights law, however, not only is justiciability not confined to adversarial forms, but in such instruments as the International Covenant on Civil and Political Rights, European Social Charter, and the International Covenant on Economic, Social and Cultural Rights, it may also be inquisitorial. Inquisitorial justiciability aims to cover violations involving more than one individual and it is worth emphasising that this mode does achieve the primary objectives of justiciability, including the identification of non-compliance by states of individual violations of human rights.

It is necessary to stress that there are also general legal principles applicable to treaty interpretation which can be used to support the justiciability of economic, social and cultural rights. First, those international treaties that embody economic, social and cultural rights, such as the International Covenant on Economic, Social and Cultural Rights and the European Social Charter, are the subject of treaty obligations and as such should be interpreted in good faith.[37] The concept of good faith in treaty interpretation requires among other things a recognition of the treaty provisions to give them their intended purpose. In other words, the interpretation of a treaty to defeat the aims and purposes of its undertaking is contrary to the concept of good faith.

The economic, social and cultural rights treaties are no exception to this rule of interpretation. Human rights treaties aim to remedy the mischief of violation of human rights and/or afford judicial support to existing rights. The ordinary interpretation of these treaties based on good faith should be aimed at achieving these purposes. The question that arises is whether justiciability is essential to the attainment of all human rights *per se* or more specifically to the aims of the economic, social and cultural rights treaties.

Justiciability as a review mechanism for the attainment of a just result, in this case the respect and protection of human rights, would seem essential to the attainment of all human rights. This conclusion, however, is not a recommendation of a particular form of justiciability. That choice is dependent on finding the most appropriate means of achieving the review without jeopardising the aims and purposes; in this case that relates to the protection of rights in a treaty. Without justiciability of human rights, there remains only a collection of rights to be enforced in any manner thought fit by the contracting parties. The absence of review of the decisions of contracting parties presupposes the finality of their decisions and provides little incentive to comply with the full terms of treaty provisions. Other forms of motivation in international law, such as reciprocity, are of rare application in human rights situations involving a state and its own citizens[38] and hence there is the need for other procedures, such as independent review.

The general interpretation of the Economic, Social and Cultural Rights Covenant is reflected to a respectable degree in state practice, albeit not in standardised and consistent forms. Most states have undertaken to make constitutional provisions for economic, social and cultural rights. Some of these constitutional provisions are stated in the non-justiciable terms of directive principles of state policy.[39] Even these at least provide a bench-mark for states. Although these provisions are expressly stated as 'unjusticiable' in themselves (as understood in the domestic legal sense), they may be the direct or incidental subjects of interpretative litigation before the courts to determine issues *inter alia* of the constitutionality of official action.[40] The point here is that the constitutional provisions on economic, social and cultural rights, although not expressly stated as creating individual rights, are in themselves recognition of the significance in constitutional litigation of governmental action affecting individuals. Certain countries have gone further than the mere provision for economic, social and cultural rights in their constitutions by making these provisions subject to the domestic law regime of adversarial justiciability.[41]

JUSTICIABILITY IN PRACTICE

There is practical evidence to support the existence of the justiciability of ESCRs in the inquisitorial as well as the adversarial mode at both international and domestic levels.

At the international level inquisitorial justiciability of ESCRs in the form of the review of state reports is not disputed. Although its effectiveness may vary from one institution to another, the underlying aim of the whole process is to ensure states' compliance with their undertakings. The independence and the expertise of the members of the review bodies deserves special mention. Under the ESCR Covenant, for instance, the review process has since 1985 been the responsibility of a new Committee[42] whose constitution and terms of reference do not differ significantly from the Human Rights Committee under the CPR Covenant (ICCPR).[43] There are similar expert committees under the European Social Charter[44] and the International Labour Organisation.[45]

The evidence of adversarial justiciability of ESCRs at the international level may be found in the case law of the European Community Court of Justice on matters such as social security and the prohibition of employment.[46] In fact, since the adoption of the Single European Act,[47] it has been argued that the European Social Charter has become part of Community law by its express reference in the preamble[48] of the Act or as part of the general principles of law recognised by the Court of Justice.[49]

The International Labour Organisation (ILO) and the African Charter on Human and Peoples Rights[50] both embody an adversarial procedure capable of encompassing the justiciability of ESCRs. The ILO procedure derives from Article 24 of the Organisation's constitution. Under Article 24 associations of workers or of employers are entitled to make representations (a term used for a complaint) to the Governing Body that a member state has failed to secure the effective observance of a Convention. This compliant is dealt with in no less adversarial a manner in terms of procedure and the independence of the review bodies involved than in ordinary courts of law.[51] Article 26 of the constitution also provides for an adversarial inter-state complaint mechanism.

Under the African Charter which embodies both ESCRs and CPRs, the independent African Commission is empowered to receive complaints from State Parties alleging a violation of any rights under the Charter by another state.[52] The Charter also provides for individual and non-governmental complaint mechanisms if a simple majority of members of the Commission so decide.[53] Naturally it follows that these petitions may be in relation to economic, social and cultural rights. Petitions have to satisfy various procedural conditions to be admissible.[54] These communications are submitted to the State Party alleged to be violating the rights for its comments before any substantive consideration of the allegations. Adversarial justiciability of economic, social and cultural rights in the African Charter is novel not only because it is subject to the same mechanism as that for civil and political rights but also because for the first time individuals may petition for the violation of their economic, social and cultural rights. The possible broadening of the dimensions of international human rights law expected to emerge from this procedure needs to be viewed with cautious optimism. Such a broadening is dependent on diverse factors, including the consciousness of the African people to bring complaints before the Commission and the question of élitism and the class structure in the determination of policy in Africa.[55] Some relevant experience may be drawn from the work of the International Labour Organisation, since that body has had a lengthy opportunity to implement economic, social and cultural rights.

The justiciability of ESCRs at the domestic level needs to be addressed differently insofar as the composite compilation of those rights in that context is rare. Nonetheless, they appear in at least one or more of three different forms. These include: as part of written constitutional provisions;[56] as part of statutory provisions dealing with ESCRs;[57] and in instances of direct application of international treaties.[58] In its inquisitorial mode and in this context the justiciability of ESCRs may take the form of Administrative Inquiries[59] set up to investigate the effect of social policies on individuals. Far more important is the adversarial justiciability of these rights which may involve disputes before courts of law or statutory tribunals involving constitutional provisions, statutes and international treaties.[60]

LIMITATIONS TO JUSTICIABILITY

There are problems associated with an obligation-based justiciability both at the philosophical and the practical level. The philosophical hurdle arises mainly from the long-standing claim that the term should be restricted to its individual-orientated, rights-based form. This makes it difficult to legitimise justiciability by other methods. Inquisitorial, obligation-based justiciability, despite its unique significance to the international protection of human rights, has to overcome this philosophical prejudice.

The second limitation arises from the practical application of obligation-based justiciability in its present form under the international human rights treaties. The review bodies have to rely primarily on information supplied by the States Parties through their reports, and this has obvious shortcomings. Other information sources may be available, such as non-governmental organisations (NGOs) and, of course, affected or concerned individuals. But, in the case of NGOs, there are not an appreciable number whose mandates permit the investigation of states compliance with economic, social and cultural rights as compared with the NGOs dealing with civil and political rights. In fact, at the first meeting of the UN Committee on Economic Social and Cultural Rights, only two NGOs – the International Commission of Jurists and the Four Dimensions Council – submitted written memoranda to the Committee.[61] There is the further difficulty of individuals being able to associate themselves directly with the effects of governments' non-compliance with economic, social and cultural rights treaties in the same way that they can for non-compliance under civil and political rights treaties. This non-association arises because of the absence in obligation-based justiciability of benefits that have immediate and direct effects on particular individuals.

Above all, there is the problem of the ability of some (mainly Third-World) states to comply fully with the terms of their treaty obligations for economic, social and cultural rights given the current international economic relations between states. The full realisation of economic, social and cultural rights depends in many ways on the rectification of the injustices that attach to international economic and social policy. Most of these issues are raised in contemporary discussions on the subject of the New International Economic Order (NIEO).[62] The relevance of this debate for the justiciability of economic, social and cultural rights lies in its call for a reduction of the relativism that is inherent in the applications of the provisions of the various international treaties.

CONCLUSION

In this chapter the question of the justiciability of human rights in international law, especially of economic, social and cultural rights, has been addressed critically. It has been shown that existing ideas relating to economic, social and cultural rights are grounded in two kinds of analysis. On the one hand there is the foundation of economic, social and cultural rights in the general historical development of human rights, through which only matters directly affecting individual persons are considered justiciable human rights. On the other hand the basis rests, in contemporary analysis, on the critique that these ideas have proved politically convenient for governments seeking to evade their responsibilities to their citizens.

The main thesis of this chapter has been the identification of the juridical issue of justiciability as achievable in one or two forms – inquisitorial and adversarial. Both forms of justiciability aim eventually at safeguarding human rights and each has its advantages and drawbacks when applied under different circumstances. The two forms of justiciability supplement each other in the process of achieving a better protection of human rights at both the domestic and international levels.

The fuller safeguarding of economic, social and cultural rights through their justiciability has, however, been restrained by a number of factors. These include the influence of domestic law conceptions of human rights' justiciability (which is mainly adversarial) which are not always applicable in international law, and the intellectual misrepresentation of inquisitorial justiciability as an inconsequential means of safeguarding human rights. In the view of the present analysis, this is a grave error. On the contrary, it is argued that the nature and significance of inquisitorial justiciability in international human rights law is that it is an independent and equally effective means of safeguarding all rights including economic, social and cultural rights.

The final conclusion is that it is possible to chronicle and to defend the adversarial justiciability of economic, social and cultural rights in both domestic and international law. The essence of the argument is to challenge the serious misconception that economic, social and cultural rights do not have an individual orientation. In domestic law evidence of the justiciability of these rights emerges from constitutional provisions such as those of the German Basic Law, and is also to be found in many states' domestic legislative instruments on a diversity of economic, social and cultural rights issues. Admittedly, not all constitutional instruments deal with economic, social and cultural rights as in the German case, but there are a number that follow similar lines. Although the future of potential universal application of a procedure remains a matter of controversy, this does not necessarily invalidate the legal significance of those that exist already. At the international level evidence of the adversarial justiciability of economic, social and cultural rights exists within the European Community and the International Labour Organisation. Further, the procedures under the new African Charter may provide additional evidence of the full justiciability (both adversarial and inquisitorial) of economic, social and cultural rights.

Appendix I

SAMPLE OF UNITED KINGDOM STATUTES AND CASES ARISING THEREFROM DEALING WITH ECONOMIC, SOCIAL AND CULTURAL RIGHTS

Social Security

Sample of Statutes

1. National Insurance Act 1965
2. Social Security Act 1986
3. Social Security Benefits Act 1975
4. Health and Social Security Act 1984
5. Social Security Act 1985

Sample of Cases

1. *Rodriguez v Rodriguez and Another* [1988] *The Times* 6 April
2. *Mono Pumps Limited v Froggatt and Radford* [1978] IRLR 368
3. *R. v National Insurance Commissioner, ex parte Mellors* [1971] 2 QB 401
4. *Secretary of State for Social Security v Solly* [1974] 3 All ER 922
5. *Metzgor v DHSS* [1978] 3 All ER 753
6. *R. v National Insurance Commissioners, ex parte Stratton* [1979] 1 WLR 1041
7. *R. v Peterborough Supplementary Benefits Appeal Tribunal, ex parte Supplementary Benefits Commission* [1978] 3 All ER 887
8. *Lees v Secretary of State for Social Security* [1985] 2 All ER 203
9. *R. v Secretary of State for Social Services ex parte Association Metropolitan Authorities* [1986] 1 All ER 164

10. *Hill v Minister of Pensions and National Insurance* [1955] 2 All ER 890

Housing

Sample of Statutes

1. Housing Act 1957
2. Housing (Homeless Persons) Act 1977
3. Social Security and Housing Benefit Act 1982
4. Housing Act 1988

Sample of Cases

1. *White v London Borough of Barnet* 21 HLR 346
2. *R. v Tower Hamlets LBC, ex parte Rouf* 21 HLR 294
3. *R. v City of Westminster, ex parte Tansey* 21 HLR 57
4. *R. v London Borough of Hackney, ex parte Evenbray* 19 HLR 557
5. *R. v Secretary of State for Social Services, ex parte Association of Metropolitan Authorities* 17 HLR 487
6. *R. v South Herefordshire District Council, ex parte Miles* 17 HLR 82
7. *R. v Ryedale District Council, ex parte Smith* 16 HLR 69
8. *R. v Surrey Heath Borough Council, ex parte LL* 16 HLR 83
9. *Restomel Borough Council v Buscombe*; *R. v Exeter City Council, ex parte Gliddon and Draper*; *R. v Southampton City Council, ex parte Ward* 14 HLR 89
10. *R. v Secretary of State for Health and Social Security, ex parte City of Sheffield* 18 HLR 6

Health

Sample of Statutes

1. Abortion Act 1967
2. National Health Service Act 1977
3. Mental Health Act 1983.

Sample of Cases

1. *Sharangdhar Prasad v General Medical Council* [1987] 1 WLR 1677
2. *Kerr v Morris* [1986] 3 All ER 217
3. *Secretary of State for the Home Department v Mental Health Review Tribunal for the Mersey Regional Health Authority* [1986] 3 All ER 232
4. *Gillick v West Norfolk and Wisbech Health Authority* [1985] 3 All ER 402
5. *Paton v Trustees of BPAS* [1978] 2 All ER 987
6. *R. v Malcherek* [1981] 1 WLR 690
7. *Selfe v Ilford and District Hospital Management Committee. The Times* 26 November 1970

8. *Royal College of Nursing v Department of Health and Social Security* [1981] A.C. 800
9. *R. v Smith* [1973] 1 WLR 1510
10. *Re B (A Minor)* [1987] 2 All ER 206

Education

Sample of Statutes
1. Education Act 1944
2. Education Act 1962
3. Education Act 1980

Sample of Cases
1. *Cumings v Birkenhead Corporation* [1971] 2 All ER 881
2. *R. v Secretary of State for Education and Science, ex parte Chance*, Unreported Judgement
3. *Plunkett v Alker* [1954] 1 QB 420
4. *Winward v Cheshire County Council* [1978] 77 LGR 172
5. *Surrey County Council v Ministry of Education* [1953] 1 All ER 705
6. *R. v London Borough of Barnet, ex parte Shah* [1980] 3 All ER 679
7. *R. v Manchester City Council, ex parte Fulford* (Divisional Court), *The Times*, 26 October 1982
8. *Watt v Kesteven County Council* [1981] 2 All ER 227
9. *Rootkin v Kent County Council* [1981] 2 All ER 227
10. *Re DJMS (A Minor)* [1977] All ER 582

Work

Sample of Statutes
1. Factories Act 1961
2. Race Relations Act 1968
3. Equal Pay Act 1970
4. Sex Discrimination Act 1975

Sample of Cases
1. *Harrison Limited v Ramsey* [1976] IRLR 135
2. *Pickstone v Freemans PLC* [1988] 2 All ER 803
3. *Duke v GEC Reliance Ltd* [1988] 1 All ER 626
4. *Greater Glasgow Health Board v Carey* [1987] IRLR 484
5. *Page v Freight Hire Limited* [1981] 1 All ER 394
6. *Hayward v Cammell Laird Shipbuilders Limited* [1988] 2 All ER 257
7. *Jenkins v Kingsgate Limited* [1981] 1 WLR 927
8. *Dugdale v Kraft Foods Limited [1976] 1 WLR 11*
9. *Marshall v Southampton and South Hampshire Health Authority* [1986] 2 All ER 584
10. *Foster v British Gas PLC* [1987] ICR 904

Appendix II

REFERENCES TO CASES IN DOMESTIC COURTS CITING INTERNATIONAL TREATIES DEALING WITH ECONOMIC, SOCIAL AND CULTURAL RIGHTS, [EUROPEAN SOCIAL CHARTER]

1. Arnsberg Administrative Court (FRG), Judgement of 1 October 1970
2. Federal Labour Court (FRG), Judgement of 21 April 1974
3. Amsterdam Court of Appeal (Holland), Judgement of 13 April 1972.
4. Berlin Labour Tribunal (FRG), Judgement of 10 October 1974
5. Council of State (France), Judgement of 8 October 1978
6. Frankfurt Regional Labour Tribunal (FRG), Judgement of 17 April 1979
7. Utrecht District Court (Holland), Two summary decisions of the Vice President on 15 June 1979
8. Federal Labour Court (FRG) Two Judgements of 10 June 1980
9. Amsterdam District Court (Holland), Summary judgement by the President on 21 October 1981
10. Utrecht District Court (Holland), Judgement of 11 March 1982
11. Utrecht District Court (Holland), Summary judgement of 4 November 1983
12. Utrecht District Court (Holland), Summary judgement of 8 November 1983
13. Utrecht District Court (Holland), Summary judgement of 29 November 1983
14. Federal Labour Court, (FRG), Judgement of 12 September 1984
15. Strasbourg Administrative Court (France), Judgement of 9 May 1985
16. Supreme Court of the Netherlands (Holland), Judgement of 30 May 1986

Source: Ph. Jaspers and Lammy Betten *25 Years. European Social Charter* (London: Kluwer Law and Taxation Publishers, 1988), p.23.

NOTES

1. I would like to thank the Commonwealth Secretariat for permission to reproduce material in this chapter which appeared in the *Commonwealth Law Bulletin*.
2. E.W. Vierdag, 'The Legal Nature of the Rights Granted by the International Covenant on Economic, Social and Cultural Rights',

in Vol. 9 (1978), *Neth. Yr. Bk. of I.L.*, p.69 – 105. See also Cranston, 'Human Rights, Real and Supposed', in D.D, Raphael (ed.), *Political Theory and the Rights of Man* (London: Macmillan, 1967) pp.43 – 53. See further, H. Kapp, 'Some Preliminary Views on the Relationship Between Civil and Political Rights and Economic, Social and Cultural Rights in the Context of Development and on the Right to Development', (Geneva Int'l Comm. of Jurists, nd).

3. H.R.W. Wade, *Administrative Law* (Oxford: Clarendon Press, 1977), p.786., Geoffrey Marshall, 'Justiciability', in A.G. Guest (ed.), *Oxford Essays in Jurisprudence* (Oxford: OUP, 1961), p.265.
4. The United States policy since Ronald Raegan has been to marginalise economic, social and cultural rights. On this see Forsythe, 'Socioeconomic Human Rights: The United Nations, The United States and Beyond', Vol. 4, 1982, *Hum. Rts. Quart.*, p.435 *et seq*. See also, attitudes to the European Social Charter in A. Ph. C. M. Jaspers and L. Betten (eds), *25 Years, European Social Charter* (London: Kluwer, 1988).
5. E.W. Vierdag, 'The Legal Nature', op. cit., p.73
6. Ibid.
7. Statute of the International Court of Justice, Article 34 (1) (New York: United Nations).
8. See Article 25 of The European Convention on Human Rights and Fundamental Freedoms (1950). Text in I. Brownlie, (ed.) *Basic Documents on Human Rights* (Oxford: Clarendon Press, 1985), p.243. See also Article 44 of The American Convention on Human Rights (1969). Text in I. Brownlie, *Basic Documents*, op. cit., p.391. See further, Optional Protocol to the International Covenant on Civil and Political Rights (1966). Text in I. Brownlie, *Basic Documents*, op. cit., p.146.
9. E.W. Vierdag, 'The Legal Nature', op. cit., p.78, where he asserts that:

   Apart from these four or maybe three provisions, the rights in the Covenant on Civil and Political Rights are directly enforceable: no special legislation is needed to amend their wording or to specify their meaning: no special funds are needed to finance their implementation. Violations of them can be judged to have occurred, or to be occurring, by courts of law or similar bodies. These are also able to afford effective redress: the violations will consist of actions or remissions by officials or private persons which can be cancelled, rectified, declared void, or lead to the payment of compensation for damage.

10. United Nations International Covenant on Economic, Social and Cultural Rights (ICESCR) (1966). Text in I. Brownlie, *Basic Documents*, op. cit., p.118
11. See European Social Charter (1961). Text in I. Brownlie, *Basic Documents*, op. cit., p.301.
12. See generally on this subject, G.J.H. van Hoof, 'The Legal Nature of Economic, Social and Cultural Rights: a Rebuttal of Some Traditional

Views', in P. Alston and K. Tomasevski (eds), *The Right to Food* (Utrecht, The Netherlands: Martinus Nijhoff/Sims, 1984).

13. Individual access to international human rights tribunals is dependent first and primarily on the ratification of the international human rights treaties and secondly on the state's express declaration recognising individual petitions (European Convention on Human Rights, but see American Convention on reverse of procedure on second issue of state declaration).
14. See note 2 supra.
15. Article 13 of ICESCR, op. cit.
16. Article 2 of Protocol 1 to ECHR. Text in I. Brownlie, *Basic Documents*, op. cit., p.257.
17. *Campbell and Cosans* Case, E.C.H.R., Series A, No. 48 (1982), *Belgium Linguistic* Cases, E.C.H.R., Series A, No. 6 (1968), *Kjeldsen, Busk-Madsen and Pedersen* Case, E.H.R.R., Series A, No. 23 (1976).
18. Article 1 common to both United Nations Covenants on CPRs and ESCRs, op. cit.
19. Article 8 of ICESCR, op. cit.; and Article 22 of ICCPR, op. cit.
20. Article 10 of ICESCR, op. cit.; and Articles 23 and 24 of ICCPR, op. cit.
21. See generally, P. Alston and G. Quinn, 'The Nature and Scope of States Parties' Obligations Under the International Covenant on Economic, Social and Cultural Rights', Vol. 9, 1987, *Hum. Rts. Quart.*, pp. 156, 159. See also G.J.H. van Hoof, 'The Legal Nature of Economic, Social and Cultural Rights', op. cit., p.101.
22. Article 9 of the International Covenant on Economic, Social and Cultural Rights provides that:

    The States Parties to the present Covenant recognise the right of everyone to social security, including social insurance.

23. International Covenant on Civil and Political Rights (1966). Text in I. Brownlie, *Basic Documents*, op. cit., p.128.
24. Ibid., Article 14.
25. Article 11 of the International Covenant on Civil and Political Rights provides that:

    No one shall be imprisoned merely on the ground of inability to fulfil a contractual obligation.

26. Article 16 of the International Covenant on Civil and Political Rights provides that:

    Everyone shall have the right to recognition everywhere as a person before the law.

27. Article 8 of the ICESCR, op. cit.
28. Ibid., Article 10.
29. Ibid., Article 13.

30. European Social Charter, op. cit., Article 1 – 19.
31. European Social Charter, ibid. Article 12.
32. E.W. Vierdag, 'The Legal Nature', op. cit., p.78. See also M. Cranston, 'Human Rights, Real and Supposed', op. cit., p.50.
33. International Covenant on Civil and Political Rights, op. cit., Article14.
34. P. Alston, 'Development and the Rule of Law: Prevention Versus Cure as a Human Rights Strategy', in *Development, Human Rights and the Rule of Law*, Report of the International Commission of Jurists Conference held in the Hague (Oxford: Pergamon Press, 1981), pp.31, 52.
35. See Limburg Principles on the Implementation of the International Covenant on Economic, Social and Cultural Rights, especially Principles 8 and 16. Text in Vol;. 9, 1987, *Hum. Rts. Quart.*, p.122.
36 See H. Kelsen, *Pure Theory of Law* (M. Knight transl.), (Berkeley, California: University of California Press, 1967) in which he asserts that:

> [T]he essential element [of a right] is the legal power bestowed upon the latter [individual] by the legal order to bring about, by a law suit the execution of a sanction as a reaction against non-fulfilment of the obligation . . . Only if the legal order confers such a legal power are we faced with a 'right' in a specific, technical sense of the word. (Ibid., p.134 – 5.)

37. The Vienna Convention on the Law of Treaties provides in Article 31(1) that:

> General Rule of Interpretation
> 1. A treaty shall be interpreted in good faith in accordance with the ordinary meaning to be given to the terms of the treaty in their context and in the light of its object and purpose.

Text in Council of Europe, Human Rights in International Law: (Strasbourg: Basic Texts, 1979), p.122.

38. For a detailed discussion of the place and role of sanction in international human rights law see J.S. Watson, 'The limited Utility of International Law in the Protection of Human Rights', 74, *Proceedings, Am. Soc. Intl. Law*, 1980, p.1 – 6.
39. See, for instance, the Constitution of India (1947); the now suspended Constitution of Ghana (1979). For further discussion of this subject in the European Context, see, C. Start, 'Europe's Fundamental Rights in their Newest Garb', Vol. 3, 1982, *Hum. Rts Law Journal*, p.103.
40. For discussion of this subject in relation to the Indian Constitution see, D. Basu, *Limited Government and Judicial Review* (Calcutta: Sarker, 1972). The United States Constitution, which does not have express references to economic, social and cultural rights, has also been interpreted as raising incidental issues on the subject before the courts. See on this F.I. Michelman, 'Welfare Rights in a Constitutional

Democracy', *Wash. Univ. L.Q.*, 1979, p.659. For a contrary perception see, R.H. Bork, 'The Impossibility of Finding Welfare Rights in the Constitution', *Wash. Univ. L.Q.*, p.595.

41. See P. Alston and G. Quinn, 'The Nature and Scope of States Parties Obligations Under the International Covenant on Economic, Social and Cultural Rights' op. cit.
42. See ECOSOC Resln. 1985/17 (1985). Text in UN Doc. E/1985/85 (1985). For further discussion of the shortcomings of the ECOSOC Sessional Working Group, see P. Alston, 'Out of the Abyss: the Challenges Confronting the New U.N. Committee on Economic, Social and Cultural Rights', *Hum. Rts. Quart.*, Vol. 9, No. 3. 1987, pp.332, 340. There is a similar state reporting arrangement in Part IV of the European Social Charter, op. cit. (Article 21 – 29).
43. Article 28 of ICCPR, op. cit.
44. European Social Charter op. cit., Article 25.
45. For a discussion of this subject see D. Vincent-Davis, 'Human Rights Law: A Research Guide to the Literature – Part III: The ILO and Human Rights', *NYUJIL & Pol.*, Vol. 15, 1982, p.211, 250 – 1.
46. Treaty Establishing the European Economic Community (1957) reprinted in Official Publications of the European Communities, Treaties Establishing in European Communities (Luxembourg, 1973) (hereinafter referred to as the EEC Treaty). Article 119 and Article 7. For a discussion of the legal significance of some of these provisions see P. D. Dagtoglou, 'Human Rights and European Community Law', *Tulane L.R.*, Vol. 56, 1981, p.294. See also, L. Marcoux, Jr., 'The Concept of Fundamental Rights in European Economic Community Law', *GA J. Int'l. & Comp. Law*, Vol. 13, 1983, p.667.
47. EEC, Single European Act.
48. A. J. Riley, 'The European Social Charter and Community Law', *E.L. Rev.*, Vol. 1, 1989, pp.80, 83.
49. A. Riley, 'The European Social Charter', op. cit., p.81. See also, *Erich Stauder v City of Ulm. Sozialamt* [1989] E. Comm. Ct. J. Rep. p.419. *Internationale Handelsgesellschaft mbH v Einfur – und Vorratsstelle fur Getreide und Futtermittel* [1970] E. Comm. Ct. J. Rep. p.419. *Internationale Handelsgesellschaft mbH v Einfuhr – und Vonatsstelle fur Getreide und Futtermittel* [1970] E. Comm. Ct. J. Rep. p.1125. *J. Nold. Kohlen – und Baustoffgropbhandlung v E.E.C. Commission* [1974] E. Comm. Ct. J. Rep. p.491.
50. African Charter on Human and Peoples' Rights, 919810. Text in 1982 *Int's Legal Mats.*, p.59.
51. E. Osieke, 'The Exercise of the Judicial Function with Respect to the International Labour Organisation', *Brit. Y.B. Int'l L.*, Vol. 47, 1974-75, pp.315, 325.
52. African Charter, op.cit., Article 47 – Article 54.
53. Ibid. Article 55.
54. Ibid. Article 56.
55. For a further discussion of this subject see, R.E. Howard, 'Law and Economic Rights in Commonwealth Africa', *Cal. West I.L.J.*, Vol. 15, 1985, pp. 607 – 32.

56. Foreign Office of the Federal Republic of Germany, Basic Law for the Federal Republic of Germany (hereinafter referred to as the German Basic Law), as adopted by the Parliamentary Council (Deutscher Bundestag) 1955. Constitution of the USSR (1977). Text in F.J.M. Feldbrugge (ed.), *The Constitutions of the U.S.S.R. and the Union Republics: Analysis, Texts, Reports* (Alphen an den Rijn: Sijthoff & Noordhoff, 1979) p.69. Syrian Constitution, Article 37. Text in A. Blaustein and G. Flanz, (eds), *Constitutions of the Countries of the World* (Dobbs Ferry, New York: Oceana, 1974). See similar provisions in the Constitution of the United Arab Emirates under Chapter Two, on Fundamental Social and Economic Bases of the State. Text in Blaustein and Flanz, *Constitutions of the Countries of the World*, op. cit., 1982. Also the Swiss Constitution as discussed in C. Stark, 'Europe's Fundamental Rights', *H.R.L.J.*, Vol. 3, 1982, p.103.
57. See United Kingdom Example, Appendix I. Also, Jaspers and Betten (eds), *25 Years, European Social Charter*, op. cit.
58. Jaspers and Betten *European Social Charter*, op. cit.
59. See Note 2 supra.
60. See Appendix II.
61. P. Alston and B. Simma, 'First Session of UN Committee on Economic, Social and Cultural Rights', *A.J.I.L*, Vol. 81, 1987, pp.747, 752.
62. See generally on this subject, General Assembly Resolution 3201 (S.VI) on the Establishment of the New International Economic Order (1974); General Assembly Resolution 3202 (S-VI) on the Programme of Action on the Establishment of the New International Economic Order (1974); and General Assembly Resolution 3281 (XXIX), Charter of Economic Rights and Duties of States (1974).

Part II
Contemporary Public Policy

6 Rights and Performance: Economic and Social Rights in the UK

Ralph Beddard

INTERNATIONAL ECONOMIC AND SOCIAL RIGHTS

The United Kingdom is a Contracting Party both to the International Covenant on Economic, Social and Cultural Rights and to the Council of Europe's European Social Charter. These, together with obligations under Conventions and Recommendations of the ILO and UNESCO make up the greater part of the code of economic, social and cultural principles to which the state is legally bound to aspire.[1] It may be relevant to take into account developments within the European Community towards social cohesion. The heated discussions on a Community Charter of Social Rights will undoubtedly raise the profile of social rights in Europe from the point of view of aspiration. Implementation of the proposed Charter, as envisaged by its supporters, could well make a notable impact upon social rights legislation within the United Kingdom but these are, and may remain matters for the future.

The Covenant on Economic, Social and Cultural Rights and its sister the International Covenant on Civil and Political Rights came into force in 1976 and comprise a major part of the United Nations International Bill of Rights. The United Kingdom ratification was forthcoming in May of that year with the result that its involvement with the treaty is, in practice, unbroken. It is now part of history that the original intention of the framers of the International Bill of Rights was a single Covenant reflecting the Universal Declaration of Human Rights but that this proved impossible, particularly, on the problems of implementation and enforcement.

Under Article 2 of the Covenant each State Party undertakes to take steps with a view to achieving progressively the full realisation of the rights recognised. This, each is enjoined to do to the maximum of its available resources and by all appropriate means, including particularly the adoption of legislative measures.

The European Social Charter, signed within the Council of Europe in 1961, was ratified by the United Kingdom the following year and came into force in February 1965. Under the Social Charter the States Parties undertake to consider themselves bound by such of the obligations as they should select. The Charter is, in fact, unusual in its format and in its 'pick and mix' approach. Part One of the Charter consists of a 19-point list of principles and the Contracting Parties are required to accept, as the aim of their policy, the attainment of conditions in which these rights and principles may be effectively realised. These aims are to be pursued, 'by all appropriate means, both national and international in character'. Part Two of the Charter proceeds to set out the 19 rights in greater detail, in much the same way as the International Covenants enlarge upon the Universal Declaration. Each Contracting Party, under Article 20 of the Charter, must, on ratification, choose at least ten Articles or 45 numbered paragraphs to which it considers itself bound, including five or more from a list of 'preferred' rights.[2] Further Articles or paragraphs can be ascribed to as and when a Contracting Party so desires and similarly, provisions exist for the denunciation of individual rights should the necessity arise. It will be noticed that it is possible under such a scheme for each state's obligations to differ from those of the other parties. The general requirement in Part One, however, obliges states to accept the principles in total.

The rights dealt with in both of the instruments cover similar ground. The Social Charter, as might perhaps be expected considering its European pretensions, describes employment rights in greater detail, including the right to collective bargaining, while the Covenant, with its additional commitment to cultural rights, contains Articles on the right to education and the right to take part in the cultural life of the community and to benefit from intellectual property rights.[3]

Both treaties are implemented by means of a system of regular reports made by the Contracting Parties and studied by one or more scrutinising committees.

Articles 16 and 17 of the Covenant make provision for reports to be furnished in stages, according to an established programme, to the Economic and Social Council. It soon became obvious that ECOSOC was ill-equipped to consider such reports in detail and in 1985 an 18-member Committee on Economic, Social and Cultural Rights, made up of independent experts and mirroring in approach and procedure the Human Rights Committee of the other Covenant, was created. The Committee receives the report of each Contracting State presented by a government representative who can be questioned and cross-examined. In this way the concerns of the Committee can be made known and perhaps transmitted to the reporting state. In the case of the Human Rights Committee there is some evidence that this has had effect in bringing about reform and it remains to be seen whether the Social and Economic Committee will find a similar pattern. It must be remembered that the implementation procedures of the Economic, Social and Cultural Covenant are limited to reporting which is more in line with the progressive nature of the undertakings, whereas the other Covenant is, at least *prima facie*, of a more immediate obligation. The major objective of the procedure envisaged by the Economic and Social Covenant is to reveal the progress, or lack of it, so that assistance from the United Nations or the Specialised Agencies can be called for or indicated. Article 19 of the Covenant permits ECOSOC to transmit the reports to the Human Rights Commission 'for study and general recommendation or . . . for information', together with any observations submitted by the appropriate Specialised Agencies. Any recommendations so made may be commented on by the reporting state or the Specialised Agency. ECOSOC reports to the General Assembly on the progress achieved and with recommendations of a general nature.

In the case of the European Social Charter a similar Committee of Experts is appointed by the Committee of Ministers. It is composed of not more than seven members who are 'of the highest integrity and of recognised competence in international social questions'. The Committee examines reports on accepted provisions which are submitted at two-yearly intervals. An interesting feature of the Charter, in line with the procedures of the International Labour Organisation, is the requirement to report to the Secretary-General, when requested, on those provisions not accepted.

The two-yearly reports on accepted provisions, together with any comments from organisations of employers and trade unions, are examined by the Committee of Experts, whose conclusions are sent to a Sub-Committee of the Governmental Social Committee of the Council of Europe, representing all the Contracting Parties, and also to the Parliamentary Assembly. Finally, the views of all these bodies are communicated to the Committee of Ministers which can, by a two-thirds majority of those entitled to sit, make to each Contracting Party any necessary recommendations.

The European Social Charter, therefore, has within it the means whereby Contracting States may be taken to task for non-fulfilment of their treaty obligations. Any shortfall, however, requires not only the conclusion of the Committee of Experts but the concurrence of the Governmental Sub-Committee, while any recommendation is dependent upon a two-thirds majority of the 23-member Committee of Ministers.

It would seem, therefore, that each of these instruments exists as a common standard of achievement with little by the way of effective implementation. The Social Charter, befitting its place, is slightly more positive in this respect. It must be remembered, however, that the reason that social rights appear in a separate Covenant and the reason the Social Charter stands apart from the European Convention is precisely because of doubts as to the feasibility of implementation by an international body. Social and economic rights have to be self-paced within each community and it is the manner in which such rights are considered, both by governments and by others, in the shape of the citizen, political parties, activists and legislators, formal or otherwise, which provides the foundation on which to build.

SOCIAL AND ECONOMIC RIGHTS IN THE UNITED KINGDOM

Any attempt at monitoring economic and social rights in the United Kingdom cannot begin, any more than in any other state, by reference to the reports made to the international scrutinising committees, except insofar as to determine any areas specifically avoided in those reports or left undisturbed. The appointment of independent committees of experts, the laying down and strict compliance with guidelines in the writing of reports and, perhaps more importantly, face-to-face questioning of government representatives can help prevent major items from being ignored, but ratification of these international instruments cannot be taken to indicate at local level much more than a desire on the part of the state to join in the general raising of standards. The breadth of scope of the instruments and perhaps the vagueness necessitated by treaty language, require that a genuine commitment in each specific area must be striven for at local level. Economic and social rights, to say nothing of cultural rights, raise questions of resources, priorities and tradition, with the result that monitoring and lobbying at national level by interest groups is essential for their promotion. The justiciability of social rights is discussed in earlier chapters,[4] but in practice such rights are not treated in this way at international level and the evaluation of social rights depends to a very large extent upon the activities of local monitoring groups. It is questionable whether the existence of international rights treaties has had anything but minimal influence in the United Kingdom. One consequence may be that it has categorised the rights and focused attention on any lacunae which may exist by introducing a more comparative approach, particularly at a European level.

If economic and social rights are properly characterised as rights, whether or not this is related to need, they should not be dependent upon political preferences nor subject to institutional pressures. Distinction is drawn by Ian Forbes,[5] in the example of women's rights, between the approach of France and Sweden. The French government set up a Ministerial Department with responsibility for women's rights, producing appropriate legislation and monitoring procedures, all of which were subject to the fortunes of the elected government. The Swedish government approached the matter from a constitutional angle and in this way brought into play the whole panoply of constitutional rights. The United Kingdom does not have the concept of constitutional rights even in the civil and political sphere. The approach in this country was of a less rights-oriented kind, with emphasis being upon fact-finding, demographic analysis and the setting up of an institution, the EOC, insulated, to some extent, from both government and the courts.

The United Kingdom attitude may be attributable not to any particular desire to be different but to historical and traditional factors which remain resistant to political and legal pressures. The Common Law, for instance, may be readily blamed. Constant reference was made in the discussions to the fact that the Common Law has developed with an emphasis on remedies rather than rights. The reluctance of many to accede to calls for a Bill of Rights or even for incorporation of the European Convention into English law may be evidence of this. Particularly notable here are the claims of the antagonists that such an approach to civil rights is contrary to the methodology of English justice and the working of the courts. The Common Law has a tendency also to emphasise property related interests. The case of *Entick v Carrington* in 1765[6] is claimed as a landmark in civil liberties but centred upon the law of trespass. The fact that the printing presses and books were held in someone's house, and the right to invade that private property, was the real subject matter of that case, not the civil rights of John Wilkes and his companions. Similarly, in *Malone v. Metropolitan Police Commissioner*, a case concerning telephone tapping which eventually reached the Strasbourg Court, Megarry's judgement was framed in terms of ownership of various property rights and may well have struck the European lawyers as quaint or even bizarre.[7] Scant reference was made in the English courts to the right of privacy which involves recognition of an interest unrelated to property for which Common-Law countries find it hard to legislate. Any question of access to information, for instance, is clearly dealing with interests of a non-property kind and can rarely depend upon Common Law but needs a statutory basis. Some Civil-Law countries, on the other hand, have constitutional notions such as the dignity of the person.

The lack of constitutional remedies in English law has, in turn, brought about a swing away from the centralism which is evident in the French pattern (indeed it is likely that the increasing trend towards centralism in this country has been primarily responsible for renewed calls for a Bill of Rights). A noticeable addition to English society, which is lacking to anything like the same extent in France, is the large number of voluntary groups and charitable organisations. It is interesting that here again the missing legal and constitutional provisions are compensated for, as in the case of women's rights, by multi-functional organisations providing a flexible, regional and pluralistic alternative.

Leaving aside the development of the Common Law, it is not always easy to speculate why Britain has developed in this isolationist way. A suggestion that some form of 'capitalist stranglehold' was responsible is not mirrored in those European countries which have a similar political complexion nor in the United States.

It may well be argued, of course, that the lack of tailored legal provisions is not in practice a bar to the achievement of economic and social rights. The forensic process is necessarily limited and it has been suggested that there is a reflection of the class system in the judges which renders them unsuitable arbiters. More effective progress might be made through the administrative approach, by administrative policy and the use of such measures as governmental grants, and such techniques as contract compliance. Indeed, Margherita Rendel pointed out that these methods had been crucial in the United States in bringing about the greater employment of women and ensuring their entry into senior posts. The litigation process is slow and complex, often requiring inordinate amounts of money, time and energy and, more often than not, incurring the necessity for professional advice and assistance with a view to interpreting complicated legal instruments. After all this, it is not always a clear legal answer that is achieved, not all economic and social rights are truly justiciable. The class action, used so successfully in the United States, is to be found in English law only as a Representative Action with the need for all claimants to have virtually identical interests, a factor rendering its use, outside landlord and tenant litigation, limited. This is not to say that there cannot be successful litigation which concerns large numbers.[8]

Where litigation has taken place there is little reference to international norms either by litigants or their lawyers. While there is an increasing reference to the European Convention on Human Rights in cases before the House of Lords, it is done in a very rudimentary fashion and invariably those cases which are cited are those involving the United Kingdom with scarcely a reference to the laws of the more than 20 other countries that are party to the Convention. Indeed in the majority of these countries the Convention is part of the municipal law and interpreted directly by the domestic courts. The Council of Europe has produced several volumes on the Convention in domestic law and a regular part of the Convention's yearbook is devoted to it. The failure would seem to lie not in the availability of the material but in the desire or competence to use it (being as it is, in most cases, beyond what is seen to be the impenetrable barrier of the Civil Law).

Development of the idea of the Ombudsman along Scandinavian lines, unfettered by the formalities which seem to hamper similar British institutions, and using investigative, judicial and advisory powers, might provide a useful complement to the courts.

Any review of economic, social and cultural rights in the United Kingdom by reference to international treaty obligations must take into account the way in which those obligations have been formulated and this is a constant theme in the succeeding chapters of this book and dominated the discussions of the workshop.

In the case of employment rights, the Covenant and the Social Charter bear a great similarity in their scope, the Charter spelling out the individual components of the rights in greater detail and including, as we have seen, the right of collective bargaining. At various stages in its lengthy procedures the scrutinising machinery of the Social Charter has found the United Kingdom lacking and Vivien Shrubshall deals with these instances in her chapter.[9] It is, however, interesting to recognise that employment law in the United Kingdom, for many decades a complex mixture of Common Law and Statute, has become, in recent years, increasingly Statute based. A major reason for this, of course, is the fact that employment law has been at the heart of much of the political wrangling of the last 20 years and illustrates well the thesis here being put. Where legislation has been a response to the decisions or recommendations of international bodies, it can often be viewed almost as a damage limitation exercise and only rarely as an acceptance of any international principle.

Education and health, taken by the group as two more examples of social rights, cause difficulty precisely because of the manner in which they are treated by the international instruments with regard to their content and extent. Julian Lonbay points out in his chapter[10] that whereas the Covenant not only outlines the objectives of education and lays down a detailed programme for the introduction and maintenance of schooling, the Social Charter, apart from a reference to vocational training, ignores the right to education on the basis, presumably that it is dealt with in the European Convention on Human Rights. The Convention, however, in its first Protocol[11] merely announces without any elaboration that no person shall be denied the right to education. It then goes on to deal with the rights of parents to choose education according to their religious and philosophical convictions. It is not easy from this to determine the content or extent of education. The 'full development of the human personality and the sense of its dignity' enabling 'all persons to participate effectively in a free society', enunciated in the Covenant, together with further references to human rights, tolerance and peace, is, with respect, of only marginal help in the creation of a national educational system. In some European countries, it was pointed out, teachers are not only treated as civil servants but are also required to take an oath of allegiance to the State. The setting of a national curriculum in the United Kingdom raises again for debate the overall purpose of education. Taken particularly in the context of ethnic, cultural and social variation, the question was raised whether more emphasis might not be given to 'useful' education in the sense of practical and vocational training. Certainly, single sex schools desired by Islamic communities in Britain produced questions that were not easy to deal with by reference to international instruments but which were sincerely posed by the cultural group concerned. Similarly, as Lawrence Lustgarten described, a series of cases relating to the teaching of the Darwinian theories of evolution had caused problems in some schools in parts of the United States. As Lonbay points out, the European Court of Human Rights in the Kjeldsen Case ruled that the curriculum is the province of the State with the condition that controversial matters should be taught 'objectively, critically and pluralistically'. The state is provided with little guidance, however, by the Covenant or the Convention, as to matters of overall balance or even content. The government's view of what should be taught in schools may therefore be opposed to those of the parents but yet again neither may be in the interests of the rights of the child. The way in which the legal system of a state treats minors is in itself an important factor in the exercise of the rights of children to education. The tendency in most European states is to give paramountcy to the wishes of the parents, and only to override these when the state, as identified in the last resort by the courts, considers that these are not in the interests of the child. In most European states the child's views count for little.

It must also not be forgotten that education is not to be interpreted as being the exclusive domain of the child. Adult basic education is specifically referred to in the Covenant while higher education is not limited in any way by age. Given, therefore, the complexity of definition, many of the problems in education occur in the provision of schooling and an educational system. A review of the programme laid down in Articles 13 and 14 of the Covenant will reveal few problems for the United Kingdom and any problems which arise are likely to concern minutiae of interpretation. For instance, does the provision of schools without thought as to the ability of destitute parents to maintain their children comply adequately with international standards? Does the right to education include the right to free books and materials?

Resources feature prominently in the provision of education. The European Court of Human Rights, as Lonbay describes,[12] interpreted 'no one shall be denied the right to education' to be limited to access to existing educational institutions. Article 27 of the International Covenant on Civil and Political Rights reads:

> In those States in which ethnic, religious or linguistic minorities exist, persons belonging to such minorities shall not be denied the right, in community with the other members of their group, to

enjoy their own culture, to profess and practice their own religion, or use their own language.

This Article, it must be remembered, is one which the Contracting States have undertaken to respect and ensure, and is not to be considered as a programme right. Nevertheless, its application would undoubtedly have to be tempered by reality and not imply the expenditure of an inordinate amount on a very small minority group. The same interpretation must *a fortiori* be applied to the provision of educational facilities under the Economic, Social and Cultural Covenant.

Very similar discussion can arise with regard to the right to health. Jonathan Montgomery, in his chapter[13] analyses the breadth available in understanding this right from the 'freedom from clinically ascertainable disease' to the World Health Organisation's definition of a 'state of complete physical, mental and social well being and not merely the absence of disease or infirmity'. Adoption of this second social model as opposed to the mechanical model was felt by some to imply the elimination of an adverse environment moving perhaps from second-to third-generation rights. The comment might be made that whereas the drafters of the European Convention sought to characterise education as a civil and political right, no attempt has been made with regard to the right to health. Indeed, in civil and political rights terms, the negative rights aspect is minimal, existing, if it does at all, in the twilight recesses of the right to freedom from inhuman or degrading treatment.

A link with earlier discussion of needs[14] arises with the historical background of both these rights in the United Kingdom. At the time of postwar discussion of the welfare state, health and education were perceived as primary needs and both became the subject of major administrative reform, co-incident with, but perhaps not formally associated with, the proclamation of the Universal Declaration of Human Rights. The government of the day believed that educated and healthy citizens would lead to the well-being of the state as a whole. It is perhaps from this perceived need that the rights to health and education in this country owe their recognition even though such recognition fails to help in defining their extent.

Concern might be expressed, and was indeed voiced during discussion, that a broader recognition of the right to health including the right to health care might, because of the practicalities involved and the necessary resource provision required, have the effect of reducing its enforceability in rights terms. Should the United Kingdom Government give priority to the National Health Service or to cleansing the environment, always assuming that it is unable to afford both?

The allocation of resources for health and health care again causes problems in a national setting because, for instance, of regional variation. Should a person in one area be able to complain on the grounds that he is less well served than another living in a different part of the country even though the needs of these areas are accountably not identical? The question of equality is here difficult to answer. It would seem unlikely that allocation of resources as between claimants could be left to the judges. The institution of the Ombudsman in health and education does not help in decisions on allocation.

Economic, social and cultural rights have been labelled second-generation rights. Generation, the dictionary tells us, is about begetting or being begotten. It is soon realised, on examination, that the analogy is inaccurate. Civil and political rights did not father social rights; in many instances the reverse is nearer to the truth. The United Nations Charter lists the solving of international problems of an economic, social, cultural and humanitarian character prior to the promotion of human rights,[15] and this would certainly be an accurate analysis at national level. So-called third-generation rights, group rights, as we have seen in some aspects of our examination of health and education, overlap with and certainly are not propagated by social and economic rights. Earlier chapters raise questions as to the suitability of a judicial approach in human rights matters.[16] The United Kingdom cannot be said to entrust the implementation of social rights to litigation, it has, so far, failed to rival the United States in this respect. While giving greater emphasis to the creation of administrative machinery, such as the Equal Opportunities Commission, it has perhaps paid less than adequate attention to the question of efficient and just dispute settlement. The Scandinavian successes in the institution of the Ombudsman have not been seriously considered while further calls for judicial intervention by the enactment of a Bill of Rights or incorporation of the European Convention have been rejected.[17]

Six says after the discussions referred to above the European Commission released the revised preliminary draft text of the European Community Charter of Fundamental Social Rights. The proposed Charter declares that the implementation of the Single European

Act must take full account of the social dimension of the Community and that the development of the social rights of citizens of the Community must be assured at appropriate levels. The rights contained in the draft Charter extend over and beyond those of the Social Charter of the Council of Europe and are to be applied, we are told in the preamble, 'according to the principle of "subsidiary"'. Implementation lies with the member states or with the European Community 'according to the circumstances' and may take the form of laws, collective agreements or existing practices. Member states commit themselves to take such steps as are appropriate and to mobilise all the resources necessary in order to guarantee the social rights contained in the draft Charter which, it reminds governments, are indispensable to the efficient operation of the internal market. Finally, the Commission is charged to present an action programme together with a set of related instruments.

Taken within its context, the draft Charter as it is presently envisaged could have a major, fundamental impact on social rights in Britain, not so much as regards the rights proposed, many of which are likely indeed to prove practically necessary in the light of the internal market, but in the manner in which the rights are to be implemented and enforced. The Council of Europe has been restrained in the area of social rights, partly on the grounds of the difficulties of justiciability of such rights. This is not likely to hold back the European Community institutions and consequently the United Kingdom government has shown less than enthusiasm for the proposals.

As we have seen, English law does not talk in terms of rights and even less in terms of constitutional rights; acceptance of the Community Charter of Fundamental Social Rights would let such provisions in through the means of European law. The general position seems to be that international treaties are referred to neither in British legislation nor in the courts. This does not necessarily detract from the value of these instruments, it does not mean that the treaties are not greatly used by lawyers and are rarely cited in litigation. They remain as a backcloth to legislation and practices rather than being part of their intrinsic fabric. Fundamental to these treaties, perhaps at danger if the Community Charter proceeds, is the necessity of monitoring. The Economic, Social and Cultural Covenant and the European Social Charter are essentially programmes for reform.

What the United Kingdom lacks is an organised means of monitoring economic and social rights. There are some areas where, undoubtedly, the courts could play a stronger role but litigation is expensive and inefficient in a programmatic context. The relatively new United Nations Committee on Economic, Social and Cultural Rights puts international monitoring of these rights in increasingly higher profile and should the European Community Charter fail to survive as presently envisaged and end up, rather like the European Social Charter, in diluted form, the need for better organised monitoring procedures would seem essential.

NOTES

1. Despite the UK's absence from UNESCO the treaties concluded during membership have not been denounced.
2. These rights are: Article 1. The right to work; Article 5. The right to organise; Article 6. The right to bargain collectively; Article 12. The right to social security; Article 13. The right to social and medical assistance; Article 16. The right of the family to social, legal and economic protection; Article 19. The right of migrant workers and their families to protection and assistance.
3. The right to education is to be found in the European Convention on Human Rights (the European Social Charter's bigger sister). It is dealt with there in a much less detailed way than in the Covenant. See chapter 9.
4. See Michael Addo, chapter 5.
5. Chapter 7.
6. (1765) 19 SE.Tr.1030.
7. [1979] Ch 344, Malone v. UK (1982) 5 E.H.R.R. 385.
8. See, for example, *Johnston v. Chief Constable of the Royal Ulster Constabulary* (case 222/84) 1986 3 All E.R. 135. £1 million damages awarded against the RUC divisible between 300 constables.
9. See Chapter 8.
10. See Chapter 9.
11. Article 2.
12. Chapter 9.
13. See chapter 10.
14. See Ian Forbes, chapter 7.
15. United Nations Charter Article 1(3). The Charter does not at this stage, however, refer to social, economic or cultural *rights*.
16. See James Fawcett's views in chapter 1, p.14.
17. See, for example, Lord Scarman's arguments in his Hamlyn Lecture. Sir Leslie Scarman 'English Law – The New Dimension' (London: Stevens, 1974).

7 Universal Rights and Public Policy: The Case for Equal Opportunity

Ian Forbes

At the heart of this chapter is the question: can there be a right to equal opportunity? Such an inquiry concerns a number of issues, ranging from the possible basis for such a right, the kind of equality of opportunity entailed, the correlative duties thereby presupposed, and the possibility for converting right and duty into a general approach to public policy and specific issues alike. It is argued here that the case can be made for a right to equal opportunity, and that this has profound implications for public policy in all its guises.

First, it does make sense to talk of rights, but only if rights are based on human need. Moreover, that connection between need and right must not be established in a foundationalist manner. Rather, the concept of need is identified in this political and philosophical discourse as a contextual and historicised, not *a priori* assumption. Need relates to human nature, expressed human agency and the real conditions for human existence, not simply some essence of humanity. Arguing from this concept of need does establish the universality of right, the existence of correlative duties or obligations on the part of others to respect those rights, and the validity of entitlements to the actions and resources necessary for their fulfilment.

The right to equal opportunity will thus be presented as a *primary* right, a right, that is, which can orientate public policy in the broadest terms. Furthermore, the relationship between this universal primary right and public policy suggests that the right to equal opportunity provides the practical and pragmatic basis for public policy *implementation*. This can be represented both as a commitment in respect of procedures (justice as means) and to underlying principle (ends imply original value stances). The important corollary to these features of equal opportunity is evaluation, whereby intent, ends and means are kept in view and in balance. In these ways, the primary right to equal opportunity can become an *effective* right.

Just as not all conceptions of rights lead to equal opportunity, so not all conceptions of equal opportunity are consistent with rights arguments. Therefore, the major approaches are reviewed in the light of the model, and some comparisons between Britain and other countries made. Radically to truncate the argument, need and opportunity are inextricably linked, and in a parallel form of connection are universality and equality. It is argued that breaches of any one threatens the primary and effective right to equal opportunity.

NEEDS AND RIGHTS

Human rights or universal rights in respect of humans only have meaning insofar as they refer to or reflect a logically prior set of assumptions and arguments about human existence. Proceeding from this assumption I follow a path marked by philosophical, normative and empirical claims concerning human beings. First, there is a set of historical needs that is common and irreducible for human persons. Second, these needs have arisen out of and are a combination of the social, physical and emotional properties of humans and their existence. Thus needs are not essential in themselves, even though they have a logical priority. Some aspects of these needs are unfortunately subjected to almost routine empirical test. Nourishment, shelter and nurture are fundamental in that the satisfaction or otherwise of these needs is clearly and closely linked in cause and effect terms with the possibility of life. Another condition for human thriving is the absence of life-threatening attack.

However, humans are not the only things to need security, nourishment, shelter and nurturance; the same could be said of some plants. Thus needs do not of themselves amount to strong claims; they do not establish the obligation to satisfy or meet needs. (This is part of the work reserved for rights). Having no special status of justification, they are not 'rock bottom' explanations. To assert a need is, after all, just as easy but no more illuminating than the bald assertion of a want or a right. But needs do form part of the logical sequence leading to claims on others, claims on resources, obligations and mechanisms for provision. The logical and moral impetus associated with the concept of need stems from the underlying valuation of life itself. Since humans value life in general and invariably in particular, we can see that needs carry the weight that they do because they represent the integration of physical and existential necessity. Using Kant's presumption about human rationality, certain conditions follow from this view of needs. The most important consequence is the realisation that humans have in common the reality and the experience of needs. Needs are universal; all humans have general and specific needs in relation to their individuality and circumstance; all humans have a limited set of needs in common. To be a needful person, therefore, entails the possibility of perceiving the common basis of human existence[1] *and with it the common conditions for its realisation.*[2]

If I believe that my needs should be satisfied, and there is no reason why a bearer of needs would not experience this wish, then logically I must express a claim relating to freedom and resources that is at once both general and particular. It so happens that only human agents are capable of doing this (even though the logical necessity of making a claim does not guarantee that the claim will actually be logical). We may therefore assume that agency is involved, and that agency is not possible without basic universal needs being met. The enjoyment of agency is dependent upon the necessary conditions of agency being fulfiled. In one agent's claim for freedom and resources, then, we see that the conditions for agency *per se* are being claimed. In other words, the conditions for agency represent an *indivisible good*. In willing the conditions of agency for myself, I will them also for all others, as do they in turn. This may be put in any number of ways, but it seems to me that the most productive yet economical way of expressing this is to say that *respect for persons* is thus activated and perpetuated.

The addition of a moral element to our self-perception, reasoning and actions is grounded in this notion of respect for persons. I do not use the term 'moral' in any evaluative sense here. Rather, morality denotes judgement and intention based on understanding and observation. It is not an empiricist claim open to contradiction and subject to the burden of falsifiability. Having identified need-based conditions of agency, we conclude that respect for persons is most consistent with the enjoyment of agency of all persons, including ourselves.

So saying we establish the moral basis for proceeding, if not the means. Implementing that understanding involves the construction of relevant and applicable injunctions on human behaviour. It is here that rights can play their part. What has to be demonstrated is that rights claims are not instrumentally or vexatiously asserted. The connection between needs and rights has to be mediated by and serve the principle of respect for persons. We are looking for 'moral rights'. As Henry Shue claims:

> A moral right provides (1) the rational basis for a justified demand (2) that the actual enjoyment of a substance be (3) socially guaranteed against standard threats.[3]

The starting point must be moral rights. Moral rights do not at this early stage of the argument have the different status of legal rights (which may or may not relate to moral rights at all), but the conversion of moral rights into legal rights may be a vital part of our intention. To make explicit the connections with a much larger argument, claims about the best way to conceive of concerted and organised political action through the agency of the state are at issue here. The available ways to see the modern state (the enforcer, the nightwatchman, the representative, the delegate, the malign or benign structure, the nation, the people) all exhibit the same flaw – the state is a geographically and administratively bounded entity which defines itself in contrast to all other states.[4] The interest and power concerns that are the key determinants of the internal structure and behaviour of states will not by definition discover and proceed on universalistic principles, so means have to be developed for incorporating approaches and procedures that will alter the state.

The move that Shue makes is to argue that we can think in terms of some basic rights as everyone's minimum reasonable demands on the rest of humanity. Those basic rights, the component of reasonableness and the involvement of all of humankind stem from the existence of universal human needs. Needs can entail rights claims; rights claims can produce legitimate demands on others and also corresponding duties. In this way, it is possible to see that rights arguments can indeed be used in a strategic way to bring about change.

Since we began with the needs for existential and physical survival and thriving as a human agent, the rights that secure the minimum conditions for need satisfaction must be both 'basic'[5] and universal. That is to say, such rights can only apply equally to all humans. Anything less, and needs would not be satisfied; any more and we would require an account of how further provision was related to the secondary or historically and circumstantially conditioned needs that were to be addressed.[6] In consideration of further needs we would see a mixture of empirical and moral judgements: what are the needs, and what is the basis for resource distribution? Moral arguments about desert, for example, would inevitably arise, creating the grounds for differentiation between individuals and groups. Were we to move directly to this terrain, however, we would find that our empirical and normative reasoning would quickly become bogged down by relativism and ethnocentrism.

In other words, universal needs and the associated universal rights should be pursued as far as is possible. Universal rights are important because they embody what Felix Oppenheim calls the empirical quality of egalitarianism.[7] This egalitarianism arises from the universal commonality and equality of human needs. Therefore the claims that spring from universal needs and rights are not related to one polity or culture, nor do they stop at the peripheries of societies. The moral nature of rights does not consist in the issue of equality but in the context of the correlative duties that are associated with the assertion, recognition, and justiciability of a right. Moreover, the principle of respect for persons requires that there be a set of rights of a so-called negative kind and the assertion, definition and defence of welfare rights follows this path.[8] Welfare rights signify the practical nature of the obligations our society and we as citizens must acknowledge.

Certain principles should attend the implementation of basic rights. First, substantial rights should be differentiated from procedural rights. Basic rights are, of course, in the former category, and they require 'initial' institutions to meet and protect these rights. Institutions of rights hold and express rights in general (procedures follow principle, procedures do not constitute principle). Second, substantial and procedural rights also need to be separated on grounds of fairness, such that procedures are not undermined and arbitrarily applied.

THE RIGHT TO EQUALITY OF OPPORTUNITY

The implementation of basic rights immediately brings into play considerations of justice and the need for judgements. Following Shue's principle of the moral minimum, I suggest that the ascription of universal needs, the derivation of universal rights plus correlative duties expressed as public policy is best consolidated in *the right to equality of opportunity*. Such a right is not a negative right, since it implies more than forbearance and is not strictly a security right. Nor is it simply a welfare right. The right to equal opportunity differs in important respects from a welfare right, especially since resources are usually but not necessarily involved. The form and content of welfare rights are in a sense secondary to the *principle* of the right to equal opportunity.

Basic rights and correlative duties, in other words, generate a *primary* right to equality of opportunity. In a strictly logical way, 'equality' endorses and realises the egalitarian nature of needs and universal rights.[9] 'Opportunity', on the other hand, involves differentiation, comparison and judgement, encapsulates the fact that resource provision may be a corollary, couples this to the moral component inherent in the concepts of duty and obligation and implies that justice must accompany procedure. Since universal needs means that we must will the ends as well as the means in relation to respect for persons, need is inextricably linked to the opportunity to realise that respect in principle and in substance.[10]

Unlike a welfare right, the primary right to equal opportunity and its associated obligation (right plus dutiful action) falls upon all humans regardless of their society or citizenship. The contingent entitlement to the primary right to equality of opportunity arises not out of our membership as citizens of this state but out of the normative responsibility of *any* state to embody the principle of respect for persons. (There is, as Bernard Boxhill argues, a case to be made for 'global equality of opportunity').[11] This in turn presupposes a public policy requirement which overrides local systems of resource allocation and justice. Provisions in respect of universal rights, therefore, inhere in much more than the traditional concerns over constitutional definitions, Bills of Rights and ratification of UN and regional Conventions. If there is a primary right to equal opportunity, then it must be reflected at every level of government, administration and social life.

A public policy establishes the basis for making decisions in respect of needs, rights, duties and procedural justice by institutionalising the primary right, setting up procedural rights in terms of justice and incorporating provisions for accountability and redress. It establishes the right to have needs met and protected, the right to a fair consideration of needs and the right to a fair consideration of interests based upon the equality of respect for persons.[12] Moreover, it enables us to make comparisons across borders and judgements about the practicability and feasibility of public policy based on the primary right to equal opportunity.

EQUALITY, OPPORTUNITY, POLICY AND POLITICS

There are three main public policy approaches to the issues of equality and social justice associated with equal opportunity. The first is the commitment to treat equals in a like fashion. Here the emphasis is on *equal treatment*; opportunities are not provided indiscriminately to all but treatment is equalised under existing patterns of resource distribution and preferment. On a simple view of justice, this promises fair procedures, but is blind to existing inequalities and the effects of advantage and disadvantage. The second approach sees *equal opportunities* as more of a starting gate approach, whereby a person is assured of an equal chance to take part in the competition for economic and social advantage. Like equal treatment, it offers fairness, but of a more sophisticated or more socially aware and pragmatic kind. However, it too may not affect the entrenched patterns of inequality in society. Consequently, this basic position is augmented, sometimes in radical ways, to take account of prior disadvantage as well as the defects and biases of the 'race' that is to be run. *Positive action* programmes, for example, may contain elements of compensation to allow for systematic disadvantage and specify in advance the criteria for success of an equal opportunity policy.

The third position sees outcomes as the best measure of policy effectivity. Here the principle of equal opportunity applying to all may well be transgressed, since it will be necessary to restrict the opportunity of some advantaged groups and individuals in order to produce a predetermined shift in economic and social advantage. *Equality of outcome* is notoriously difficult to achieve and defend on both practical and theoretical grounds. Defining specific outcomes is fraught with political difficulty; once defined, the policy defies orderly implementation given unforeseen events. Also, it will almost certainly require *positive discrimination*, which violates commonly agreed (if Western) principles of justice.

Each of these positions is associated with a particular ideological approach, but policy selection and mode of implementation of equal opportunity taken in its broadest sense are not necessarily linked to the political complexion of a government in power. Four responses do stand out.[13] The first, minimalist position proceeds from the assumption that choice, selection and preferment throughout society will be procedurally just and reasonably meritocratic, given, at the most, public pronouncements to that effect. This is to have no policy at all. The second approach seeks actively to secure procedural justice where appropriate, namely between those in direct competition. The third strategy is related to the conservative and liberal interpretations of equal opportunity; there is the determination to strive for procedural justice combined with the insistence that all individuals be included in the competition for advantage. Reforms are necessary to equalise starting positions. Finally, proponents of radical equality of opportunity go further; they recognise the importance of social factors, the existence of group disadvantage and the need to implement policy by means of positive action. Change to structures and policies must therefore be made to realise equality and a just end-state. This fourth position is often denounced as an unjustifiable attempt to impose equality of outcome.

POLICY AND PRACTICE

The implementation of equal opportunities, consistent with a right to equal opportunity, is conditioned by ideological considerations as well as the overwhelming domination of political and administrative structures by men. Typically, governments and administrations may adopt a range of policy measures which draw on the available models and approaches according to a mixture of circumstances, applicability and preference. In general, equal opportunities implementation should have four elements: investigation to understand the degree and kind of change required; implementation of policy and procedures; evaluation of effectiveness; review of goals and procedures. All participating parties should be included in this managed change process, and it should be properly resourced.

However, this model comes into conflict with popular assertions that economic decision-making and activity are best left unencumbered by political processes and administration. The robust version suggests that individuals are by nature inclined to self-sufficiency, independence and self-help. On this account, *any* collective regulatory initiatives are perceived as running counter to forces and impulses which will produce natural and desirable outcomes. Instead, market forces are supposed to lead to significant gains in efficiency without an equivalent loss of equity and justice, while our ends as individual consumers and producers are met through largely self-governing means.[14] The implementation of equal opportunity policy against this background produces a definite kind of outcome. That outcome can be judged in empirical terms and normatively assessed in respect of the preceding argument concerning universal needs and rights. Here we see that a right to equal opportunity can be in conflict with government belief and state practice.

The neo-liberal approach to public policy is most developed in the UK, which nevertheless does have legislation and administrative structures in respect of equal opportunity. A comparison with France and Sweden shows the varying nature and intensity of implementation of the right to equal opportunity. Sweden has one of the best records in the area of equal opportunities this century, a substantial claim well supported on a variety of measures.[15] The variations between Western European countries establishes that there is considerable room for manoeuvre within the liberal democratic state tradition, and that the general limitations on political action associated with the distinction between negative and positive rights need not in fact preclude public policy to respect the right to equal opportunity.

An analysis of the institutional apparatus and policies developed by Britain, Sweden and France leads to specific conclusions about the efficacy of different procedures and methods of implementation, the importance of political commitment and the impact of alternative perceptions of social organisation on outcomes.[16]

FRANCE AND POLITICAL MOTIVATION

In the case of France, the Ministry of Women's Rights created under the first Mitterrand government reflected a firm political commitment to improve the situation of women. This public policy strategy highlights the benefits of government, administration and a united women's movement in close cooperation and the value of positive action. Although much was achieved, a telling limitation within the French model stems from the practice that women in the civil service are not affected by the provisions of the Bill. It is not unusual for government agencies to be exempt from social and civil regulation, but this case does seem to fall outside any justifiable category for such exemption. The state, in other words, in this case was setting the legislative agenda for, but not an active example to the wider society. It thereby violates the primary right to equal opportunity of women in principle and in terms of some procedures.

Nevertheless, the Roudy Act of 1984 did establish the principle of and need for longitudinal monitoring of organisations. This has emerged as the only realistic means of taking equal opportunities beyond mere lip service and tokenism. Responsibility for the implementation of equal opportunities principles must reside with each organisation just as much as it is a general social concern. Without monitoring, it is practically impossible to form anything but the most indefinite claims and targets for action. Quite apart from its educative function, monitoring is vital if any evaluation of performance is to be possible.

Put another way, monitoring is one component of the logical consequences of the identification of needs and the obligation on society that arises out of the specification of a right. The other element, equally important, is a programme of positive action designed to rectify existing inequalities of employment, status and situation. Some progress has been made in the fields of training, employment and promotion with provision for 'remedial measures' incorporated into the Roudy Act.[17] Other advances relate to maternity arrangements and child care provision. In this respect, France provides rather more than any other EC country, certainly much more than Britain. Over a quarter of two-year-olds attend pre-school; at three and then four this rises to 80 and 97 per cent respectively. In fact, of the one million plus children under three who are cared for or supervised in the European Community, fully two thirds of places are provided in France. France has historically stressed the national need for a regular supply of French citizens, with the full support of the Church, so it is no great surprise that it lays a greater emphasis on 'parental involvement in day-nurseries and children's centres, including networks of mothers with part-time playgroup jobs'. Associated with this is a statutory entitlement to generous parental and family leave provision (not confined to women) with protection for social security rights, and the public sector allows a basic six days per year for the care of a sick child or for temporary child-minding. In this last respect, Sweden provides ten times this amount and extends it to cover sickness of the person normally caring for the child.[18] Such levels of provision are unknown in Britain, where the meagre arrangements in existence have been under an almost constant threat. This is a clear case where need and opportunity are linked by virtue of a common resource requirement, and where right is clearly connected to practical policies.

In terms of implementation, the French experience does demonstrate the value of the formal political, governmental and administrative recognition of women's situation, the need for monitoring of positive action, and the pertinence of child care and welfare policies. The Ministry model of change ensures a level of dynamism and access to centres of power. However, such a route to change is vulnerable to fluctuations in party fortunes, and dependencies arising from electoral exigencies and constant caucusing detract from the focus on the needs of women. Women's groups, too, are not always united in their support for the government, and women in general react in conventional ways to economic downturn, despite any moves to improve their situation. While France has exhibited some commitment to procedures associated with equal opportunity, it has not acted to recognise and entrench the primary *right* to equal opportunity. Indeed, the Constitutional Convention has resisted attempts to incorporate the principle of equality into core state documents.

SWEDEN: STATE FEMINISM

There is a radical difference between the efforts of Sweden and those of France and the United Kingdom. Compared to them, Sweden is in another category altogether; and in that (Scandinavian) category it is an acknowledged leader. Effectively, 'state feminism' is in place in Sweden.

State feminism consists of four things. First and foremost, equality for women 'is official government policy', written into the definitions of state responsibility.[19] Second, this is a non-partisan public policy, and there is evidence of a determination to transcend rather than adjust discrimination. Third, Sweden's seven active instruments of implementation ensure that the policy is practically embodied in a range of Acts, institutions and procedures in the public and private sectors of the economy. Fourth, Sweden is regarded as 'the pioneer country in matters of positive action'.[20] As such, Sweden comes close to a *de facto* adoption of a primary right to equal opportunity, since the principle of equality is both a generator and defender of public policy.

Swedish initiatives combine executive and legislative action to enhance the effectiveness of the commitment to equal opportunities. This approach, which integrates progress in economic and social respects with fiscal and development policy, is markedly absent in Britain. In practice, Swedish action is wide-ranging and positive. It goes well beyond the legal-rational view of equal opportunities implementation, and makes attempts to tackle the presumptions behind the social barriers to women's equality.

Sweden has also shown itself to have a general resistance to the erosion of social welfare policies (with widespread negative consequences for women and the poor) under the onslaught of economic exigencies. According to Roger Lawson, Sweden is a prime example of a 'strong welfare state', 'highly committed to social security and welfare and capable of preventing mass unemployment in the face of worldwide economic crisis and with a low rate of economic growth'.[21] In the area of equal opportunities, it is has been through the voice and influence of 'wage-earner solidarity, rather than through a more abstract appeal to individual rights, that gender inequalities have been reduced'.[22] By repudiating the notion of rights as properties of individuals, the Swedish approach is consistent with the argument developed at the beginning of this chapter. Only if equal opportunity is seen as a *primary* right can responsibility for creating the conditions for the realisation of that right be held to be a common social concern and duty.

A combination of the presumption that individuals have clear social responsibilities and a corporatist approach to public policy-making has done more than lead to progressive legislation and social policy. It has served to resist the 'social disarmament' that has so adversely affected the situation of less powerful groups elsewhere in the 1970s and 1980s. Whatever the criticisms that can be made of the Swedish example, it is proving capable of sustaining the advances it has made, when those all around it are steadily reducing the choices of and undermining the autonomy of women, especially less advantaged groups of women.[23]

INTERNATIONALISM AND THE EUROPEAN COMMUNITY

The EC, by definition and intent, seeks to act in a supranational manner on agreed principles. It is, therefore, ideally placed to endorse the primary right to equal opportunity and promote appropriate public policies. Indeed, in recognition of the rights of individual citizen members of the European Community, the EC sees itself as 'a driving force in the implementation of the programme for equal opportunities'.

However, it has been very slow to implement such policies within its own organisational structure.[24] Community claims to have advanced equal opportunities policies and practices have also to be discounted against Sweden's achievements, where progress has been secured without the 'benefit' of Community membership and the encouragement and sponsorship of various Directives. There is a great deal of similarity here between Britain, France and the EC; all have introduced equal opportunities legislation but have failed in some measure to apply the principles behind those policies to themselves and to address endemic structural and administrative features over which they have some measure of control and considerable responsibility. Nevertheless, European sanctions do come into play, especially against Britain, and its reluctance to honour both the letter and spirit of EC initiatives and law.

Unfortunately, the most recent Action Programme of the European Community may narrow its vision by entrenching the view that rights holders are individuals. Explicitly, the Commission intends to legislate 'with a view to a progressive individualization of rights'.[25] This is a retrograde step, since it will cut the link between needs and rights by assuming that individuals are the possessors of an abstract set of rights. This means that rights-claims become restricted and formal rather than relative to other humans and entailing social obligations of a complex kind. The EC, in other words, is failing to act in a supranational way in respect of the supranational right to equal opportunity.

UNITED KINGDOM: COMMISSIONING EQUALITY?

Britain's legislative and administrative initiatives on equal opportunity have brought about a reliance on the formal qualities of quangos and the vigour of local government. Much of the legislation has been forced upon it by membership of the EC, and there is very little evidence of a state commitment to equality of opportunity. Some change has been produced through the agency of the Equal Opportunities Commission (EOC) and the Commission for Racial Equality, but these technically powerful bodies are severely restricted by dint of inadequate resource levels, the idiosyncrasy of the legal charters and the system within which they operate, and the minimal ability to affect government legislation changes or alter administrative practices. The government could provide legislative leadership and exercise enormous influence given a commitment to basic procedural aspects of equal opportunity, namely, equality of access and equality of treatment, and to the aims of economic independence, full rights and educational and social fulfilment. This presupposes extra resources and changes in established practices across the whole range of government provision of services, but government policies have only increased the disadvantages of women since 1979. Its legislative record is nothing short of disgraceful.

The major offsetting influence stems from local authorities, a substantial number of which have implicitly begun with the presumption that there is a right to equal opportunity enjoyed by all individuals in their constituencies. In many cases, local authorities are faced with diverse communities, where the generalities of citizenship rights can be in contrast to the particularities of differences between ethnic communities and the varying experience of people within them. They have recognised their responsibility to respect and realise these differences and yet act in a universal way even at the local level. To proceed, they have acknowledged their potential for bringing about change by developing and implementing equal opportunities policies.

Implementation is seen as a complex process, requiring considerable all-party political support, a corporate approach to policy-making, utilisation of existing personnel with skills and experience relating to equal opportunities issues, and a commitment to community involvement and consultation.[26] It has become necessary to function at a variety of levels, in recognition of the shortcomings of bureaucratic consultative and policy-making structures and the need to reconcile national and local party differences.[27] It is also argued that 'unless the implementation structures are robust enough', they will fall victim to economic efficiency arguments supported by values 'that discriminate against the very people the policy is designed to help'.[28] Moreover, local authorities are themselves subject to economic pressure arising out of political objectives.

The national government response to economic difficulties (first under Healey, then Howe, Lawson and Major) has been to restrict economic activity and to reduce budget deficits, with marked effects on opportunities in terms of employment, education and human fulfilment. British government action over the past ten years has been wilful in its antagonism to the interests of women, ethnic minorities and the poor and in its resistance to legally-binding decisions against its legislative and administrative shortcomings. There is no 'Bill of Rights' even on the horizon. Existing Conventions receive scant respect. This means more than a rejection of rights claims, of course, because of the connection that I have established between universal human needs and entitlements against the state. In this respect, the institutional and practical role of the state has been increasingly restricted instead of being developed as a creative and positive influence on social issues. The state has been 'minimalised'; market values have taken over the role of allocation of resources and preferences, and individuals are being left to accept the consequences of the reduction and withdrawal of state services.

The paradox is that Britain is becoming an increasingly strong state, based on the requirement that the individual make her and his solitary way in the world. The new-found strength stems in part from relinquishing activities and responsibilities which had become so troublesome – corporate economic planning, full employment, continued growth in social services – and in part from ignoring the demands of historically important interest and pressure groups. Most important here are women, trades unions and ethnic minorities.[29] The corollary to this kind of strong state is that only certain individuals are recognised. Such individuals have no claim to social or state security; they must secure their own future in the market place. Such a market place is to be protected from the depredations of government and bureaucracy. Equal opportunities policies are therefore frowned upon because they will, like any other regulation, restrict the efficiency and room for manoeuvre of entrepreneurs. Also, 'social' legislation disturbs the allocative working of the economic market to the detriment of all individuals by virtue of the attempt to impose a predetermined outcome. However, the primary right to equal opportunity still applies to, even though it does not presuppose, the 'individual' of neo-liberal thought, and lip-service is often paid to procedural equality of opportunity.

CONCLUSION

The comparison of states shows that the primary right to equal opportunity and the secondary procedural implementation of that right is a legitimate and practical possibility. Equal opportunity has been shown to be heavily dependent upon the particular actions of government and the orientation of the state in general. French progress was most swift under the sponsorship of a specific party political initiative with the support of an identifiable cohort of supporters and practitioners. At the level of the state, however, the right to equal opportunity has been rebuffed. British implementation has enjoyed no such sustained or coherent efforts by central government. What progress has been made has arisen out of the tenacity of individuals and groups who have tried to realise the potential inherent in the creation of a limited but fundamentally sound and quite powerful institutional structure. The greatest effect has been achieved at local-authority level; even large private firms, keen to enhance their personnel development, have not been slow to adopt equal opportunities practices.[30]

While French progress is restricted by a mixture of institutional inertia and fluctuating party fortunes, the implementation of equal opportunity in Britain is being actively frustrated. Far from there being an infrastructure of state feminism, the rhetoric of the British government advances the view that women belong in the family while its actions produce a mass of changes prejudicial to the interests of women. Yet the implications for implementation of the British model augment the French experience. The formation of an autonomous Commission does provide protection from electoral swings, and enforcement of the Act and anti-discriminatory work can be effective. There are major drawbacks, however. The EOC is prevented from formulating decision-making in reference to crucial areas of social policy that affect specific groups of women, and must respond on the basis of the cases of individual women (and men). It lacks, in other words, the position and influence of a Ministry, or the grass-roots contact of the local authority. Thus, experience suggests that the French and the British do not offer alternative models of implementation; there is a very good case for employing both of the centralised means for the policy ends, and for encouraging work at the local level.

Apart from the resolve of government and the efficacy of implementation methods, equal opportunity is most affected by general economic and social policy. In this respect, countries can be judged according to whether they develop the responsibilities of the state and community in such a way as to enhance access to resources, status and benefits in society. The 1980s have seen a widespread and systematic move to diminish the role of the state. This 'social disarmament' is a sin of commission, with direct and quantifiable effects on those whose right to equal opportunity is being violated. It is much more easily countenanced and implemented where social obligations and responsibilities (common citizenship) have been systematically negated. Where they have been supported and developed, as in Sweden, expectations regarding equal opportunities policies will not be based on individual wants, but on the basis of group needs and the demands for social progress.

Sweden clearly deserves its reputation for achieving change. It outperforms the United Kingdom and France in terms of commitment to progress and level of end-state achievement on every count. State feminism in Sweden is buttressed by institutional and structural arrangements and the commitment of women is further protection against regressive change. This also means that policies can be developed and implemented more readily because such policies are at the very least consistent with underpinning conceptions of social justice, and are more likely to be seen as logical and proper social actions. Corresponding to this social background and the stated commitment to equality of opportunity, Sweden's implementation is based on the full range of measures necessary to meet claims and duties arising from the primary right. Again, Sweden's approach is not counterposed to the mechanisms found in Britain and France; rather, they provide a range of insights to the way that a universal right impinges upon public policy. In other words, implementation by norms, statements of principle, party campaigns or through formal legal equality can never take the place of enforcement and enactment in public policy arenas of the correlative duties implied by human needs, universal rights and the primary right to equal opportunity.

NOTES

1. Acknowledgement of that common basis is not so simple or rational a matter. The non-rational grounds of discrimination and prejudice can nevertheless be made subject to rational procedures (viz anti-discrimination legislation).
2. 'Common' gestures towards such problematic but central concepts as equality, fairness and objectivity.
3. H. Shue, *Basic Rights* (Princeton: Princeton University Press, 1982) p.13.
4. For a Foucauldian discussion of the nature of the state in respect of other states, see my 'Beyond the State' in I. Forbes and M. Hoffman (eds), *International Relations, Political Theory and the Ethics of Intervention*, (London: Macmillan, 1991).

5. Shue argues for finding the 'moral minimum' in order to clarify responsibilities and to deal effectively with the host of arguments against respecting basic rights.
6. Here we must acknowledge that there is a vast range of definitions of thin and thick theories of the good within and between societies.
7. F. Oppenheim, *Political Concepts: A Reconstruction*, (Oxford: Basil Blackwell, 1981); see chapter 6.
8. See chapter 2, R. Plant, 'A defence of Welfare Rights'.
9. Taken at face value, universality and equality have common roots for liberal and socialist or radical thought, and emerge in similar ways in public policy if not institutional organisation.
10. An associated argument has been conducted over the concepts freedom and ability. Neo-liberals argue that freedom is not necessarily conditional upon ability; others establish both logical and substantive grounds for their connection.
11. His argument is based on the difference principle and addresses the issue of immigration possibilities and the way that states can act to restrict or increase equality of opportunity. 'Global Equality of Opportunity and National Integrity', in E.F. Paul *et al.* (eds), *Equal Opportunity* (Oxford: Basil Blackwell, 1988).
12. See R. Dworkin's *Taking Rights Seriously*, (London: Duckworths, 1979).
13. Forbes, I. 1988, 'Equality of Opportunity: Radical, Liberal and Conservative Critiques', Political Studies Association Annual Conference, Plymouth.
14. Forbes, I., 'A Market Policy for Socialists?' *Economic Affairs*, Vol. 7, No. 6, 1987 (Aug./Sept.), and Plant, R., 'The Social Limits of Markets', *Economic Affairs*, Vol. 7, No. 6, 1987 (Aug./Sept.).
15. See my 'Unequal Partners: The Implementation of Equal Opportunities in Sweden, France and the UK', in *Public Administration*, Spring 1989; A. Mazur, 'New Issues, Agendas, and Policy Outcomes: Equal Opportunities in France 1970 – 1989: Policy, Practice and Outcome', European Consortium of Political Research, April 1989; D. Sainsbury, 'Welfare State Variations, Women and Equality: On Varieties of the Welfare State and their Implications for Women', European Consortium of Political Research, April 1989. Information on the qualitative nature of women's employment, the percentages of work that is part-time and low paid, the degree to which they have been allowed to assume high office and positions of authority, the level of support they can expect in dealing with what are (still) seen as traditional role functions, such as child-bearing and rearing, and levels and kinds of violence against women also places the 'progress' achieved by these countries in a less favourable light.
16. I. Forbes, 1988; A. Michel, 1986. 'Positive Action for the Benefit of Women', *Preliminary Study for the Committee for Equality Between Women and Men*. Strasbourg: Council of Europe; E. Vogel-Polsky, 'National institutional and non-institutional machinery established in the Council of Europe member states to promote equality between women and men', *Study for the Committee for Equality between Women*

and Men, Council of Europe, Strasbourg, 1985.
17. A. Michel, ibid. 1986, pp.10 – 11.
18. *Equal Opportunities Commission*. 1984. Submission to the Select Committee on the European Communities of the House of Lords on the Proposed Directive on Parental Leave and Leave for Family Reasons (Com (83) 686 Final), EOC/POL/SEPT/84, pp.26, 35 – 40.
19. J. Scriven, 'Women at Work in Sweden', in M.J. Davidson and C.L. Cooper (eds), *Women at Work* (London: Wiley & Sons, 1984), p.153.
20. R. Nielsen, 'Equality Legislation in a Comparative Perspective: Towards State Feminism'. *Women's Research Centre in Social Science* (Copenhagen, 1983) p.2.
21. R. Lawson, 'Welfare State Strategies and Crisis Management', Paper prepared for Social Administration Association Conference, Edinburgh, 1987, p.1; also published as R. Lawson, 'Gegensaetzliche Tendenzen in der sozialen Sicherheit: Ein Vergleich zwischen Grossbritannien und Schweden', in *Zeitschrift fuer Auslendisches und Interntionales Arbeits – und Sozialrecht*, Vol. 1, 1987.
22. R. Lawson, ibid. 1987, p.8.
23. M. Eduard, *Sweden*, in Joni Lovenduski and Jill Hills (eds), *The Politics of the Second Electorate* (London: Routledge & Kegan Paul, 1981), pp.224-6; Scriven, 1981, p.176.
24. *European File*, 'Equal Opportunities for Women', 10/87, 1987, p.10.
25. *Bulletin of the European Communities*. Medium-term Community Programme, 1986-90, Supplement 3/86, 1986, p.15.
26. W. Ball, 1987, 'Local Authority Policy-Making on Equal Opportunities: Corporate provision, co-option and consultation', *Policy and Politics*, Vol. 15, No. 2, pp. 101 – 10; 1987. I. Stone, 'Equal Opportunities in Local Authorities', *EOC Research Series* (London: HMSO, 1988).
27. Ball, ibid. 1987, pp.108 – 9.
28. R. Means, P. Burton, T. Davies and S. Fenton, 'Implementation of Social Goals in Labour Market Policy: The Case of Black Youth, Equal Opportunities and the Youth Training Scheme', *Policy and Politics*, Vol. 13, No.1, 1985,. p.82.
29. As John Solomos writes in respect of ethnic minorities, 'equal opportunities are both a political issue and a legal administrative question'. 'Equal opportunities policies and racial inequality: the role of public policy', *Public Administration*, 67/1, Spring 1989, p.91.
30. 'Managerial imperatives will demand an equal opportunities policy which will have the effect of attracting and retaining an adequate workforce.' Joni Lovenduski, 'Implementing equal opportunities in the 1980s: an overview', *Public Administration*, 67/1, Spring 1989, p.18.

8 The European Social Charter: Employment, Unions and Strikes

Vivien J. Shrubsall

The European Social Charter was signed in Turin in 1961 and took effect in 1965. The Charter guarantees certain social and economic rights (including basic employment rights) and complements the European Convention on Human Rights which protects civil and political rights. The Charter sets out in Part I a declaration of aims towards which contracting parties should strive and those aims are particularised in Part II. The Charter is binding on 14 of the Council of Europe's 21 nations and the United Kingdom accepted all but ten of the 72 specific obligations in Part II of the Charter.

The main employment rights in the European Social Charter are:

Article 1 – the right to work;
Article 2 – the right to just conditions of work;
Article 3 – the right to safe and healthy working conditions;
Article 4 – the right to a fair remuneration;
Article 5 – the right to organise;
Article 6 – the right to bargain collectively;
Article 7 – employment protection for children and young persons;
Article 8 – employment protection for women;
Article 9 – the right to vocational guidance;
Article 10 – the right to vocational training.

Each Article in subdivided into specific undertakings. The United Kingdom accepted all of these specific undertakings except Articles 2(1), 4(3), 7(1) (4) and (7), 8(2) and (3)[1] in its original acceptance of the Charter in 1962.

Enforcement of the Charter's provisions is by a system of supervision. There is no procedure for individual petition as there is under the European Convention. Contracting parties to the Charter present biennial reports to a Committee of Independent Experts concerning the application of the undertakings which they have accepted. That Committee is an independent body with seven members appointed by the Committee of Ministers. Five of the seven present members are academics. The Committee of Independent Experts does not include a national from all contracting parties and so there is not necessarily present an expert on the law and practice of a state whose report is being examined. The Experts consider the national reports and prepare Conclusions on them, Article by Article. Because of the delay between the end of the report period and the consideration of the reports by the Experts the situations described in the national reports are often overtaken by events. Often the Experts postpone a Conclusion pending clarification in the next national report.

The next stage is that the national reports and the Expert's Conclusions are submitted to the Governmental Committee, a committee of civil servants who represent and are appointed by their respective governments. Each contracting party appoints one representative to the Governmental Committee. That Committee prepares its own Report for the Committee of Ministers. Of course, the Governmental Committee often differs from the Experts over the interpretation of the Charter's undertakings and the degree of compliance and violation. The time lag between the report period and the Governmental Committee's deliberations facilitates argument that law and practice have been modified in the meantime.

The Expert's Conclusions and the Governmental Committee's Report are then forwarded to the Parliamentary Assembly which adopts an Opinion. The final stage in the supervisory system is reference of the three documents to the Committee of Ministers which is empowered to make 'necessary recommendations' to a contracting party. The recommendations must be by two-thirds majority of the Committee of Ministers and as 'recommendations' they are not binding. In any case there has been a marked absence of recommendations. The Committee of Ministers prefers instead to 'bring to the attention' of the states concerned 'cases not entirely in conformity with the Charter' by referring them to the appropriate passages of the Experts' Conclusions, the Governmental Committee's Report and the Assembly's Opinion. The 1988 Resolution which completed the ninth cycle of supervision (for the period 1 January 1982 to 31 December 1983!) illustrates the point clearly. It contains a general recommendation that governments should take account of the documents' observations but no particular state is specifically recommended to change its law or practice.

Contracting parties to the European Social Charter now report in two groups. The United Kingdom is in the first group of seven states. The tenth cycle of supervision is now proceeding based on reports for the period of January 1984 to December 1985. The national reports of the first group were examined by the Experts between October 1986 and June 1987. Their Conclusions on these reports were published towards the end of 1987, some 20 months after the end of the reporting period. The Experts found that the United Kingdom was not fully complying with 11 of the total of 62 undertakings which were accepted. Five of those 11 were in respect of the employment-related rights of Articles 1 – 10. The Governmental Committee Report (July 1988) found only two failures to comply. Those are in respect of Article 6(4), the right to collective action including the right to strike, and Article 1(2), effective protection of the right to earn a living in an occupation freely entered upon.

COMPARISON OF THE CHARTER AND NATIONAL LAW AND PRACTICE

The Right to Strike

Article 6(4) obliges contracting parties to recognise the right of workers to collective action, including the right to strike.

Save for exceptional circumstances (for example, sect. 5 Conspiracy and Protection of Property Act 1875, sect. 53 Police Act 1964)[2] which would anyway be within restrictions permitted by Article 31[3] of the Charter, there are no national criminal sanctions incurred by strikers merely because they break their contract of employment. However, with one delegation dissenting, the Governmental Committee Report on the tenth cycle for group one, took the view that the absence of criminal sanctions against strikers was not sufficient compliance with Article 6(4). The majority held that a state did not comply with Article 6(4) if its legislation or practice enabled the employer to take legal action against strikers for economic damage of if the employer could dismiss and refuse to take back a striker. Is our national law and practice consistent with such an interpretation? In theory a UK employer could sue striking employees for economic loss but in practice it does not happen. The realistic aim of most employers is the resolution of any industrial dispute and the resumption of normal working. An employer who did resort to law would be more likely to sue the union or union officials rather than the individual employees and anyway the measure of damages would not be easy to establish. It is the absence of protection against dismissal of strikers which is the real stumbling block to compliance by the United Kingdom. Under sect. 62 Employment Protection (Consolidation) Act 1978 no employee who is dismissed for participating in a strike or other industrial action can complain of unfair dismissal unless the employer 'picks and chooses' by not dismissing all such employees. If the employer dismisses all the strikers no one of them can complain of unfair dismissal. It is only if dismissals are selective that unfair dismissal actions can be brought. It was that provision which enabled more than 5000 striking printing workers to be dismissed without remedy in January 1986 during the 'Wapping Dispute', that is, the dispute between News Group International Ltd and the National Graphical Association over the move of production of *The Times, the Sun* and so on from Fleet Street to Wapping.

The industrial action need not necessarily be in breach of contract for section 62 to apply. The Court of Appeal held in *Power Packing Casemakers v Faust*[4] that employees who were dismissed for refusing to work non-contractual overtime were engaging in 'other industrial action' and so could not complain of unfair dismissal. The Court of Appeal held that the employees were participating in action with the object of putting pressure on the employer and therefore the action was 'industrial action' within the meaning of section 62. It followed that since all participants were dismissed none of them could pursue actions in unfair dismissal, even though they had not refused to do anything required of them by their contracts. The Court of Appeal refused to imply the earlier definition of irregular industrial action short of a strike which depended on the action being in breach of contract. National law also denies protection in unfair dismissal to any dismissed striker who is not re-engaged even where other strikers are taken back. An employer has only to wait three months and then he is free to re-engage selectively, for example, he can re-engage all but those he regards as militants. That is the effect of a Conservative government amendment to section 62 which was enacted in 1982. Even within the three months he can discriminate against those employees he does not want back by offering them less favourable terms of re-engagement (*Williams v National Theatre Board Ltd*).[5]

The United Kingdom representative of the Governmental Committee purported to justify national law on the grounds that it was not appropriate to prolong job vacancies indefinitely when it was clear that no agreement could be reached between employer and employees. It was argued that that kind of situation would threaten the existence of the firm and would be contrary to the obligations elsewhere in the Charter to maintain as high and stable a level of employment as possible. However, the blanket exclusion of strikers from unfair dismissal protection does not depend on breach of procedure agreements or breakdown of negotiations and there is no time qualification; *immediate* dismissal is a legitimate employer reaction to a strike. Even if the strike action was occasioned because of the employer's own breach of contract the blanket exclusion applies and the merits of the dispute are never litigated.

With the exception of one delegation (presumably that of the United Kingdom) the Governmental Committee concluded that the United Kingdom did not satisfy the undertaking in Article 6(4) and 'hoped that the standards applied in the United Kingdom would move towards fuller compliance with the Charter'.

The right to work

Article 1 of the Charter refers to the responsibility of contracting parties to achieve and maintain as high and stable a level of employment as possible and to protect effectively the right of the worker to earn his living in an occupation freely entered upon.

Information in biennial reports from the UK showed a high rate of unemployment (12.1 per cent to 13.2 per cent over the report period) and unequal geographical distribution. Part of the reason for the rise in unemployment was said to be the rise in the birth rate during the 1960s and the increased numbers of female part-time workers, particularly in service industries. The Experts made no observation on the UK's compliance with that part of Article 1 but did find breach of Article 1(2), that is, effective protection of the right of the worker to earn his living in an occupation freely entered upon. The Experts noted with satisfaction the amendments in what became the Sex Discrimination Act 1986 (removal of exemptions for small firms and private households and the rendering void of discriminatory provisions in collective agreements). However, the Experts found that sections 30 and 89 of the Merchant Shipping Act

1970 were in breach of Article 1(2). In fact section 89, which made it an offence for a merchant seaman to desert from a UK registered ship, is repealed by the Merchant Shipping Act 1988. Parts of section 30 are also repealed but it remains an offence for a merchant seaman to combine with others to disobey commands, neglect duty or impede the progress of any UK registered ship whilst at sea.

In fact the supervisory agencies of the Charter concentrate on the freedom to work, that is, the absence of coercion on the worker, rather than the worker's access to work. National law continues to regard the contract of employment as not specifically enforceable against the employee; section 16 Trade Union and Labour Relations Act 1974 prevents any court making an order which compels an employee to work. The usual arguments of mutuality of obligation and mutuality of trust and confidence would be used to prevent specific enforcement of an employment contract against an employer. However, it is possible for an industrial tribunal to order the re-instatement or re-engagement of an employee who has been found unfairly dismissed. Statistics and published research show that in fact such orders are very rarely made and the usual remedy awarded is damages. *Effective* protection of a right to work would make re-instatement of any unfairly dismissed worker the usual remedy.

That aspect of the law of unfair dismissal is reflected in judicial attitudes to ordinary breach of contract actions. A worker has the right to be paid but no right to perform the work itself, as a general rule. Exceptions are where work and wages go together (piece rates) or where the enhancement of the employee's skill or reputation as a result of performance of the contract is regarded as part of the contractual remuneration (for example, actor, singer, writer). There was an attempt made by Lord Denning in *Langston v AUEW*[6] to argue that an ordinary worker has a right to work as well as a right to contractual wages but there exists little other indication of that argument receiving general judicial endorsement. It may be that where an employer is 'starving-out' an employee, in the sense of gradually taking away his work so as to encourage him to resign, he acts in a repudiatory breach of contract for the purposes of constructive dismissal even though he continues to pay wages or salary. However, such a view merely enables the employee to seek a remedy in unfair dismissal, namely, in damages.

The right to union membership and participation in union activities

Article 5 requires contracting parties to ensure and promote the freedom of workers and employers to form local, national or international organisations. The Article permits national restriction of this right for the police and members of the armed forces.

The Experts found that the UK compulsory affiliation of police offices below the rank of superintendent to the police staff association did not infringe the Article because there is no obligation to pay subscriptions and no penalty for non-payment. They also found that the Trade Union Act 1984, which requires secret ballots for the election of union governing bodies, the taking of industrial action and the existence of political funds, did not adversely affect the exercise of the right to organise.

The Committee of Independent Experts found more difficulty with the ban on union membership of staff employed at the Government Communications Headquarters at Cheltenham. The Employment Protection (Consolidation) Act 1978 removes from protection Crown employment except for the purpose of safeguarding national security. The House of Lords held in *Council of Civil Service Unions v Minister for the Civil Service*[7] that once the minister produced evidence that the exception was for reasons of national security any right of the employees or their representatives to judicial review of that exception was overridden. That was so even though the regular consultation procedures had been ignored. The International Labour Conference Committee, adjudicating on the enforcement of ILO Conventions, found that the ban was in breach of Convention No. 87 on the freedom of association and protection of the right to organise. The European Commission of Human Rights held that the unions' complaints under Articles 11 and 13 of the European Convention were ill-founded.[8] The Convention contains an exception in Article 11(2) for restrictions 'necessary in a democratic society in the interests of national security or public safety' and the Commission found that the ban on union membership at Cheltenham was justified under that exception.

Applying the provisions of the European Social Charter, the Committee of Experts postponed a conclusion on whether the ban was in breach of Article 5. Article 31 of the Charter permits restrictions necessary for the protection of public interests, national security, public health or morals. The Committee wondered whether the ban was a restriction within Article 31, or a total abolition of the right to organise which would be contrary to the Charter. Pending further information about the replacement staff association, its functioning and the way in which representatives were elected, the Experts reached no immediate conclusion.

Since the right embodied in Article 5 is a freedom to organise it follows that enforced membership under a closed shop would be a violation. National legislative provisions on dismissal for non-membership of a union have changed radically in the decade 1978–88. The Employment Act 1988 completes the removal of restrictions to the principle that dismissal for membership *or* non-membership of a union is an unfair dismissal. The same principle applies to dismissal for participation in the activities of a trade union. Protection against action short of a dismissal is provided by section 23 of the Employment Protection Consolidation Act 1978. The Court of Appeal held in *National Coal Board v Ridgeway & Fairbrother*[9] that 'action short of dismissal' included the denial of a wage increment to members of a particular trade union.

The right to information and consultation

The Charter does not contain any specific undertakings concerning the right of unions or employees to information and consultation. Article 5 includes a general undertaking not to impair the freedom to organise and Article 6 obliges contracting parties generally to promote joint consultation and negotiation machinery. However, an Additional Protocol to the Charter was adopted by the Council of Europe's Committee of Ministers in November 1987 and was open for signature from 8 May 1988. The Protocol does contain specific information and consultation undertakings. Article 2 of the Protocol contains obligations similar to those of the draft EC 'Vredeling' Directive (1983). It recognises that workers should be informed regularly about the economic and financial situation of the employing undertaking and should be consulted in good time on proposed decisions which could substantially affect the interests of workers. Article 3 of the Protocol recognises the right of workers to take part in the determination and improvement of working conditions and the working environment.

The United Kingdom has not signed the Protocol and the government has stated that it is unable to accept the minimum obligation required of acceptance of any of the Articles to the Protocol. The objections were similar to those raised to 'Vredeling', namely, though it was in an employing undertaking's best interests to inform and consult employees that situation was much better achieved by a voluntarist policy rather than by legislative intervention.

Existing national provisions relating to consultation and the disclosure of information for collective bargaining purposes are in section 17 Employment Protection Act 1975 (with the accompanying ACAS Code of Practice), section 99 of the same Act and the Transfer of Undertakings (Protection of Employment) Regulations 1981. Those oblige employers to inform and consult on certain matters with *recognised* trade unions but there is no longer any procedure under which an employer can be required to grant recognition and anyway the exceptions are extensive. The ubiquitous 'national security' exception appears in relation to disclosure of information and there are others for confidential and sensitive information. UK law already encourages worker participation in respect of health and safety matters by providing for the appointment of safety representatives and the establishment of statutory safety committees.

Sections 27 and 28 of the Employment Protection (Consolidation) Act 1978 provide for reasonable time off for trade union officials and members to enable participation in trade union duties (time off with pay) and activities (time off without pay). These provisions have been restrictively interpreted by courts and tribunals and an official's 'duties' have been held to include only those matters having a proximate relationship to industrial relations between the particular employer and his employee, that is, time off to attend general instructional or policy-making meetings at national level will not be within the provision if there is no link with negotiation at the particular employer level. (*Sood v G.E.C. Elliott Process Automation Ltd*[10]). In *British Bakeries Ltd v Adlington*[11] the Court of Appeal held that union officials were entitled to paid time off to attend a meeting about the repeal of legislation restricting hours of work in the baking industry. The Court of Appeal held that the tribunal were entitled to conclude that on the facts of the case there was an exceptionally close connection between the repeal of the legislation and relations between the employer and the union members. The case does not undermine the principle behind the interpretation of an official's 'duties' but it does suggest a wider application of that principle.

NOTES

1. The obligations not accepted are as follows: the provision of public holidays with pay, the right of men and women workers to equal pay for work of equal value, minimum age of employment to be 15 years, limits on working hours and holidays for persons aged 15 – 18 years, protection against dismissal during maternity leave and time off for nursing mothers.
2. Section 5 of the Conspiracy and Protection of Property Act 1875 makes it an offence for any person wilfully and maliciously to break a contract of service knowing or having reasonable cause to believe that the probable consequence will be to endanger human life or cause serious bodily injury. Section 53 of the Police Act 1964 makes it an offence for any person to cause disaffection amongst the police or to induce any member of the police force to withhold his services.
3. Article 31 makes the rights contained in the Charter subject to restrictions and limitations 'necessary in a democratic society for the protection of the rights and freedoms of others or for the protection of public interest, national security, public health, or morals'.
4. [1983] 2 All ER 166.
5. [1981] IRLR 5. In this case the employer made the offer of re-engagement to certain dismissed strikers subject to the condition that they would be regarded as being at the final stage in the disciplinary procedure so that one further step out of line would have meant dismissal. The Employment Appeal Tribunal held that the offer was still an offer of re-engagement and there was no breach of the 'no-discrimination' rule! The Employment Appeal Tribunal refused to compare all the terms and conditions of the respective offers of re-engagement.
6. [1974] 1 All ER 980.
7. [1984] 3 All ER 935.
8. [1988] EHRR 269.
9. [1987] IRLR 80.
10. [1979] IRLR 416.
11. Court of Appeal. 15.2.89.

9 Implementing the Right to Education in England

Julian Lonbay

INTRODUCTION

This chapter analyses the right to education as enshrined in the International Bill of Rights and other human rights treaties adhered to by the United Kingdom. It then assesses how the UK, particularly England, has implemented the international norms.

The International Covenants on Human Rights, comprising State-agreed definitions of human rights, are universal.[1] One might therefore expect them to be vague, in order to accommodate the different types of social organisation to be found in different states.[2] Conversely it might be expected that, because of the homogeneity of Western Europe and its relatively common legal traditions, the European Convention on Human Rights and the European Social Charter would enshrine the more specific rights.[3] In fact the reverse is the case when one comes to consider the right to education. There are several possible explanations as to why this is so.

First, the implementation of human rights, especially those protecting economic, social or cultural rights should, in theory, allow individuals, armed with their rights, to divert or insist on 'specific resource allocation' within a state to support their 'rights'. Western states, in particular, were wary of so arming their citizens and thus allowing them to insist on particular state expenditure.[4]

Second, if the right is given internal legal force in the municipal legal order then its exercise potentially short-circuits traditional channels of political change. The political agenda may, in effect, have been set in signing the Treaty. The West was extremely cautious in permitting such back-door 'socialism'. In the drafting of the Covenants and the European Convention om Human Rights and its first Protocol Western countries fairly consistently argued against wording that appeared to imply state obligations when the rights could also be legitimately and effectively fulfiled by private action.[5]

Thirdly, the idea of education is a complex one involving the notion of equality of opportunity as well as involving both state and private provision. It poses particular additional difficulties for international enshrinement as a human right as it is also closely involved with national culture as well as contentious political, religious, linguistic and ethnic compromises. It is also heavily dependent on state financial and other resources.

An additional factor complicating the issue of a right to education is that education is generally considered to be mainly applicable to the young, although, especially in times of rapid technological change, it has been recognised as important to older generations as well. As children are involved this poses difficulties relating to their exercise of legal rights. The problem of parent–child conflicts arise[6] alongside those of parent–state.

The right to education was also recognised to be of the greatest importance to the individual, his family, and in the West at least, as a determinant of success. Thus at the end of the day it was firmly included in the list of rights protected in international treaties.

The inclusion of the right to education reflected not simply the factors outlined above but also the fact that human rights law is based on respect for the individual. The principles of equality and non-discrimination are fundamental in international law, many arguing that these ideas form part of *jus cogens*. These principles are strongly endorsed in the international human rights treaties.[7]

DEFINITIONS OF EDUCATION

Education involves learning. As teaching is an imprecise science and learning capacities vary it is difficult to set an 'outcome'. A right to education cannot therefore mean a right to a specific level of learning or knowledge. It is not a commodity that all are capable of absorbing. Thus, for example, attempts in the United States to find a 'property interest' in high school diplomas have fallen on stony ground.[8]

In a wide sense education involves upbringing and socialisation. Its content is thus variable according to the society's aims. In a narrow sense education is associated with 'schooling'. Education can be regarded as a 'family of processes whose principle of unity is the development of desirable qualities in someone'.[9] Thus to assure a 'right to education' the individual must be granted access to the 'family of processes'. What amounts to a 'desirable quality' depends on each society. But one could expect international human rights norms to establish common minimum aims for education.

THE PURPOSE OF EDUCATION

Shklar considered the purpose of education to be 'the right to be socially successful if one is able'.[10] The aim of education would thus be for the individual to develop the abilities and talents that are necessary for 'success'. Pluralistic outcomes are thus inevitable as individuals have widely differing goals and aspirations.

Education can be seen as a method of distributive justice. From this viewpoint education is to be used to help compensate individuals for environmental or other disadvantages. The Coleman Report in America and the Swann Report in the UK must make one cautious about the extent that schools can effectively support social change.[11]

The purposes of education are defined in the human rights treaties. The International Covenant on Economic, Social and Cultural Rights in Article 13(1) declares:

> The States Parties to the present Covenant recognise the right of everyone to education. They agree that education shall be directed to the full development of the human personality and the sense of its dignity, and shall strengthen the respect for human rights and fundamental freedoms. They further agree that education shall enable all persons to participate effectively in a free society, promote understanding, tolerance and friendship among all nations and all racial, ethnic or religious groups, and further the activities of the United Nations for the maintenance of peace.[12]

A series of Conventions seek to disallow discrimination in education and promote the ideal of equality of opportunity.[13]

REALISATION OF THE RIGHT TO EDUCATION

The International Covenant of Economic, Social and Cultural Rights[14] prescribes that primary, secondary and higher education be made available in order to realise the right to education. Primary education is to be 'compulsory and available free to all'. Secondary education is also to be made generally available '. . . in particular by the progressive introduction of free education', and higher education 'shall be made equally accessible to all, on the basis of capacity'. The States Parties are bound by article 13(2)(e) to pursue actively the development of schools at all levels.[15] There are no equivalent provisions in the European Convention on Human Rights and the European Social Charter.

The Covenant carefully does not dictate that the state alone should provide the educational infrastructure. Article 13(4) makes quite clear the 'liberty of individuals and bodies to establish and direct educational institutions'. This liberty is made subject to respecting the purposes of education (outlined in article 13(1)) and must 'conform to such minimum standards as may be laid down by the State'.

ALLOCATING EDUCATIONAL RESOURCES/OPPORTUNITIES

The right to education should help to determine how educational resources are to be distributed. Both liberals and egalitarians agree on 'basic' education.[16] Beyond this level resource distribution can be based on egalitarian ideals or according to desert (contribution).

Though difficult to settle on agreed 'outcomes', all West European states, including the United Kingdom, have established a basic minimum education, and enforce it by compulsory schooling.

Decisions as to the detailed scope and content of education have traditionally been controlled by parents. Parental rights are still much in evidence and are expressly recognised in the Universal Declaration of Human Rights (Article 26(3)), the International Covenant on Economic, Social and Cultural Rights (Article 13(3)),[17] the Convention against Discrimination in Education (Article 5(1)(b)) and in the European Convention on Human Rights (Article 2 of Protocol 1). The parental role in choosing non-state schooling is recognised,[18] as is their right 'to ensure the religious and moral education of their children in conformity with their own convictions'.

In recent years there has been increasing recognition of the interests of the children receiving education. The Declaration on the Rights of the Child 1959 recognised the importance of the development of the child.[19] The 1988 Draft Convention on the Rights of the Child[20] goes further and in numerous articles seeks to balance the parents' rights 'in a manner consistent with the evolving capacities of the child'.[21] In Article 14 it states:

(1) States Parties shall respect the right of the Child to freedom of thought, conscience and religion.

(2) States Parties shall respect the rights and duties of the parents . . . to provide direction to the child in the exercise of his or her right in a manner consistent with the evolving capacities of the child.[22]

This Article, if adopted in its present form, will have the effect for those states that will be parties to the new Convention of modifying the treaty rights of parents, granted in earlier human rights treaties, to direct the religious and philosophical education of their children.

Exactly who may control the detailed content of education is not explicitly established in the treaties, which only deal with the overall aims of education.[23] The European Convention on Human Rights despite the brevity of its treatment of the right to education, has in fact, through the development of its norms, gone the furthest in exploring this question.

THE EUROPEAN RIGHTS

One might expect that the European human rights treaties would be more explicit in dealing with the right to education,[24] but, for the reasons outlined above, the European treaties are in fact less specific than the UN-sponsored treaties. The European Convention on Human Rights was essentially designed to protect civil and political rights with the European Social Charter dealing with economic, social and cultural rights.

Article 2 of the First Protocol (hereafter Article 2P) was phrased negatively but contains no limiting clause. The *travaux préparatoires* make it clear that the negative phrasing of the right was adopted to block any particular education according to parental preference.[25] The Contracting States were more interested in ensuring freedom from governmental coercion and to protect non-state educational provision than in granting parents rights over the content of instruction (with the exception of respecting parental philosophical or religious convictions).

Is there a duty on the State to provide a schooling system?

In the *Belgian Linguistic cases*[26] the European Court of Human Rights ruled that Article 2P did enshrine a right, but that there was no obligation on the state to establish a general official education system. It considered that Article 2P

(1) guaranteed access to existing educational institutions (the scope of the educational system may vary from country to country);
(2) allowed one to draw profit from the education so received, through official recognition of studies completed in accordance with national law;
(3) allowed a right to be educated in a national language.

The limited nature of this judgement can at least be partially explained on the grounds that it was only the sixth judgement of the Court and was on a matter of great sensitivity in Belgium.

In the *Kjeldsen, Busk Madsen and Pedersen*[27] case the Commission considered that article 2P gave all children a right to education.[28] In the *Campbell and Cosans*[29] case the European Court of Human Rights considered that the first sentence of Article 2P gave rise to a separate issue and ruled in effect that any conditions of access that violated any right enshrined in the Convention would amount to a denial of the right to education and thus be contrary to the first sentence of article 2P.[30] The import of this element of the judgement was emphasised by the later Article 50 judgement awarding Jeffrey Cosans £3000 damages as:

> the applicant must be regarded as having suffered some non-pecuniary loss . . . his failure to complete his schooling perforce deprived him of some opportunity to develop his intellectual potential.[31]

The Content of education: A minimum guarantee?

There must be a core of education provided to allow socialisation of the child to take place. The European Court of Human Rights is well-placed to survey and to determine this basic core.[32]

In the *Belgian Linguistics cases* M. Petren in the Commission Report considered that a core would include 'an elementary education'.[33] In *Kjeldsen* the Court ruled that in principle decisions on curriculum fall to the state, but, if controversial, topics must be taught 'objectively, critically, and pluralistically'. The Court again is the final arbiter of this.[34] The interest of the child in receiving an accurate knowledge concerning sexual matters was recognised. This amounts to the reverse side of the state's right to ensure a minimum necessary education. Parental objections could not disallow the child from receiving the knowledge that the state, supported by the European Court of Human Rights, thought necessary.

The content of this 'core' could also be determined by reference to the recipient of education. in the *Campbell & Cosans* case the Court gave a very wide definition of education:

> It is the whole process whereby, in any society, adults endeavour to transmit their beliefs, culture and other values to the young, whereas teaching or instruction refers in particular to the transmission of knowledge and to intellectual development.

The Court found that

> [t]he use of corporal punishment . . . is an integral part of the process whereby a school seeks to achieve the object for which it was established, including the development and moulding of the character and mental powers of its pupils.[35]

Education so widely defined clearly gives scope for the recipient to determine the core content. It must be directed to the aims mentioned.[36]

In the European Social Charter there is no direct endorsement of the right to education. But articles 9 and 10 support the notion of the individual influence over the curriculum. In particular they recognise that the development of the abilities of the recipient, and the recipients rights to seek his/her appropriate career, are for the individual to determine, and for the state to help implement even to the extent of giving 'financial assistance'.

THE UNITED KINGDOM

Provision of Schooling

Implementation of the right to education as proclaimed in international law is not very demanding for the UK in terms of educational infrastructure.[37] The general obligation in the International

Covenant on Economic, Social and Cultural Rights to provide basic (elementary education) is clearly fulfiled in the UK.[38]

Parental Rights

Non-state sector provision and choice thereof

The specific obligations as regards parental rights in the International Covenants are also relatively easy to fulfil. There is a freedom for parents to chose non-state sector schooling and no legal impediment to block individuals from establishing independent schools that conform to the minimum standards laid down by the state.

Religious instruction

As regards religious instruction the situation is slightly more complex. Until the implementation of the national curriculum the only compulsory subject that had to be taught in schools was 'religion'. The law on religious education has now been overhauled by the Education Reform Act 1988.[39] By section 2(1) every maintained school[40] must have a curriculum that includes 'provision for religious education for every registered pupil at the school'. Section 9 allows pupils to be excused from such instruction at the request of a parent. The child may be withdrawn from the school to attend alternative religious instruction.[41] The Act also requires a collective act of worship; again exemption on parental demand is possible.[42] This fulfils the obligations under existing international law, but the situation is arguably not in accord with the draft Convention on the Rights of the Child (see below, the section on children's rights).

Minorities

Under the compromise that brought Church schools more fully within the state sector such schools received considerable financial assistance with capital and daily running costs.[43] There are increasingly vocal demands from the Muslim community (amongst others) who seek a similar level of aid for their (currently private) schools.[44] No application for such a voluntary aided status has yet been approved. A government minister speaking in Coventry in April 1989 ruled out the prospect of Muslim schools receiving voluntary status (and thus benefitting from state financial support).[45] This rules out the 'opting-out' solution[46] and is contrary to what the UK representative had promised when defending the UK report on the implementation of the Covenant on Economic, Social and Cultural Rights to the sessional Working Group (of Governmental Experts) on the implementation of the International Covenant on Economic, Social and Cultural rights.[47] As Christian and Jewish schools have been granted voluntary status, one must question whether this position is in conformity with the general principle of non-discrimination espoused by international law. Muslims, not being a racial group,[48] cannot benefit from the provisions of the Convention on the Elimination of Racial Discrimination[49] but the position falls squarely under article 3(d) of the Unesco Convention Against Discrimination in Education which under Article 3 provides:

> In order to eliminate and prevent discrimination within the meaning of this Convention, the States Parties thereto undertake: . . . (d) Not to allow, in any form of assistance granted by the public authorities to educational institutions, any restrictions or preference based solely on the ground that pupils belong to a particular group; . . .[50]

It also raises difficult questions as regards the rights of children dealt with below.

Children's Rights

The increasing recognition of the rights of the child will cause more difficulties for the United Kingdom (should it adhere without reservations to the draft Convention on the Rights of the Child as it now stands). Educational statute law has yet to catch up properly with the implications of the *Gillick*[51] case for children's rights. On Lord Scarman's view in this case 'parental rights must yield to a child's right to make his own decisions when he reaches a sufficient understanding and intelligence to be capable of making up his own mind on the matter requiring decision'.[52] For example, the Education (No. 2) Act 1986 forbids anyone under 18 years of age from being a school governor. As Maureen Grenville[53] shows there may also be problems in relation to enforcing the parental duty to 'ensure efficient full-time education'[54] when the 'mature' child wishes to take a job, for example, that might include a training element. The same difficulty will be raised where a child has religious views that differ from those of his parents. Currently the parents have statutory rights in this area, and these will prevail in the common law recognition of the child's interests. This will not accord with the position in international law. The child may not wish to be 'privately' educated, or perhaps will object to the religious instruction, or form of collective worship that his parents want.

CONCLUSION: ENFORCEMENT OF EDUCATIONAL RIGHTS IN ENGLAND

Essentially in England the law provides statutory duties on the Secretary of State for Education to promote the education of the people,[55] on Local Education Authorities, *inter alia*, to ensure an efficient education system[56] (that is, schools and other facilities)[57] and on parents[58] to ensure that a child receives a 'suitable education'.

An aggrieved parent, as is well-known, must normally seek the specific remedy provided in the various Education Acts. These are either in the form of appeals to the Secretary of State for Education,[59] or in the form of a special Appeals procedure.[60] Parents seeking remedies beyond this have had difficulty in receiving a sympathetic hearing in the courts.[61] There is the possibility of judicial review if the LEA acts unreasonably, but given the wide discretion granted to LEAs in fulfiling their duties, and the notorious reluctance of English courts to interfere by substituting their own opinions for those of the executive,[62] the chances of a parent succeeding in an action are not good.[63] There is also the risk of differing judicial opinions.[64]

Perhaps the best illustration of judicial reluctance to engage itself on behalf of parents and children in the educational sphere comes from the way the courts have dealt with the 1981 Education Act. This Act was essentially designed to promote the education and integration of children with special educational needs. Learned commentators have noted that:

> There is no doubt, however, that the Act requires a redistribution of resources in favour of children with special; educational needs.[65]

We have seen that the education provisions of the international human rights treaties are designed to help promote the full development of the individual. In *R v Surrey Education Committee ex p. H*[66] parents sought special school education for their child. The LEA and Appeal Committee rejected their request. They appealed to the Court of Appeal, where Slade LJ, ruling that the Appeals Committee had given adequate reasons for their decision, said that there was:

> . . . no question of Parliament having placed the local authority under an obligation to provide a child with the best possible education. There is no duty on the authority to provide such a utopian system, or to educate him or her to his or her maximum potential.[67]

The reluctance of courts to get involved in this area forms part of their general reluctance to interfere with executive decision-making by substituting their own opinions for those of the executive.

To end more cheerfully one must point out that there have been successful changes to educational provision in the UK resulting from application of the international human rights treaty norms. In particular the banning of corporal punishment after the case of *Campbell & Cosans*[68] in the European Court of Human Rights can be cited as a successful outcome for international law within the domestic forum.[69]

The difficulties over children's rights are stored up for the future. Both the government and the courts must welcome any guidance that international law can provide for drawing the delicate balance to be struck between the aspirations of children and the wishes of their parents in such sensitive cultural areas as religious education.[70]

ANNEX I

EXTRACTS FROM RELEVANT HUMAN RIGHTS TREATIES

The Universal Declaration of Human Rights

Article 26

(1) Everyone has the right to education. Education shall be free, at least in the elementary and fundamental stages. Elementary education shall be compulsory. Technical and professional education shall

be made generally available and higher education shall be equally accessible to all on a basis of merit.
(2) Education shall be directed to the full development of the human personality and to the strengthening of respect for human rights and fundamental freedoms. It shall promote understanding, tolerance and friendship among all nations, racial or religious groups, and shall further the activities of the United Nations for the maintenance of peace.
(3) Parents have a prior right to choose the kind of education that shall be given to their children.

The International Covenant on Civil and Political Rights

Article 18

. . . (4)The States Parties to the present Covenant undertake to have respect for the liberty of parents and, when applicable, legal guardians to ensure the religious and moral education of their children in conformity with their own convictions.

International Covenant on Economic Social and Cultural Rights

Article 13

. . .
(2) The States Parties to the present Covenant recognise that, with a view to achieving the full realisation of this right:
(a) Primary education shall be compulsory and available freely to all;
(b) Secondary education in its different forms, including technical and vocational secondary education, shall be made generally available and accessible to all by every appropriate means, and in particular by the progressive introduction of free education;
(c) Higher education shall be made equally accessible to all, on the basis of capacity, by every appropriate means, and in particular by the progressive introduction of free education;
(d) Fundamental education shall be encouraged or intensified as far as possible for those persons who have not received or completed the whole period of their primary education;
(e) The development of a system of schools at all levels shall be actively pursued, an adequate fellowship system shall be established,

and the material conditions of teaching staff shall be continuously improved.
(3) The States Parties to the present Covenant undertake to have respect for the liberty of parents and, when applicable, legal guardians, to choose for their children schools, other than those established by the public authorities, which conform to such minimum educational standards as may be laid down or approved by the State and to ensure the religious and moral education of their children in conformity with their own convictions.
(4) No part of this article shall be construed so as to interfere with the liberty of individuals and bodies to establish and direct educational institutions, subject always to the observance of the principles set forth in paragraph 1 of this article and to the requirement that the education given in such institutions shall conform to such minimum standards as may be laid down by the State.

UNESCO Convention against Discrimination in Education

Article 4

The States Parties to this Convention undertake furthermore to formulate, develop and apply a national policy which, by methods appropriate to the circumstances and to national usage, will tend to promote equality of opportunity and of treatment in the matter of education and in particular:
(a) To make primary education free and compulsory; make secondary education in its different forms generally available and accessible to all; make higher education equally accessible to all on the basis of individual capacity; assure compliance by all with the obligation to attend school prescribed by law;
(b) To ensure that the standards of education are equivalent in all public educational institutions of the same level, and that the conditions relating to the quality of education provided are also equivalent;
(c) To encourage and intensify by appropriate methods the education of persons who have not yet received any primary education or who have not completed the entire primary education course and the continuation of their education on the basis of individual capacity;
(d) To provide training for the teaching profession without discrimination.

Article 5(1) states:
1. The States Parties to this convention agree that:
a) . . .
b) It is essential to respect the liberty of parents and, where applicable, of legal guardians, firstly to choose for their children institutions other than those maintained by the public authorities but conforming to such minimum education standards as may be laid down or approved by the competent authorities and, secondly, to ensure in a manner consistent with the procedures followed in the State for the application of its legislation, the religious and moral education of the children in conformity with their own convictions; and no person or group of persons should be compelled to receive religious instruction inconsistent with his or their conviction;
c) It is essential to recognise the right of members of national minorities to carry on their own educational activities including the maintenance of schools and, depending on the educational policy of each State, the use or the teaching of their own language, provided however:
(i) That this right is not exercised in a manner which prevents the members of these minorities from understanding the culture and language of the community as a whole and from participating in its activities, or which prejudices national sovereignty;
(ii) That the standard of education is not lower than the general standard laid down or approved by the competent authorities; and
(iii) That attendance at such schools is optional.

(2) The States Parties to this Convention undertake to take all necessary measures to ensure the application of the principles enunciated in paragraph 1 of this article.

Convention of the Elimination of all forms of Discrimination Against Women

Article 10
States Parties shall take all appropriate measures to eliminate discrimination against women in order to ensure to them equal rights with men in the field of education and in particular to ensure, on a basis of equality of men and women:

(a) The same conditions for career and vocational guidance, for access to studies and for the achievement of diplomas in education tional establishments of all categories in rural as well as in urban areas; this equality shall be ensured in pre-school, general, technical professional and higher technical education, as well as in all types of vocational training;
(b) Access to the same curricula, the same examinations, teaching staff with qualifications of the same standard and school premises and equipment of the same quality;
(c) The elimination of any stereotyped concept of the roles of men and women at all levels and in all forms of education by encouraging coeducation and other types of education which will help to achieve this aim and, in particular, by the revision of textbooks and school programmes and the adaptation of teaching methods;
(d) The same opportunities to benefit from scholarships and other study grants;
(e)The same opportunities for access to programmes of continuing education, including adult and functional literacy programmes, particularly those aimed at reducing, at the earliest possible time, any gap in education existing between men and women;
(f) The reduction of female student drop-out rates and the organisation of programmes for girls and women who have left school prematurely;
(g) The same opportunities to participate actively in sports and physical education;
(h) Access to specific educational information to help ensure the health and well-being of families, including information and advice on family planning.

European Convention on Human Rights

Article 2 of Protocol 1

No person shall be denied the right to education. In the exercise of any functions which it assumes in relation to education and to teaching, the State shall respect the right of parents to ensure such education and teaching in conformity with their own religious and philosophical convictions.

Draft Convention of the Rights of the Child

Article 5

(3) States Parties shall respect the responsibilities, rights, and duties of parents or, where applicable, members of the extended family or community as provided for by local custom, legal guardians, or other persons legally responsible for the child, to provide, in a manner consistent with the evolving capacities of the child, appropriate direction and guidance in the exercise by the child of the rights recognised in the present Convention.

Article 28

(1) States Parties to the present Convention recognize the right of the child to education and, with a view to achieving this right progressively and on the basis of equal opportunity, they shall, in particular:
(a) make primary education compulsory and available free to all;
(b) encourage the development of different forms of secondary education, including general and vocational education, make them available and accessible to every child, and take appropriate measures such as the introduction of free education and offering financial assistance in case of need;
(c) make higher education accessible to all on the basis of capacity by every appropriate means;
(d) make educational and vocational information and guidance available and accessible to all children;
(e) take measures to encourage regular attendance at schools and the reduction of drop-out rates.
(2) States Parties shall take all appropriate measures to ensure that school discipline is administered in a manner consistent with the child's human dignity and in conformity with the present Convention.
(3) States Parties shall promote and encourage international co-operation in matters relating to education, in particular with a view to contributing to the elimination of ignorance and illiteracy throughout the world and facilitating access to scientific and technical knowledge and modern teaching methods. In this regard, particular account shall be taken of the needs of developing countries.

Article 29

1. States Parties agree that the education of the child shall be directed to:

(a) The development of the child's personality, talents and mental and physical abilities to their fullest potential;
(b) the development of respect for human rights and fundamental freedoms, and for the principles enshrined in the Charter of the United Nations;
(c) the development of respect for the child's parents, his or her own cultural identity, language and values, for the national values of the country in which the child is living, the country from which he or she may originate, and for civilizations different from his or her own;
(d) the preparation of the child for responsible life in a free society, in the spirit of understanding, peace, tolerance, equality of sexes and friendship among all peoples, ethnic, national and religious groups and persons of indigenous origin;
(e) the development of respect for the natural environment.

2. No part of this article or article 28 shall be construed so as to interfere with the liberty of individuals and bodies to establish and direct educational institutions, subject always to the observance of the principles set forth in paragraph 1 of this article and to the requirements that the education given in such institutions shall conform to such minimum standards as may be laid down by the State.

NOTES

1. For the full texts see: International Covenant on Economic, Social and Cultural Rights (New York: 1966); International Covenant on Civil and Political Rights (New York: 1966); *Human Rights in International Law: Basic Texts*, (Strasbourg: Council of Europe, 1985).
2. For instance, some states may wish to exercise more central power than others (which may have more liberal tendencies). Equally the problems of mass illiteracy in the Third World might cause one to think that the International Covenants would provide a lower target than that found in Western Europe.
3. For full texts see Council of Europe, *Human Rights in International Law*, op. cit. Both the International and European human rights treaties have enforcement mechanisms (of varying strength) and the norms that they enshrine have therefore evolved.
4. The UK was particularly concerned, as is evidenced by its reservation to Article 2 of Protocol 1, to the European Convention on Human Rights. For the text of Article 2 of Protocol 1 see Annex 1.
5. In Ireland, for example, the state directly owns only 14 national (that

is, primary) schools. See Dail Eireann, *Debates* Cols. 76 – 78 (11 October 1978); generally Lonbay, J., *The right to education*, Doctoral thesis, chapter 11, pp.867-1014.

6. Namely, the type of issue raised by the *Gillick* case. This is increasingly likely to cause difficulties. See below the section on Childrens' rights.
7. Universal Declaration of Human Rights Articles 1, 2; International Covenants Articles 2, 3. See *Human Rights in International Law*. Council of Europe, op. cit.
8. In the USA *Goss v Lopez* 419 U.S. 565 (1975) established a property interest in education that could not be denied without the appropriate 'due process'. However on the question of the imposition of academic sanctions (lowering 'grades' [that is, marks]) for disciplinary infractions there has been no consistency. Some courts have allowed the practice and others have not. See *Knight v Board of Education of Tri-point School District* 38 I11.App. 3d 603, 348 N.E. 2d 299 (1976); *Hamer v Board of Education Twp. High Sch. District No.13*, 383 N.E. 2d 231 (I11.App. 1978) and *Katzman v Cumberland Valley School District* 479 A.2d 671 (Pa. Cmwlth. 1984). In the *Belgian Linguistics cases* ECHR Ser.A., No.6 the European Court of Human Rights emphasised the right to draw benefit from education by recognition of diplomas. In Application 9270/81 (7 December 1981); Council of Europe, *Digest of Strasbourg Case-law relating to the European Convention on Human Rights*, vol. 5 (Berlin: Heymanns Verlag, 1985), p.784. The European Commission on Human Rights concluded that the European Convention on Human Rights protected no right to pass an exam.
9. R.S. Peters, 'Education and the Educated Man', *Proceedings of the Philosophical Society of Great Britain*, vol. 4, no.5, 1970, esp. at p.13.
10. J. Shklar, 'Injustice, Injury, and Inequality: An Introduction', in F. Lucash (ed,), *Justice and Equality here and now* (New York: Cornell University Press, 1986) 13 at p.21.
11. Most famously in the Coleman Report: Coleman, J.S. *et al.*, *Equality of Educational Opportunity* (Washington DC: US Government, 1966), p.312. See M. Warnock, 'The concept of equality in Education', *Oxford Review of Education*, Vol. 1, p.3, 1975; H.J. Eysenck, 'Equality and Education: Fact and Fiction', *Oxford Review of Education*, Vol. 1, 1975, p.51; A. R. Jensen, 'The Price of Inequality', *Oxford Review of Education*, Vol. 1, 1975, p.59; A. H. Halsey, 'Sociology and the Equality Debate', *Oxford Review of Education*, Vol.1, 1975, p.9; R.H. Ennis, 'Equality of Educational Opportunity', *Educational Theory*, Vol. 26, p.3; *Education for All*, The Swann Report, *Cmnd. 9453* (London: HMSO, 1985), especially at pp.82 – 6.
12. This article expands Article 26(2) of the Universal Declaration on Human Rights. For the relevant texts see Annex I.
13. The Convention against Discrimination in Education (1960), especially articles 4 and 5; the International Convention on the Elimination of All Forms of Racial Discrimination; Convention on the Elimination of Dis-

crimination against Women (Article 10, 14(2)(d)). For the full texts of these Conventions see UN, *A Compilation of International Instruments* (NY. 1988). For the articles mentioned here see Annex I.

14. See also the Universal Declaration of Human Rights Article 26(1); the Convention against Discrimination in Education, Article 4. Text in Annex I.
15. Article 14 requires that States Parties that have not yet secured 'compulsory primary education free of charge' should adopt a plan of action (within two years) to achieve that aim 'within a reasonable number of years'.
16. Shue does not include it in his list of basic needs as its absence would not cause pain, although it would seem to fit his definition of a basic right. H. Shue, *Basic Rights: Subsistence, Affluence, and U.S. Foreign Policy* (Princeton, New Jersey: Princeton University Press, 1982), pp. 19 – 20.
17. See also Article 18(4) of the International Covenant on Civil and Political Rights, Annex I.
18. Article 13(3) of the International Covenant on Economic, Social and Cultural Rights. For the text see Annex I.
19. In Principles 2,4,5,6,7,9,10. See UN., *A Compilation of International Instruments*, op. cit. p.366 for the text of the Declaration of the Rights of the Child, G.A. Res. 1386 (XIV) of 20 November 1959.
20. Currently the draft has only been approved by a Working Group of the Commission on Human Rights. See UN Doc. E/CN.4/1989/29 (30 December 1988). The Report of the Working Group on the draft Convention on the rights of the child is found in UN Doc. E/CN.4/1989/48 (2 March 1989).
21. Notably in article 5 which sets out the balance to be achieved between parent and child. For the text see Annex I.
22. UN Doc. E/CN.4/1989/29, p.8.
23. See Article 29(1) of the draft Convention of the Rights of the Child. For text see Annex I.
24. Generally see J. Lonbay, op. cit., Chapter 7, pp.436 – 659.
25. Ibid., p. 528.
26. *The cases relating to certain aspects of the Laws on the use of Languages in Education in Belgium*, Ser.A No.6 (23 July 1968).
27. *Case of Kjeldsen, Busk Madsen and Pedersen*, Ser.A No.23 (7 December 1976).
28. Commission Report, Ser.B Vol.21 p.43.
29. *Campbell and Cosans*, Ser.A No.48 (23 February 1982).
30. Ser.A No.60 (22 March 1983) Para 41.
31. *Campbell & Cosans*, para. 26
32. As it has done in other fields, for example, *Tyrer v U.K.*, Ser. A No.26 (1978).
33. Series B, *Belgian Linguistic cases*, Vol.1, p.340.
34. *Dudgeon v U.K.*, Ser.A No.45 (1981).
35. Ser.A No.48, para. 33.
36. Article 29 of the draft Convention on the Rights of the Child is the latest expression of international will as to what the aims of

education should be. See Annex I for the text.

37. See paragraph 21 of the First Report of the UK, UN Doc. E/1982/3/Add.16.
38. The UK's first report on the implementation of articles 13 to 15 of the International Covenant on Economic Social and Cultural Rights, UN Doc. E/1982/3/Add.16 (30 March 1982), noted that the requirements of Article 14 had been met since 1944. Recent reports of children with no primary educational facilities in some areas of London would amount to a clear violation of the Covenant. See *The Times Educational Supplement*, 25 November 1988, and 17 and 24 February 1989.
39. The Education Reform Act 1988, c.40.
40. Section 25 of the Education Reform Act, 1988 defines 'maintained school'.
41. Subject to the conditions set out in section 9(4) and (6).
42. Though different religious groups may now have separate 'collective acts' of worship (s.6(2)), as the Act requires collective acts of worship to be 'wholly or mainly of a broadly christian character', with various permitted exceptions (ss.7, 12).
43. These are the 'voluntary-aided schools'. Voluntary-controlled schools allow 'state' control with only a small role for the original owners.
44. For instance, in Kirklees, *Times Educational Supplement*, 3 February 1989, p.A10.
45. Timothy Renton, *Times Educational Supplement*, 21 April 1989, p.A3.
46. Whereby under chapter IV of the Education Reform Act 1988 schools can opt for grant-maintained status, be supported directly from central government and seek a change of character (s.89) subject to the Secretary of State's approval.
47. UN Doc. E/1982/WG.1/SR.21 p.6, Mr Chatterjie responding to a question by Mr Allafi (Libyan Arab Jamahiriya) on this point.
48. As distinct from other 'groups' that might be considered racial, for example, Sikhs, cf. *Mandla v Dowell Lee and Another* [1983] 1 All ER 1062.
49. Article 5(e) (v). For text see Annex I.
50. It might be considered that the Muslim aims of separate education for girls contradicts the aim of the Convention on the Elimination of all Forms of Discrimination against Women, Article 10. See Annex I for text.
51. *Gillick v West Norfolk and Wisbech Area Health Authority* [1985] 3 All E.R. 402.
52. Lord Scarman, in *Gillick*. 1985 3 All ER 402 at 422. Note though the differing view of Lord Fraser in this case. See S. Cretney, 'Family Law' 1985 All ER Rev. 171, and M. D. A. Freeman, 'England: the trumping of parental rights', *Journal of Family Law*, Vol.25, 91, 1986–87.
53. M. Grenville 'Compulsory School Attendance and the Child's Wishes', *JSWL* 4, Vol. 4, 1988.
54. Education Act 1944, s.36.
55. Education Act 1944, s.l.

56. Education Act 1944, s.8.
57. Including adequate sports and recreation facilities, Eduction Act 1944, s.53.
58. Education Act 1944 s.36.
59. For example, Education Act 1944 ss.68, 99.
60. As set our in the 1980 and 1981 Education Acts and the Education (No.2) Act 1986.
61. *Watt v. Kesteven CC* [1955] 1 All ER 473; *Cumings v. Birkenhead Corp.* [1972] Ch.12; [1971] 2 WLR 1458.
62. In *Chief Constable of the North Wales Police v Evans* [1982] 3 All ER 141 the Chief Constable had acted 'unlawfully and in breach of his duty' (p.155) but the House of Lords refused to sanction the issuance of an order of mandamus (even though it was recognised that this order was appropriate in the circumstances [per Lord Brightman p.156]), for fear of usurping power, in this case of the Chief Constable.
63. *Meade v London Borough of Haringey* [1979] 2 All ER 1016. Note that in the case Eveleigh LJ (1027) considered the LEA's action not to be unreasonable.
64. In *R v Oxfordshire Education Authority, ex p. W, The Times*, 22 November 1986, it was held that there was no duty on a Council to provide speech therapy, it not being irrational to decide that speech therapy was 'non-educational provision'. In *Muller v. Lancashire CC*, the *Independent*, 8 November 1988, it was held that as the LEA considered speech therapy an educational need, there was therefore a duty to provide it.
65. Goacher B., *et al.*, *Policy and provision for Special Educational Needs*, (London: Cassell, 1988), p.165.
66. [1985] 83: LGR 219.
67. Milman concludes that: 'The prospect of a parent successfully challenging the educational provision offered by an LEA are bleak', D. Milman, 'The Education Act 1981 in the Courts', (1987) *JSWL* 208 at 215; 1987.
68. cf. J. Lonbay, 'Rights in education under the European Convention on Human Rights', *MLR*, Vol. 46, 1983, p.345.
69. See sections 47 and 48 of the Education (No.2) Act 1986.
70. This arena looks set to become highly politicised with the two main parties adopting opposite stances.

10 Recognising a Right to Health

Jonathan Montgomery

It is a necessary condition for the pursuit of virtually any human project that the subject has at least a minimal level of good health. The importance of a right to health is not, therefore, in issue and it is recognised in the fundamental documents of the human rights movement. The Universal Declaration sets out in Article 25 that:

> Everyone has the right to a standard of living adequate for the health and well-being of himself and of his family, including food, clothing, housing and medical care and necessary social services . . .

The International Covenant on Economic, Social and Cultural Rights recognises (Art.12) 'the right to enjoyment of the highest attainable standard of physical and mental health'.

In the abstract, therefore, the existence of such a right is accepted and is clearly part of the established rhetoric of human rights. But there is considerable disagreement about its nature. The concept of 'health' is said by some to be so vague as to preclude discussion of any supposed right to health. This is a serious difficulty, but it is wrong to hold that it makes any exploration of the right to health pointless. It may be true that abstract arguments about the right to health cannot be sustained because there is inadequate agreement about its content. However, further consideration of what it might mean to recognise a right to health may clarify the meaning of the abstract right sufficiently to expose the grounds of disagreements. In turn this may assist them to be resolved. The aim of this chapter, therefore, is to explore the implications of realising a right to health in the context of the English legal system. For current purposes, the existence of a core right to health will be assumed. The issue concerns the concrete legal rights which can be derived from it.

This exploration comprises four aspects. The first stage is to examine the concept of health. I shall suggest there are two competing traditions by which it is understood, which will generate rather different conclusions about the legal rights which can legitimately be derived from a right to health. Once the appropriate conception of health has been chosen it will be necessary to specify the obligations which would serve to promote it. A person can be said to have a right when their interests justify imposing an obligation on another,[1] but not all duties which might serve these interests can legitimately be imposed. Further, the legitimacy of coercion is not the only issue. Clarification and specification of the proposed obligations themselves must take place before it is possible to ask which of them it is permissible to impose.

Such clarification is also necessary in order to make the meaning of the 'right to health' intelligible. To talk of rights as two-term relations between persons and things is only the first step in specifying the content of rights. Rights must then be translated into three-term relations where it is made clear who is obliged, to whom, to do what.[2] Parts two and three of this chapter are therefore concerned with sketching a typology of obligations which would promote health and with identifying the appropriate persons or classes on whom such duties should be put. The right to health requires such specification, not only in terms of the relationship between the individual and the state, but also between citizens. While it may be acceptable to conceive of some rights as held against the state only, the health of members of the community is so intricately interdependent that their relationships with each other must also be considered.

Finally, it will be necessary to ask what constraints must be brought to bear on the use of the law to promote health. These constraints will differ as to the identity of those who bear the obligations. The implications of possible conflicts between the interests of individual citizens must be considered: how far is it a necessary incident of society that some risks to health are accepted? So too must issues of paternalism and freedom: is there a right to be ill? Then there are questions related to the limits of the claims which individuals properly have against the state. There is no upper limit to good health; we can always live longer and run faster no matter how old or quick we already are. It is implausible to suggest that there can be a 'right' that this ever-receding line is attained. A distinction between those obligations which would serve to promote a maximal level of health and those which are justified in terms of respecting basic health needs to be considered: a distinction which may elucidate the differing force of the right to health under disparate political theories.

The final stage makes no attempt to deal comprehensively with the conditions which make coercion acceptable. Rather, it tries to show the importance of the distinctions drawn in the first three parts of the chapter. I shall suggest that they clarify what is at stake and therefore contribute to our understanding of the use of the law in the name of health.

An analytical project of this sort cannot hope to resolve many disputes about what right we (should) have to health. Nevertheless, a clearer idea of what it might mean to recognise a strong conception of the right to health may well serve to pinpoint the ground over which the disputes are fought and elucidate their origins. In the end arguments about the scope of the right to health are about the nature of rights in society and the nature of society itself.

TWO SENSES OF 'HEALTH'

The meaning of 'health' is a political issue. The views taken by doctors tend to be at odds with those of other health workers in the battle for professional power. So too the understanding of the word will tend to vary between conservatives and socialists. A convenient example of the two main schools of thought is, therefore, provided by the working party set up by a Labour health minister to consider inequalities in health in 1977. The Black Report was published (just, on a bank holiday with a very small print run) in 1980 by the Conservatives. Its first chapter chronicles two different models of health. The traditional 'engineering' model on which modern medicine has been based is summarised as 'freedom from clinically ascertainable disease'. The second much broader social model embraces many positions, but for convenience the definition adopted by the World Health Organisation was taken as representative: 'a state of complete physical, mental and social well-being and not merely the absence of disease or infirmity'.[3]

On the first model a right to health will be concerned primarily with two aims. The first is the provision of health care to repair the defective human machine; where people have fallen ill they must be cured. The second will be to control the causes of the initial breakdown. Because the model more easily accommodates the idea of disease than other aspects of ill-health (which cannot be cured in the same way) the paradigm case will be the prevention of the spread of infectious diseases. Environmental concerns, conditions which make the spread of disease more likely and people more vulnerable to stress and other health hazards, are peripheral to the mechanical model of medicine. These latter issues are, however, central to the promotion of health as conceived by the social model. Strong correlations can be shown between poor health and poverty, poor housing and lower socio-economic class. On the social model these are health issues. The poor health which they produce must be tackled, and prevention rather than cure is the primary component of a right to health under this model. The two main aims of the narrower model will be viewed as secondary to these social concerns.

In a developed nation such as the United Kingdom, most sophisticated models of health, whether based on the engineering or social premises, will cover much the same ground. The vast improvement in the nation's health and the eradication of many endemic diseases has required even those who favour the narrower model to expand their view in order to explain the role of medical services. Nevertheless, there is a fundamental distinction between the essentially negative assumptions from which it proceeds – that respect for health involves ensuring the absence of constraints on its existence – and the positive conception of the right to health – the promotion of improvements in health – which underpins the social model.

The account of the right to health which follows is based upon the social model. This reflects a preference for that model, but in addition it enables a fuller explanation of the right to health to be provided. Legal rights required by the narrower model will almost certainly also be required by the broader one. The converse is not necessarily true. By examining the rights derived from the one and then considering how many of them can be generated by the other, it may be possible to show which rights should gain widespread support and which will be controversial.

THE CLAIMS MADE IN THE NAME OF THE RIGHT TO HEALTH

The specific incidents of the right to health can be discussed under four categories. They cannot be rigidly defined, nor can they be said to be mutually exclusive. However, they crystallise out the distinction between the two models of health and that which separates negative from positive claims. Thus, the negative aspect of the mechanical model of health is the right not to have the efficiency of the body threatened by some external force. Its positive counterpart requires the provision of assistance to restore the body to working order. The social model reaches somewhat further. Even in its negative aspect it can found a claim to protection from environmental factors which contribute adversely to the state of a person's health. The positive aspects of the right to health on the social model can extend even further and provide a justification for requiring actions designed to improve even an acceptable level of health. The nature of the obligations to which these four categories give rise can be shown by example.

Protection from disease and accidents

The first class of obligations which follow from the core right to health requires the protection of the right-holder from incidents which will impair the efficiency of the human body. This involves the prevention of the spread of diseases through the community; prophylactic measures such as the vaccination of children will come under this umbrella, as will measures taken to confine contagion to particular individuals or communities. This prevention may be achieved through the exercise of coercive powers such as quarantining or indirectly through a system of deterrence, criminal and/or civil. The spread of disease may thus be punished by the state as a breach of a public duty to the community as a whole, or may result in a private claim for compensation arising in the person who has contracted it against the person who has contaminated them.

The second main direct cause of breakdown in the health of an individual is physical injury. The provisions of the criminal law penalising violence can therefore be seen to protect the right to health (among other rights). So too can the rules of law which allow compensation for the victims of accidents. Compensation provides both a deterrent effect and also protection from the consequences of breaches of the right to health.

Protection from adverse environmental factors

The second class of obligations which follow from the right to health concern the control of the environment in which the right-holders live and work. This includes duties on employers to provide safe systems of work, both at common law and under statutory provisions.

It also covers the eradication of factors which are connected with the deterioration of health. It is now clear that health is more likely to break down in conditions of poor housing, stress and unemployment (among other adverse factors). Occupational diseases are often linked with work conditions even when their exact causal contribution is unclear. Statistical correlations between environmental factors are often presented well before explanations of the links are available, if at all. Full recognition of the right to health would need to embrace the minimisation of such known risks. Smoking is beginning to emerge as a testing area, with an established increase in the probability of ill health for both active and passive smokers, but without the reasons being clear.

Promotion of a healthy environment

While the last category of duties was concerned with eradicating threats to health, the third set deals with steps aimed at increasing standards of health. One example of such measures would be provided by the provision of free school milk, designed to ensure that all children benefit more fully from the protection which comes from good dietary regimes. Preventative services would also come into this category: the provisions of leisure services; control of the use of additives in food; screening for conditions such as cancer. A maximal right to health would embrace measures aimed to promote health. But to many thinkers these would be outside the scope of such a right. Although possibly still justifiable in economic terms such as their impact in reducing the overall cost of health services, they could not be claimed by individuals as a matter of right.

The relationship between the first three categories can perhaps best be illustrated by way of example. The history of the control of water supplies can provide examples of all three. Water-borne disease made a significant contribution to death-rates in the UK in the nineteenth century. The last cholera epidemic in Britain, for example, was in 1865 and since then its contribution to mortality rates has been negligible. This is best explained by improvements in the cleanliness of water supplies isolating the disease.[4] This would come under the first category of controlling spread of infection. The emergence of provisions relating to the pollution of water goes further than the isolation of suspect supplies and seeks to eliminate the conditions which allow infectious diseases to become established. This comes under the category of protection from adverse environmental factors. The next stage in the history of the control of water supply from the point of view of health is its fluoridation, undertaken in order to improve the quality of teeth amongst children. Fluoridation secures no benefit to mature humans, but promotes improved dental health for subsequent generations.

Provisions of health care services

Finally the right to health also covers the right to health care. Ill-health cannot be avoided completely, but its effect can be mitigated and good health can often be restored. Thus, a health care system is an essential component of the means by which a society recognises the right to health. The Universal Declaration and the European Social Charter make explicit reference to the provision of medical services. Controversy in this area arises over the efficiency and extent of such services. If the right to health is held by all citizens equally, then it follows that access to health care should be comprehensive, although the source of that provision need not be uniform for all citizens.

There is also an issue as to the way in which this right becomes a legal one. The National Health Service Act 1977 provides

> 1(1) It is the Secretary of State's duty to continue the promotion in England and Wales of a comprehensive health service designed to secure improvement –
> (a) in the physical and mental health of the people of those countries, and
> (b) in the prevention, diagnosis and treatment of illness . . .

It goes on to lay down in Section 3 that there is a duty to provide facilities of specified types 'to such extent as [the Secretary of State] considers necessary to meet all reasonable requirements'. There can be no doubt that the Act imposes duties on the executive to protect and promote the health of citizens. However, this duty does not give rise to legally enforceable rights in any individual. Instead, it seems that breaches of this duty can only be challenged through the parliamentary channels of ministerial accountability and by electoral choice. Neither avenue is renowned for its efficiency on narrow issues.

Individual citizens who have felt that their health care needs have not been met have sought to argue that there has been a breach of duty before the courts. But their actions have been unsuccessful. In 1979 a group of orthopaedic patients who were denied treatment because of lack of facilities sought to force the Secretary of State to proceed with plans to extend hospital buildings in their health district. They claimed that there had been a breach of the statutory duty under Section 3 of the 1977 Act on the basis that, because their claims to be treated were reasonable, the Act required that they be met. The Court of Appeal refused to consider whether their claim for these facilities was in fact reasonable. Instead they held that unless the Secretary of State had taken a decision that no reasonable minister could have reached his word was final. Without evidence that there had been bad faith in the taking of the decision the patients had no case.[5]

The essence of the case was that the government had promised to provide comprehensive health care but was refusing to fund it. More recently the same issue has been brought to the courts by a different route, but with no more success. The 'Baby Barber' case in 1987 was an attempt to force a health authority to perform an operation which it lacked the resources to perform.[6] The Courts declared that the issue of funding was non-justiciable and political rather than legal.

There may be other legal routes allowing individuals to challenge decisions to withhold health care resources from them. Judicial review has been accepted in principal for some grounds of refusal. In one case the judge suggested that refusal of access to health care on the basis of sex or race might be struck down by the courts.[7] An obligation on hospitals and health authorities to take reasonable care in offering the care which they hold themselves out as providing may offer some hope,[8] although its usefulness may be limited in respect of financial restraints.[9] As the law stands, however, it cannot be said that there is any established route giving individual citizens the means to enforce their right to health.

This is not to suggest that there is no legal right to health care in England and Wales. There is clearly a legal obligation on the Secretary of State which serves to promote the health of each individual citizen. But the strength of that right is greatly reduced by the absence of effective means of enforcement. A maximal concept of individual rights to health care would include the individual having access to some means to protect their right. The identity of those who can enforce the legal rights which serve people's health is an important variable in the realisation of the moral/political right.

DUTIES AND DUTY-HOLDERS

Within each of the four broad types of right which serve to protect different aspects of a maximal sense of the right to health a distinction can be drawn in respect of the identity of the persons on whom legal duties are to be imposed. Three classes of duty-holders can be identified. Some duties will arise in the state. Some will be held by individual citizens. Others will be imposed on classes of persons carrying particular statuses such as employers, manufacturers, teachers and doctors.

Accidents, infection and their avoidance

In relation to rights to protection from the spread of disease and accidents, specific provisions exist by which the state is empowered to control the actions of persons who carry infectious diseases. Their very existence is implicit recognition of the public's right to protection. The Public Health (Control of Diseases) Act 1984 is the latest in a series of statutory frameworks dealing with the area. It allows for the compulsory testing, removal to hospital and detention in hospital of those who present a risk to public health because they suffer from a notifiable disease. The scope of these powers is very wide, and some conditions such as HIV/AIDS have been brought only within the scope of some of them.[10] In the interests of civil rights, various safeguards exist to protect the interests of those against whom the powers are used. The right to health is not the only fundamental value which is at stake here.

Obligations to prevent the spread of diseases are also placed upon private individuals by the law. The common law offence of public nuisance includes cases where infectious persons are knowingly and unnecessarily exposed in public places. The intentional passing of virus may be a crime, although the problems of proof are very great.[11] It is arguable that someone who knows that they are carrying a contagious disease and fails to take reasonable steps to protect others from it might be liable in negligence should they be infected.[12] There is little evidence, however, that the legal duties themselves (as opposed to financial liabilities which may follow from their breach) actually have significant effects in practice. This is particularly the case in relation to more intimate behaviour.[13]

In the 'private' context, therefore, the systems which provide compensation for those who suffer ill-health are more significant. Here there is a general responsibility for negligent actors to compensate those who suffer from carelessness. Some statuses, such as employer and manufacturer, give rise to duties of care which are more onerous than those at large, sometimes as a result of statute and sometimes because of particular developments of the common law. The essential principal is that the person suffering ill-health will receive compensation, if, and only if, they can prove that their disability has been caused by some unlawful event for which the defendant can be held responsible.

Jane Stapleton's study *Disease and the Compensation Debate* (Oxford: OUP, 1986) has demonstrated how the rules by which the tort system operates make it very difficult for whose who suffer non-traumatic injuries to recover compensation. She identifies three classes of disablement, arranged according to cause as: accidents, man-made diseases and natural diseases. Recognition of the right to health in its fullest sense would imply protection from all three categories of disablement through financial compensation to reduce their impact. In England the third class is dealt with as part of the welfare provision. The first is tackled by the tort system and insurance, sometimes compulsory as with motor accidents.[14] The second however, is poorly covered. The causes of non-traumatic injury are often difficult to trace, they may not be clearly attributable to individual fault because of possible intervening causes. The law relating to the limitation of actions through the lapse of time provides greater problems in this area because of the difficulty of pin-pointing the exact time of injury.

These problems are deeply rooted in the conceptual structure of English law. It is not clear whether they can be remedied by reforming that structure, or whether it would be necessary to replace it. Two recent House of Lords decisions have brought promising developments in the field of causation to a halt by reasserting orthodoxy.[15] It seemed that the tide was flowing in favour of victims of man-made disease, but it has been turned back. The reason for this would seem to be the involvement of two private interests in fault-based compensation which means that to improve the position of victims is also to make that of defendants worse.

I have suggested that compensation for all those injured, rather than just those whose injuries are the fault of another as the present English system allows, is required by the fullest conception of a right to health. This probably depends on accepting that the obligations which arise out of the right to health in the context of bearing the loss of ill-health fall fully upon the state. The current tort-based system assumes that such obligations arise only upon private individuals, and uses the concept of fault to identify which ones. The general position in English law is that support for the victims of disease and accidents is a state issue only so far as general social insurance is accepted, and in relation to the provision of health care. Indeed the state is generally protected more fully than private individuals from suit rather than less.

This can be illustrated by the case of *D.H.S.S. v. Kinnear*,[16] which arose out of the incidence of brain damage caused by a whooping cough vaccine widely administered to children in the late 1950s and early 1960s under a Departmental policy. Some of the victims brought an action against the DHSS claiming that it was responsible for their injuries because it was negligent to recommend the immunisation programme. The court struck out the claim as failing to contain any reasonable cause of action. Mere negligence was insufficient, there had to be bad faith or *ultra vires* (stepping beyond their statutory powers) before any state obligation to individuals arose. Had an individual doctor prescribed the drug in a negligent manner, either to an unsuitable patient or without proper care to see that it was safe, they would clearly have been liable. So, too, a manufacturer would have to bear the cost of injuries caused by negligence in the production of a vaccine. Nevertheless, no such duty to take care was accepted on the part of the state.

The general point is therefore clear. In the special case of vaccination Parliament accepted that there was a responsibility on the state to support the victims of the DHSS policy. The Vaccination Damage (Payments) Act 1979 provides them with compensation. But it is less extensive in its scope than general liability in tort would be. It deals only with some injuries and there are strict limits on the amounts payable. One major advantage has become apparent, however. The acceptance of responsibility by the state has also led to the relaxation of the strict rules of causation which present so much difficulty to disease victims. The 1979 Act set up tribunals rather than courts to adjudicate on claims. In these tribunals, where there is no defendant as such, it has been widely accepted that the whooping cough vaccine caused the injuries and compensation has been forthcoming for the victims. In the courts, however, where the manufacturers of the vaccine have been sued, the same causal link has not been accepted.[17]

As the burden is on the plaintiff to prove the causation, the lack of scientific knowledge about the exact causal process means the failure of the case. Spreading the losses across all citizens by having the state bear the cost of ill-health therefore creates a system which is better able to support the victims of disease.

There is an intermediate position which can be taken. Rather than obligations to support the victims of ill-health arising on the state they may be placed on those whose status justifies them bearing more of the loss than the public at large. This often goes under the label of 'enterprise liability'. The argument is that some people make money out of enterprises, such as the manufacture of drugs, which also lead to losses to individuals. These losses may occur without anyone being at fault. Even after the most extensive testing of new drugs some dangerous side-effects may remain undetected. Even so the losses would not occur if the drug companies were not operating and it is unclear why they should reap the commercial benefits of their business but pass the losses to individual customers.

This approach to the problem of drug-induced injuries has been taken up by Sweden. Two schemes to provide no-blame compensation for the victims of medical injuries have been set up.[18] The Patient Insurance Scheme has been in existence since 1975. It is operated by a consortium of Swedish insurance companies and funded by premiums from doctors and dentists who are in private practice and local councils (who play the role of our health authorities). Patients can claim compensation without relinquishing their rights to legal action. The second mechanism is the Pharmaceutical Insurance Scheme, which was set up in 1978 and is funded entirely by the drug companies, in proportion to their turnover. It provides compensation for injuries caused (on the balance of probabilities) by drugs, irrespective of fault. Here, minor injuries are excepted, and to claim from the Scheme the victims must cede their right to sue. Nevertheless, while the number of victims compensated through the courts prior to the scheme was minimal, thousands benefit from the insurance schemes annually.

The crucial point about the Swedish schemes for present purposes is that they are not examples of the state shouldering the burden of compensation. Those who benefit financially from the activities which provide the context in which the accidents occur are the people who bear the costs of compensation. Both Sweden's insurance schemes are voluntary. However, there is no reason why the principle could not be used in compulsory schemes.

Environmental concerns

The range of environmental factors affecting health means that generalisations about the appropriate duty-holders are of only limited use. Save for a long-standing reluctance in the common law to make Englishmen their brothers' keepers, difficulties arise primarily in debates about the legitimacy of specific proposals, not about whether duties are acceptable in principle.

The status approach has long been accepted in relation to health and safety at work. Employers are expected to take steps to ensure that conditions meet minimum levels, set by statute and policed by inspectors and which form the basis of compensation claims. The health and safety interests of workers are also pursued by the issue of advice and information which goes beyond these mandatory standards. Similarly, tenants have been protected by environmental health provisions designed to protect them from the extremes of landlords with the upper hand in the 'free' market. These provisions also provide for specialist enforcement agencies.

Obligations on individuals to promote environmental conditions which do not compromise the interests of others in achieving good health present more difficulties. Here the problem arises because the English common law is traditionally reluctant to impose positive obligations. Liability in tort is readily accepted in relation to acts which adversely affect others. But the suggestion that I am responsible for losses which occurred as a result of my failure to look after another's interests will be met with disbelief. Without some prior relationship omissions will not be actionable, but the existence of such a relationship makes it a status-based obligation.

Like status-based obligations, government involvement in controlling the environment also has a long pedigree. Some areas, such as planning controls can only very poorly be exercised in the private sector,[19] but are nevertheless important in preserving a healthy environment (amongst other things). In others obligations can be placed on individuals and bodies, but effective enforcement needs to be by government agencies.[20] In yet others, a flexible system of regulation, rather than strict and general rules, is necessary which requires the creation of special bodies. While self-regulation is possible, and currently in vogue, for it to be obligatory government sponsorship of some sort is called for.

The important issues in relation to the identity of duty-holders in the context of environmental protection or promotion of health are, therefore, about efficiency and privacy. The coercion of individuals is conceived as a specific example of the problem of liberty. Obligations imposed on the basis of status and upon the state will be attacked for failing to produce the intended benefits, or for overstepping the limits of permissible state activity; general problems for political theory rather than ones uniquely rooted in health.

The provision of health care

This issue has already been discussed as a duty held by the state. Here the issues are about how rather than whether there should be obligations. Attention must also be given to obligations on others. As with the environmental concerns, the common law's reluctance to require individuals to act restricts the scope of legal obligations to care for others. For the judges, the 'Good Samaritan' acts out of goodness, not obligation.[21]

English law does recognise duties based upon status, however. While usually not even health care professionals would be bound by the law to help an injured passer-by, general practitioners are bound by their contracts of employment to assist anyone within the geographical area for which they are responsible. Those working in accident and emergency departments have an obligation to provide their services to anyone who presents themselves.[22] Obligations to take positive steps to search out health problems, and not merely to react to them, have also been recognised on the basis of status. One case required an employer whose business necessitated employees' exposure to known carcinogens to instigate a screening programme in order to escape negligence.[23]

THE LIMITS OF COERCION

The aim of the earlier parts of this chapter has been to elucidate the concept of a right to health. I have sought to identify the sorts of duties which would serve to promote the health of citizens. I consciously eschewed questions dealing with their acceptability and tried to limit the discussion to general features distinguishing different types of obligation. This fourth section is intended to begin to move from the largely value-free questions about what rights we might recognise towards asking what rights we should recognise. It remains, however, an exploratory exercise. I shall not try to solve the problems but to show how the various features exposed by the earlier sections give rise to significant distinctions when the question whether or not duties should be imposed is tackled. Three sets of debates can illustrate this.

Health and paternalism

If an interest becomes a right when it justifies the imposition of obligations on another, be it another person or the state, then questions about the limits of the right to health will turn primarily on considerations of the position of persons other than the right-holder. Nevertheless, the general issue of individual liberty is still relevant to the area of health. Some would argue that measures which affect large numbers of citizens are taken indiscriminately without the consent of those affected and thus impose a view of their own well-being which they would not accept. One of the main principled objections voiced in the House of Commons against the Water (Fluoridation) Act 1985 was that it would not allow individuals to choose whether to drink fluoridated water.[24]

In the context of the first and fourth category of obligations, the anti-paternalist position can be pushed more strongly. We do not generally force health care upon patients. Consent is required before any procedure is carried out on their bodies.[25] They are entitled to withhold that consent irrationally.[26] Although in serious cases which involve crimes, society takes on the role of enforcer, breaches of the obligation to refrain from injuring another's health are usually enforceable only where the injured party chooses to do so. There is therefore a right to be ill in these contexts, realised by ensuring that the holder of the moral/political right is also the person able to enforce the legal obligations which protect it.

The objection based on paternalism is more complex in the context of preventative measures designed to alter environmental conditions. It is hard to argue for the complete separation of individuals into autonomous agents when environmental health issues are at stake because it is impossible to provide a selective environment which will promote one person's health but have no effect on others. This does not remove the need to consider the way in which legal obligations are set out. Opponents in Parliament were concerned both about the absolute issue, to fluoridate or not to fluoridate, but also with provisions promoting democratic participation in the debates. For some, on both sides of the House, the crucial point was that the decision would be taken by unelected water authorities. Neither local democracy, by referenda, local councils or health authorities, nor central democracy in the form of parliamentary decision would determine whether any particular water source would contain fluoride. To meet these concerns a concerted but unsuccessful effort was put into forcing public choice into the Bill at report stage.[27]

Health and power: professionalism and vested interests

A second area of concern in relation to judging the acceptability of imposing measures designed to promote health is with the implications for the power of sections of society. The production of an environment designed to maximise health places us all in the hands of those who claim expertise to determine the definition of health and the efficiency of means to promote it. The notion of a 'therapeutic society' where citizens' lives are overseen and controlled by such professionals is a matter for much concern when the provisional and controversial nature of professional knowledge is considered.[28]

Health care professionals are not, of course, the only people with vested interests. Environmental issues have a significant impact on the economics of industry. Proposals for health promotion by improving the environment generally mean that the costs of manufacturers are increased. Their resistance to them is, therefore, unsurprising. Two of the major contributors to ill health in the UK are tobacco and alcohol.[29] Both have powerful lobbies behind them, a fact which goes a long way towards explaining the meagre steps taken to reduce their use.

A consideration of the nature of the legal measures aimed at furthering the cause of good health indicates that these worries are more significant in some areas than others, and that the risks can be reduced by using the right types of obligation. The politics of health will provide more controversy in relation to obligations derived from the social model of health than that based on the functioning of the human machine. There is less agreement as to its content, making individuals more vulnerable to group interests. Uncertainty will also tend to be greater when environmental issues are at stake.

One way to reduce the potential for abuse is to ensure that those able to enforce the relevant duties have the maximum detachment from that politics. This may require the individual whose health is in issue to be able to choose whether to enforce their right. This would seem attractive where the issues are relatively clear, and biases may arise because of the personal advantages which some courses of action offer to the person responsible for promoting the other's health. In cases where the difficulty arises from the complexity or technicality of the decisions, then specialist enforcement agencies may be appropriate. Sometimes it may be necessary to impose extra duties on those with vested interests in order to counteract or minimise their effect.

The status of health care claims

Some writers argue that however much the recognition of certain claims might benefit citizens' health, it is nevertheless inappropriate to give them the status of rights. Claims arising out of the social model of health are most likely to meet this type of objection, and those relating to the use of the environment actively to promote health are particularly prone to rejection.

Such objections are usually based on stances taken on general political issues. Most common will be two related issues. The first deals with the problem by asking whether claims can be derived from whatever bases (if any) are accepted as founding human rights. Norman Daniels, for example, argues that a distinction must be drawn between wants and needs. Only the latter, defined by reference to normal species functioning, can achieve the status of rights.[30] Theories of human rights which depend on 'lowest common denominator' standards of this type will clearly find it difficult to accommodate some of the implications of the social understanding of health.

A similar reluctance will be exhibited by theorists whose model of society conceives its members as wholly autonomous entities who should not be held responsible for the well-being of their fellow citizens. From this perspective the identity of the duty-holders will be of great importance. Measures aimed at promoting health will be more acceptable if they impose no burden on other individuals. General understandings of the role of the state will also be crucial. A nightwatchman state will be able to play very little part in anything other than cases where the citizen's physical integrity is threatened because other aspects of the right to health assume more active government than that theory allows. This has little to do with health as an idea, but will have a strong impact on the degree to which obligations based on health are accepted.

CONCLUSION

I have not tried to justify any particular content for the right to health. This seems to me to be fraught with difficulties. Without clarification of what such a right might mean it seems foolish to begin such a project. Nor does there appear to be sufficient common ground between theories of moral or human rights to make a general theory of the right to health possible. Instead, I have begun from the assumption, based on the international documents, that there is a consensus that a right to health should be recognised in the abstract, but no agreement as to what it means to do so in practice. I have, therefore, sought to sketch a map of the field of choice so that the range of possible concrete legal rights which might be derived from a right to health can be identified.

I have suggested a series of variables. First, a contrast between the social and engineering models of health. Second a division into four categories of claim: those relating to the prevention of or compensation for specific actions which cause ill-health; the removal of adverse environmental conditions; the creation of a health-promoting context; and the provision of health-care services. Third, variations in terms of the means by which duties can be enforced: whereby there can be rights inherent in individuals; specifically created enforcement agencies; or government responsibilities for which accountability depends on the political process. Finally, three categories of duties: those imposed on individuals; those based on specific statuses; and those arising in the state or its organs.

Save for the use of the environment actively to promote improvements in health above a minimum functional standard, where a social model of health is implied, any combination of these variables may probably be exhibited in measures taken in order to recognise rights to health. I have tried to illustrate how each of these variables tends to carry with it different implications for different understandings of society and in relation to general issues of political theory. I have also suggested that objections may be minimised by choosing carefully the appropriate way to impose obligations. If by the end of this essay the complexities of the task of recognising a right to health appear more clearly, then it has served a useful purpose.

NOTES

1. J. Raz, 'On the Nature of Rights', *Mind*, Vol XCIII, 1984, pp.194–214.
2. J. Finnis, *Natural Law and Natural Rights*, (Oxford: OUP, 1980), pp.218 – 21.
3. DHSS (1980), *Inequalities in Health*: Report of a Research Working Group Chaired by Sir Douglas Black.
4. T. McKeown, *The Role of Medicine: Dream, Mirage or Nemesis*? (London: Nuffield Provincial Hospitals Trust, 1976).
5. R v Sec. State for Social Services, ex p. Hincks discussed in J. Finch, *Health Services Law* (London: Sweet & Maxwell, 1981).
6. In re Walker *The Times*, 26 November 1987, *Independent*, 25 and 26 November 1987.
7. R v St. Mary's Hospital, ex.p Harriott [1988] 1 FLR 512. See R Singh, 'Infertility Treatment and the Courts', *Fam. Law* 1988 299. See also the attempt to use anti-discrimination concepts to deal with the denial of treatment to victims of HIV/AIDS in Taunya Lovell Banks, 'The Right to Medical Treatment', in H.L. Dalton, S. Burris *et al., AIDS and the Law* (New Haven, Conn: Yale University Press, 1987).
8. J. Bettle, 'Suing Hospitals Direct: Whose Tort was it Anyhow?' *NLJ*, Vol.137, 1987, p.573.
9. J. Montgomery, 'Suing Hospitals Direct: What Tort?', *NLJ*, Vol. 137, 1987, p.703.
10. Public Health (Infectious Disease) Regulations S.I. 1988, No 434.
11. I am grateful to Professor A.T.H. Smith for this point, explored in an unpublished paper, 'Aids and the Criminal Law'.
12. See F. Kaganas, 'Compensation for AIDS victims', *AALR*; Vo. 16, 1987 p.117.
13. R. Porter, 'History says no to the policeman's response to AIDS', 293 *BMJ*, 1986, 1589 – 1590; see also R. Porter and D. Porter, 'AIDS: law, liberty and public health', in P. Byrne (ed.), *Health, Rights and Resources*, (London: King's Fund, 1988).
14. This should not be taken as indicating complacency about the need for reform; see, for instance, A. Simanowitz, 'Medical Accidents: the problem and the challenge', in P Byrne (ed.), *Medicine in Contemporary Society*, (London: King's Fund, 1987).
15. Hotson v E Berkshire AHA [1987] AC 750, Wilsher v Essex AHA [1988] AC 1074.

16. (1984) 134 NLJ 887.
17. Loveday v Renton *The Times*, 31 March 1988.
18. M. Brahms, 'The Swedish "No Fault" Compensation System for Medical Injuries', 138, *NLJ*, 1988, 14 and 31.
19. P. Polden, 'Private Estate Planning and the Public Interest', 49 *MLR* 1986, 195.
20. G. Richardson, A. Ogus and P. Burrows, *Policing Pollution* (Oxford: Clarendon Press, 1982).
21. Shapo, *Duty to Act* (1977). J.M. Ratcliffe (ed.), *The Good Samaritan and the Law* (Gloucester, Mass: Peter Smith, 1981).
22. Barnett v Chelsea and Kensington Hospital [1969] QB 428.
23. Stokes v Guest Keen, 1 *WLR*, 1968, 1776.
24. HC Vol 71 Col 74 ff.
25. Chatterton v Gerson [1981] All ER 257.
26. Sidaway v Bethlem RHG [1985] 1 All ER 643, 666 per Lord Templeman.
27. HC Vol 73 Col 953 ff.
28. See E. Friedson, *Profession of Medicine* (New York: Dodd, Mead & Co, 1970).
29. DHSS *Prevention and health: everybody's business* (1976).
30. N. Daniels, 'Health Care Needs and Distributive Justice', in R. Bayer, A. Caplan and N. Daniels (eds), *In Search of Equity: Health Needs and the Health Care System* (New York: Plenum Press, 1983).

Index